ALSO BY MICHAEL MANDELBAUM

THE ROAD TO GLOBAL PROSPERITY

MICHAEL MANDELBAUM

SIMON & SCHUSTER
NEW YORK LONDON TORONTO SYDNEY NEW DELHI

Simon & Schuster
1230 Avenue of the Americas
New York, NY 10020

First Simon & Schuster hardcover edition March 2014

SIMON & SCHUSTER and colophon are registered trademarks
of Simon & Schuster, Inc.

For information about special discounts for bulk purchases,
please contact Simon & Schuster Special Sales at 1-866-506-1949
or business@simonandschuster.com.

The Simon & Schuster Speakers Bureau can bring authors to your live event.
For more information or to book an event contact the Simon & Schuster Speakers
Bureau at 1-866-248-3049 or visit our website at www.simonspeakers.com.

Interior design by Akasha Archer
Jacket design by Tom McKeveny
Jacket photographs: globe © pavilalistock;
golden apple © Ragnarock/Shutterstock

Manufactured in the United States of America

1   3   5   7   9   10   8   6   4   2

Library of Congress Cataloging-in-Publication Data

Mandelbaum, Michael.
The road to global prosperity / Michael Mandelbaum. —
First Simon & Schuster hardcover ed.
pages cm
1. Capitalism 2. International trade. 3. International economic relations.
4. Economic development 5. Financial crises. I. Title
HB501.M31364 2014
337—dc23

ISBN 978-1-4767-5001-9
ISBN 978-1-4767-5003-3 (ebook)

*To Robert J. Lieber, Charles H. Lipson, Rajan Menon, and Michael B. Oren:
gentlemen and scholars;*

*and to Anne Mandelbaum,
with my love and admiration*

ACKNOWLEDGMENTS

I owe a debt of gratitude in the writing of this book to my home institution, The Johns Hopkins University School of Advanced International Studies, where I have taught since 1990. Its curriculum emphasizes economics, and graduating students take an oral examination in two fields: the one in which they have concentrated and international economics. I have therefore taken part, with a number of economist colleagues as the other examiner, in many such examinations, which contributed to this book in two ways: first, they encouraged my long-standing interest in economics and inspired me to learn more on my own by reading what economists write, particularly for noneconomists; second, what I heard in those examinations inspired the conviction—which reading and discussions deepened and which is a major theme of *The Road to Global Prosperity*—that at the root of the major economic issues the world will face in the years ahead lie political considerations.

I am immensely grateful to my stellar agent, Esther Newberg of International Creative Management, whose encouragement, unerring judgment, and wise counsel make her all an author could wish a literary agent to be. It has been a privilege to work with my editor at Simon & Schuster, Alice Mayhew, and her colleague Jonathan Cox, whose editorial suggestions improved this book in significant ways.

I am indebted to Thomas L. Friedman of *The New York Times* for many conversations on the subjects covered in these pages.

I am most deeply grateful of all to my wife, Anne Mandelbaum, for her astute advice and for the sustenance I draw upon daily from her unwavering support, her uncommon sense, her wit, and her love.

CONTENTS

Economics may propose but politics dispose.
—MARTIN WOLF

A single headline rarely signals a dramatic change in the history of the world, but *Time* magazine's February 15, 1999, cover did exactly that. It showed three American economic officials—Alan Greenspan, chairman of the Federal Reserve Board, and Secretary of the Treasury Robert Rubin and his deputy secretary Lawrence Summers—with a bright yellow headline calling them "The Committee to Save the World." The accompanying story described their efforts to keep the ongoing financial crisis in Asia from worsening and spreading around the globe.

In the past, headlines about saving the world referred to political leaders grappling with issues of war and peace, not financial officials coping with markets. When the world needed saving, the threats came from the aggression of kings, emperors, and dictators, not from the weakness of national currencies under assault from investors and speculators.

By early 1999, however, things were different. The attention of national leaders had shifted to economic matters. As recently as 1971, when informed of the latest problems with the ever-volatile Italian currency, President Richard Nixon had responded, "I don't give a shit about the lira." Four decades later, neither President Barack Obama nor any other national leader would have considered adopting Nixon's view of the lira's beleaguered successor, the euro. The difficulties of the European currency that threatened to plunge Europe's economy into a severe downturn had the potential to drag the American and global economies down with it. Between 1971 and 2011 economic issues—above all, the health of the global economy—replaced matters of war and peace as the major focus of national leaders because economic matters came to have greater effects on the countries they led.

At first, this shift seemed very good news indeed. In economics, unlike in war, everyone can be a winner; and from 1991 to 2008 virtually every country gained enormously from participating in the global economy. Then came the great financial crisis in September of that year and the deep, punishing global economic downturn that it triggered. These disasters gave rise to the impression that the days of worldwide economic growth had come to an end and that the results of the great shift from war to commerce were not destined to be as favorable as they had first seemed.

The message of this book is that this post-2008 impression is wrong. The global economy will continue to grow. Its growth will make people everywhere richer. While not inevitable, this is the likely future. Political obstacles stand in the way, as they always do; but they are likely to be circumvented or overcome, to the benefit of the vast majority of the world's 7 billion inhabitants. Despite the economic disasters of the recent past, in the decades ahead most countries and most people most of the time will travel the road to global prosperity.

•   •   •

The rise of the international economy as the major influence on the future of nations and their governments and on the daily lives of people everywhere has four main causes. The first is the sharp decline in the importance of large-scale war. While armed conflict has not disappeared entirely, major conflicts, like the two world wars and the Cold War that followed, are now extremely unlikely.

The conquest of territory and the defense of borders have

ceased to be the chief concern of governments almost everywhere and have been replaced by the promotion of economic growth. This is the second reason for the shift in the hierarchy of issues in international affairs. Of course, governments' pursuit of economic gain did not begin in the twenty-first century. Regimes have striven from time immemorial to increase their wealth, but did so, for most of history, for the purpose of enhancing their military strength. In the wake of the Cold War, however, the primary motive changed: governments have sought wealth in order to improve the material well-being of those they governed because virtually every government's prospects for remaining in power depend on its success in doing exactly this. Political legitimacy has come to depend on the delivery of prosperity.

Third, prosperity is widely understood as requiring a free-market economy. This was not always so. In the second half of the twentieth century many countries organized economic life in ways that minimized the role of the market, and therefore of globalization. Where Communist parties ruled, central planning of economic affairs by government bureaucrats held sway. Other countries, many recently released from European imperial rule, adopted the economic strategy known as import-substitution. Under this approach they sought to develop powerful domestic industries and supported them with protective tariffs, subsidies, government guidance of loans and investment to favored firms, and official control over foreign currency—policies inconsistent with the free cross-border exchange of goods and capital. By the end of the century, however, communism had collapsed and import-substitution had been discredited. The countries that had practiced them almost all embraced free markets. Once free markets are the rule, immersion in global trade and investment follows naturally: where markets are concerned, bigger is better. In the twenty-first century, international economic integration became truly global in scope.

The fourth cause of the rise of the international economy to a position of supreme importance in world affairs has been the advance of technology. Beginning with the steamboat, the railroad, and the telegraph in the nineteenth century, continuing with the automobile, the airplane, and the telephone in the twentieth, and including the cheap satellite communication, cell phones, and Internet of the present day, innovations in transportation and communication have bound free-market economies, and the people living and working within them, ever more tightly together. Goods, money, and people move in ever-larger volumes, and ever more quickly, across national borders. Globalization is an increasingly important part of the daily life of more and more people. What the Russian revolutionary leader Leon Trotsky once said about war now applies to the global economy: you may not be interested in it, but it is interested in you.

All this means that, in 2014 and beyond, while the future of the world, its almost two hundred independent countries, and the 7 billion people within them will depend on many things, the single most important influence will be the health and stability of the global economy. The future of the global economy is the subject of this book.

Such a book implicitly promises two things. The first is an empirical focus. More than a few volumes have been written about how the global economy *ought* to work. This one describes how it *is likely* to work. The second promise is that the reader will get a picture of the forces that will *shape* the future. No one can say what precisely the future will be, but it is possible to specify the factors on which the future will *depend*, and that is what this book does. The future of the global economy will depend on politics. Politics will determine how smoothly it will function and how wealthy the world, its different countries, and the people living in them will become.

The major concerns of this book, economics and politics, differ in basic ways. The heart of politics is power; the aim of economics is wealth. Power is inherently limited. The quest for power is therefore competitive. It is a "zero-sum game:" one player's gain necessarily imposes a loss on another. Wealth, by contrast, is limitless, which makes economics a "positive-sum game" in which everyone involved can gain simultaneously. This key difference means that political activity is by definition contentious and competitive, whereas in economics, while competition is essential, cooperation is the rule. Further, while the main institution of politics, government, is hierarchical, centralized, and can involve coercion, the comparable institution for economics, the free market, is far more egalitarian, decentralized, and voluntary. The government, to cite a final important difference, serves as the vehicle for collective decisions and collective action; the market is the forum par excellence for individual initiative.

These polar opposites are illustrated by the Chinese concept of yin and yang, represented by a circle divided into two identical, complementary, teardrop-shaped sections, each nestling within the other and usually depicted in black and white. Yin and yang describe how seemingly contrary forces are interconnected and mutually influential, and so it is with politics and the global economy in the twenty-first century. They are distinct but interdependent. Neither can exist in its contemporary form without the other. To be sure, economics is not entirely the creature of politics. Market forces operate spontaneously, at their own pace, and according to their own logic; but they can only do so within politically established limits. In the future, politics will shape the global economy in four major ways, each of which is the subject of one of the chapters that follow.

Economic activity does not occur in a vacuum. It requires a stable political framework, one that protects it against disruptive intrusions from the outside—war being the most disruptive of all—and assures that the buying, selling, and investing at the heart of economic life can proceed dependably. In the first era of globalization, from the middle of the nineteenth century to the outset of World War I, Great Britain did more than any other country to protect global commerce. Over the ensuing three decades, which were marked by two world wars and the Great Depression, the necessary framework was absent and global economic activity sputtered at best. In globalization's second era, from the end of World War II to the end of the Cold War, the United States succeeded Britain as the guarantor of the global marketplace; and that American role carried over into the third and current era. But the tranquility necessary for cross-border trade, investment, and immigration is not guaranteed to continue, nor are the economic services, which also support cross-border economic activity, that the United States has furnished to other countries. The prospects for their continuation in the years ahead is the subject of this book's first chapter.

For national economies it is the domestic government that supplies the shelter within which markets operate. Although Britain in the nineteenth century and the United States in the twentieth did provide some elements of global governance, the world as a whole has no governing body. While markets are increasingly global in scope, the authority of governments remains confined within national borders. This mismatch between politics and economics means that people and firms operating in global markets have less assurance of reliable protection than is ideal; and this mismatch will affect the workings of the global economy in other ways as well, which are discussed throughout this book.

When global markets do function smoothly, a different political issue arises. Cross-border flows of merchandise, of capital, and of human beings cause economic, political, and even cultural disruption to the societies that receive them: while economics is more benign than war and politics, it is not entirely benign. The disruptions invariably generate political backlash, as the injured or threatened parties respond angrily and fight back, seeking to restrict whatever cross-border flows injure or threaten them. As a result, the global economy, when it is working successfully—indeed, *because* it is working successfully—cannot help but provoke opposition to its workings, which in turn produces political conflicts. Conflicts over trade, investment, and immigration arose in the nineteenth and twentieth centuries and continue in the twenty-first. How they play out will do a great deal to determine how much trade, investment, and immigration there is in this century. The inevitable political backlash against globalization is the subject of Chapter Two.

Trade, investment, and immigration administer to the body politic the equivalent of what Hamlet calls "the thousand natural shocks that flesh is heir to." Some shocks are bigger than others, however, and the biggest come from the least substantial item that passes across borders: money. Indeed, of the three components of global economic activity—goods, money, and people—money is the most dangerous. If the world's economy were a human being, money would be its Achilles heel. It is no accident that the three great crises of the two decades following the end of the Cold War—the East Asian and euro crises and the near-meltdown of the American financial system in late 2008—all had their roots in international finance. Financial systems are inherently fragile; the increasingly international scope of financial markets makes them even more vulnerable. Their instability has an economic and ultimately a psychological basis, but it is politics that determines just how vulnerable to financial upheavals the international economy is and how quickly and effectively financial crises are brought under control when they do erupt. The book's third chapter addresses this particular political determinant of the global economy's future.

The single most important feature of that future will be the rate of economic growth. Growth is the chief goal of almost all national economies and therefore of the international economy as a whole. One major source of growth is adding more resources. (The other is making more effective use of existing resources: that is, increasing productivity.) A key economic resource is labor. National economies tend to grow when their populations grow. Similarly, the global economy has grown when national economies that had previously existed outside it became part of it. In globalization's first era Japan, Germany, and the United States joined Great Britain and western Europe; after 1945 southern Europe and a number of countries in East Asia became part of the integrated international economic order. More countries brought more workers, more consumers, more specialized production, more products, and lower prices to the global market. They brought, in short, economic growth. Today, the most important new members of the global economic order are often called "emerging markets." The most prominent of these are Brazil, Russia, India, and China—known collectively as the BRICs.

The global economy's performance will depend heavily on the growth that each of the BRICs is able to achieve, which will in turn depend on yet another kind of political issue, the subject of the book's fourth and final chapter. In all four BRICs, a particular feature of the country's political history is crucial for its future growth: Brazil's political tradition known as populism; the impact of Russia's energy reserves on its political life; India's democracy; and China's autocratic political system. Each feature has contributed to the country's economic success in the past, but each has now become an obstacle to its continued success. All four countries must overcome their respective obstacles in order to maximize their rates of economic growth and thus their contributions to the global economy.

The global economy will therefore be decisively affected in the years ahead by the answers to four questions:

- Will the world be stable and peaceful enough to permit trade, investment, and immigration on a large scale?
- How strong will the unavoidable political backlash against these cross-border flows be, and what will be the consequences of that backlash?
- How frequent and how severe will global financial crises, of the kind that swept East Asia in the late 1990s, the United States in 2008, and Europe in 2010, turn out to be?
- Finally, how effectively will Brazil, Russia, India, and China cope with the political obstacles to future economic growth that each confronts?

The most important question for the twenty-first century, which encompasses the four questions to which this book is devoted, is whether the peoples and governments of the world will sustain a high level of cross-border economic activity in the years ahead. The answer is yes. While nothing in politics is certain, individuals and governments are likely, in most countries, on most issues, most of the time, to make political decisions that will serve to sustain and expand rather than to set back globalization, the ongoing process of cross-border economic integration. Since its origins in the middle of the nineteenth century, globalization has made those engaged in it richer. Becoming richer will be an even more important and widespread goal in the future than in the past. Governments are therefore likely to adopt policies that enhance economic growth and to avoid those likely to produce the opposite result. Globalization will endure, but not without challenges, complications, and potential pitfalls, all of them rooted in politics. Those challenges, complications, and pitfalls are the subject of the pages that follow.

CHAPTER ONE

THE ROOF

It may be true in one sense that Trade ought not to be enforced by Cannon Balls, but on the other hand Trade cannot flourish without security, and that security may often be unattainable without the Protection of physical force.

—LORD PALMERSTON, 1860[1]

Ultimately, someone has to shoulder the responsibility for peace, security, and the framework of laws and regulations that makes trade possible.

—DANI RODRIK[2]

The history of civilisation is a history of public goods. The more complex the civilisation, the greater the number of public goods that needed to be provided. . . . Unless there is a global economic collapse, an increasing number of the public goods demanded by our civilisation will be global or have global aspects.

—MARTIN WOLF[3]

The Three Pillars of Stability

In post-Communist Russia private businesses need what Russians call a *krysha*. The word means "roof," and refers to the protection that these businesses buy, usually from illegal, Mafia-like organizations. Just as in a house lacking a roof the inhabitants would spend almost all their time and energy protecting themselves from the elements and do little else, so, too, businesses cannot function without protection from the forcible interruption of their activities. Indeed, not only individual businesses but entire markets, whether local, national, or international, need such protection.

Normally, government provides it. Supplying protection is the first duty of government, the reason it is established in the first place.[4] Russian businesses are forced to buy protection privately because the government is too weak, or too corrupt, to furnish it.

Protection is one example of what economists call "collective" or "public" goods. Others are police and fire protection and clean air. Society needs public goods, but individuals or small groups will not supply them. It is government that must do so,[5] which means that international public goods are rarer, and more difficult to generate, than public goods within individual countries because the international system lacks a government. Here the global economy is in the same predicament as Russian businesses. Yet just as Russian firms are able to do business without effective local and national government, the global economy does function despite the absence of global government.

The world as a whole does not entirely lack public goods. It has had enough security for international economic activity to flourish for most of the time since the mid nineteenth century—between the repeal of the British Corn Laws and the outbreak of World War I, and then again since the end of World War II. The world has thus enjoyed one of the benefits of government without actually having one. It has received this crucial governmental service from its wealthiest and most powerful country, first Great Britain, then the United States.

In both cases the protection of cross-border trade, investment, and immigration, which worked to the advantage of all countries, emerged as the not-fully-intended consequence of British and

American policies designed to protect their own national economic and political interests. The two countries acted in the fashion of the owner of the largest and most expensive house in a neighborhood who hires private security guards to protect his home against burglary. The guards' presence will keep burglars away from the other houses in the neighborhood as well, even though their owners pay nothing. Similarly, British and American policies protected the commerce of other countries.[6]

American-provided security continues in the present, so the future of the global economy depends heavily on whether the United States sustains this global role. While American military power is important for the continued functioning of the global economy, however, the globalized international economy of the twenty-first century, unlike its nineteenth-century predecessor, has two other sources of protection. The roof that shelters trade, investment, and immigration is sturdier today than it was then because it rests on three pillars rather than only one. The two others are the political legitimacy of market capitalism and cross-border economic transactions—the legitimacy, that is, of globalization—and the historically unparalleled illegitimacy of the practice against which British and American protection have shielded the global economy: war.

A government is legitimate when it is constituted according to established principles and operates in a proper way. Like ballast on a ship, legitimacy reinforces stability. A government possessing it is less likely than one without it to be actively challenged by, and more likely to command the active support of, those it governs. In traditional societies a legitimate ruler was one who was descended from a legitimate ruler. The ruling family usually owed its legitimacy to a proclaimed association with a deity. Twenty-first-century political legitimacy comes from popular sovereignty—the selection of the government by the people in free elections in which all adults may take part.

The globalized international economy also possesses legitimacy, not by virtue of its design but because of its results. It enjoys what political scientists call "performance legitimacy" through the prosperity it has delivered. Since 1846, and especially since 1945, globalization has built up a stockpile of goodwill and trust among people and governments around the world. A worldwide consensus has formed in favor of the twin propositions that economic self-sufficiency is bad and markets are good.

The legitimacy it has earned through past performance does not make the integrated international economy immune to criticism or even opposition. From the 40,000 people who rallied (and in some cases rioted) against globalization at the 1999 meeting of the World Trade Organization in Seattle (which was convened to launch new global trade negotiations) to the first round of the French presidential elections in April 2012 when candidates receiving upward of 40 percent of the popular vote expressed severe reservations about, if not outright opposition to, full-fledged French participation in the global economy,[7] scarcely a day has passed without some public manifestation of unhappiness with international trade, or finance, or immigration—or all three. The consistent, widespread, and sometimes powerful distaste for the workings of the international economy does not, however, pose a serious threat to its continuation because its legitimacy rests on something besides performance.

There is no credible alternative to it. No method of organizing economic life on the planet other than internationally integrated free markets commands anything like the political support necessary to displace the current system. No collection of rules, institutions, and practices that is new, different, and promising is available. The alternative to the current global economic order is . . . nothing. The Great Depression of the 1930s gave rise to two replacements for global capitalism: the fascist version of import-substituting industrialization, and centrally planned communism. The great recession triggered by the American financial crisis of 2008—the worst global economic downturn since the Great Depression—has not inspired or raised to prominence any alternative at all.

The legitimacy that the current configuration of the global

economy enjoys has accumulated through its own success and the failure of its rivals complements the support it receives from the policies of the United States. Legitimacy protects global economic integration from resistance from within. In the twentieth century it suffered severe damage from attacks from without in the form of the two world wars, the equivalents of a tornado that blows off the roof of a house and wrecks its contents. Now globalization has acquired a historically unprecedented source of protection from that threat.

For almost all of recorded history war was considered a normal, indeed inevitable human practice. War was like winter: it might be delayed, it might be mild, but sooner or later human communities were bound to experience it. In the twentieth century that attitude began to change. War came to be seen as not only undesirable but also avoidable. It was increasingly regarded—more in some places than in others—as a senseless and obsolete custom. It was put in the same category as foot-binding or dueling: once entirely legitimate but now less and less so—and a good thing, too.[8]

This new aversion to war has three sources.[9] One is economic. People and their governments discovered that they could do far better economically by trading and investing with their neighbors than by attempting to conquer them.[10] At the same time, because economic growth has made people richer, they have more to lose through war than did their forebears. The same trend that has made global economic integration popular has made war unpopular.

Political change in the decades since World War II has also contributed to the rise of war aversion. The major illiberal ideologies of the twentieth century, fascism and communism, made war central to their visions of political life. The fulfillment of their designs for remaking the world required conquest. These ideologies have all but disappeared. The closest contemporary equivalent, Islamic fundamentalism, while virulent and dangerous, has no chance of taking over powerful countries, as did fascism and communism. It will surely provoke international conflict—as it already has—but not on the scale of the two world wars or the Cold War.

In addition, more and more countries have become democracies, and democracies tend not to go to war with one another.[11] Democracy goes hand in hand with an emphasis on the rights of individuals. War, because it kills people, violates individual rights in the worst possible way.

Finally, war-aversion has technological roots. The ongoing Industrial Revolution has generated ever-more-powerful machines for a wide variety of activities, including war. As war has become more destructive, it has become less legitimate. The prospect of a war using the most powerful of all armaments, nuclear weapons, is especially forbidding because a nuclear exchange on any but the most modest scale would destroy the countries waging it.

Because of the rise of war-aversion, with its diverse sources, armed conflict has become both less frequent and less deadly.[12] Sovereign states have built up a resistance to it in something like the way that human beings have acquired immunity to deadly diseases. That resistance affords a measure of protection to international economic activity that supplements the protection it receives from American power and the legitimacy of globalization.

Just as disease has not vanished, however, war has not become, nor will it become, entirely extinct. The absence of a formal, effective, global government means that there is no supreme authority to prevent sovereign states from fighting each other. The kinds of political conflicts that triggered war in the past have not disappeared. War remains possible, and therefore a possible influence—in the worst case a very powerful influence—on the future of the global economy. That future thus depends on the kinds of wars that are fought during the decades ahead.

Major War

Beginning in 1996, an estimated 5 million people died in fighting in the Congo, in Central Africa.[13] That terrible conflict illustrates two features of the world of the twenty-first century. One is that the rise of war-aversion does not make large-scale killing a thing of the past. The other is that the impact of twenty-first-century wars, large or small, beyond those directly involved depends very much on their location. Not all wars are equally important, or, to the rest of the world, important at all. Deadly though it was, the Congo war changed nothing outside Central Africa. Elsewhere it barely attracted any attention. It had no discernible effect on buying, selling, and investing in the rest of the world.

War in Africa does not matter, or at least thus far has not mattered, to the global economy. What would matter are wars in the most economically dynamic regions of the world, of which Africa is not one, and especially wars involving large countries that play major international economic roles. Three such countries, Russia, India, and China, could go to war, with damaging economic consequences, in the years ahead. In all three, war-aversion is weaker than in western Europe and North America, where it has put down deepest roots.[14] Each of the three has political interests that are or could be in jeopardy in the years ahead, interests for which it has fought in the past.

During the Cold War a conflict between the Russian-dominated Soviet Union and its chief adversary, the American-led Western coalition, could have visited more damage on the international economy than even the two world wars. In the twenty-first century that conflict has disappeared, but Russia's location, bordering on the European Union, China, and the Middle East, means that any war it fights could disrupt international commerce; and post-Soviet Russia does not lack causes of conflict.

As a recently imperial power, it is susceptible to the impulse to reclaim its former territories. In some of them, notably Ukraine and Kazakhstan, millions of ethnic Russians were left outside the borders of the new Russian state when the Soviet Union collapsed, and the Russian government has proclaimed a special responsibility for protecting them. Post-Communist Russia has fought a war against one of its new neighbors, in August 2008, with the former Soviet province and now independent country of Georgia.

While the rhetoric of Russia's leaders has sometimes tended toward the bellicose, however, the Russian impulse for war is far from overpowering. If reluctantly, most Russians seem to have resigned themselves to the end of their country's career as a great Eurasian empire.[15] More importantly, Russia is militarily weak, especially in comparison with the strength of the old Soviet Union. Its armed forces did not distinguish themselves against tiny Georgia.[16] Weakness, and the leadership's awareness of it, constrain Russian foreign policy even where war-aversion does not. Russia is a declining power, something that cannot be said of India.

Before the twenty-first century, in global economic significance India ranked closer to Africa than to Europe. Its embrace of global integration, however, and consequent rapid growth after 1991 have made its conflict with neighboring Pakistan a threat to economic well-being beyond South Asia. That conflict centers on the Muslim-majority Indian province of Kashmir. The province's Hindu ruler opted to join India rather than Pakistan when British India was divided into the two countries in 1947. Pakistan objected and attempted, unsuccessfully, to reverse the decision by force. The two countries fought again over the province in 1965 and 1999.

Kashmir's status is important enough to both countries to be a cause of war because each sees the territory as integral to its national identity. For Pakistan, a country created as a home for South Asian Muslims, its separation from adjacent Kashmir violates its very reason for existence: if large groups of Muslims can live comfortably in India, after all, why should there be a Pakistan? The Pakistani military and its security services have an additional interest in sustaining the conflict with India; it ensures that they remain politically powerful and handsomely funded. India, by contrast, was established as an explicitly secular country. Including within its borders Kashmir, its only constituent state without a Hindu majority, validates that principle. Furthermore, India, like virtually every other country, is loath to surrender territory that it already governs.

The issue remains explosive. True, as a full-fledged democracy, India has incorporated some of the democratic inhibitions against war. It is also stronger than Pakistan. But although it has been stronger since 1947, this has not prevented Pakistan from attempting to pry Kashmir away from India militarily. Pakistanis have also planned and launched terrorist attacks within India, notably a 2001 attack on the Indian national parliament in New Delhi and a deadly assault on the Indian city of Mumbai in 2008, which thus far have not triggered war but could do so in the future.

Magnifying the potential global economic damage of another Indo-Pakistani conflict is the fact that, since 1998, both countries have possessed nuclear weapons. South Asia is probably the likeliest site of the world's next, and second, nuclear war—the first being the American nuclear attacks on the Japanese cities of Hiroshima and Nagasaki at the end of World War II. The next nuclear shot fired in anger would cause a psychological shock far beyond South Asia, with unpredictable but hardly positive effects on the world's markets. A global-economy-shaking war on the Asian subcontinent is not inevitable, but as long as the status of Kashmir remains contested, it is possible.

Also possible, and with wider ramifications for the global economy than a conflict waged by India or even Russia, is a war involving China. China has the second-largest economy in the world, is a leader in international trade and manufacturing, and owns the largest store of foreign-currency reserves. If anything, those rankings understate China's significance. It stands at the center of the multinational manufacturing networks known as supply chains, as the assembly point for many of the world's manufactured products. A war involving China could disrupt these networks, with severe consequences for all the countries that are part of them and that buy their products.

How likely is such a war? According to one version of international history, it is all too likely. This view, encapsulated by the term "Wilhelmine China," sees history as the ongoing rise and fall of powerful countries,[17] with conflict breaking out when a rising power confronts one already ensconced in a dominant position. Germany under Kaiser Wilhelm was a rising power at the outset of the twentieth century, and its growing strength, combined with its expanding ambitions, led to a conflict with the incumbent dominant power, Great Britain. The result was World War I.[18]

Happily, the world has changed in the century since the outbreak of the First World War and the present. The three ingredients of war-aversion—the economic gains from peace, the war-repelling features of democratic government, and the enormous destructive power of modern weapons—were far weaker then than they are now. Economics in particular affects China's foreign policies. The Chinese have a great deal to lose from anything that injures the global economy, as a war in which they took part surely would.

On the other hand, like Germany a century ago, China in the second decade of the twenty-first century has achieved rapid economic growth, has used some of its new wealth to build up its armed forces, and harbors ambitions for greater power and influence—certainly in its home region and ultimately, perhaps, beyond East Asia. A civilization as old and proud as China's is not likely to consign itself permanently to a mere supporting role in world history. Moreover, several issues have the potential to entangle China in hostilities with its neighbors and with the United States.

China claims sovereignty over waters off its coast that conflict with the claims of Japan, Korea, Vietnam, Thailand, Brunei, Malaysia, and the Philippines. The parts of the seas and oceans over which sovereign states assert control are called their "territorial waters." That is, countries consider them parts of their territory, and the defense of territory remains a universally accepted reason for going to war. Although stopping short of outright conflict, China's armed forces have, in asserting its claims, bumped up against the military forces of rival claimants. The Sino-Japanese dispute over the ownership of five tiny uninhabited islands in the East China Sea, which the Japanese call the Senkakus and the Chinese the Diaoyu, became particularly heated in 2012 and 2013.[19] Nor do these competing claims have merely symbolic significance. Under the disputed waters lie valuable mineral deposits, including oil and natural gas.

To protect the offshore acreage that it claims, China deploys a "white-water" navy, one capable of patrolling coastal regions but not operating in the open seas. It has good reason to develop a wider-ranging "blue-water" navy for patrolling the world's oceans because it depends heavily on seaborne commerce. Ships carry the petroleum that China needs, and the products it makes and sells, over great distances and far beyond the Pacific Ocean. An interruption of that commerce would stifle the Chinese economy; yet, lacking the requisite naval forces, China has no way of preventing this.

To protect its economic lifelines China depends on the world's leading naval power, the United States. If China were to build a fleet comparable to the American one, complete with aircraft carriers, it would pose a serious threat to American naval supremacy, for naval power is a zero-sum game. Either the United States controls the world's sea-lanes or China does; sharing control is not feasible. The German decision to build a high-seas fleet to challenge that of Great Britain contributed to the political tension that led to World War I.[20] A comparable twenty-first-century Chinese decision would raise the specter of a Wilhelmine China. Despite the dangers, China has strong incentives to avoid relying on American naval power to safeguard its maritime trade. The two have radically different political systems, which feeds mistrust on both sides, and the Communist authorities suspect the United States—correctly—of wishing to promote the "peaceful evolution" of the Chinese regime in a democratic direction. Even more importantly, on an issue of central importance to the Chinese—a fundamental territorial issue, as they define it—they are at odds with the United States.

The government in Beijing insists that the island of Taiwan, one hundred miles off the southern China coast, is Chinese territory. The Taiwanese do not accept this claim. Taiwan was declared a province of China only in 1885, was captured by Japan ten years later, and has not been governed from the mainland in the thirteen decades since. The losing side in the Chinese civil war, the Kuomintang, took control of it in 1950. Thereafter, Taiwan became an American ally, an economic dynamo, and, in 1996, a democracy.

For the Communist government of the mainland, and apparently for many of the 1.3 billion people it governs, Taiwan's de facto independence is illegal and unacceptable, the last vestige of the humiliating historical era in which foreigners seized parts of Chinese territory.[21] For their part, the Taiwanese do not wish to be ruled from Beijing and certainly not by a Communist government. This has led to the use of force in the past: in the 1950s the Communist government shelled islands Taiwan controlled in the Taiwan Strait, and as recently as 1996, on the occasion of the island's first democratic presidential election, conducted military operations near Taiwan.

No status for the island would satisfy both sides. The Taiwanese would prefer formal independence, but Beijing has repeatedly said that it will go to war to prevent this. For reasons of prudence, and at the insistence of the United States, the Taiwanese government has refrained from declaring itself fully sovereign, thereby remaining in a kind of limbo: effectively but not officially independent.

The island, the mainland, and the rest of the world have lived with this status for more than six decades and perhaps can live with it for the indefinite future. Peace between China and Taiwan, and therefore the stability of the global economy, depend on its continuation. But it is not certain to continue. The military balance between China and Taiwan is a dynamic one. China is steadily increasing its military might; Taiwan needs American weaponry to counterbalance Beijing's power. Either side upon concluding that the balance was tilting against it—or in its favor—could conceivably be tempted to try to change the status quo: China by attacking, Taiwan by declaring independence.

Moreover, if China's economic success and the growth of its military power could trigger an armed conflict, so, too, could its economic failure. A severe economic downturn would threaten the legitimacy of Communist rule, which, like that of global integration in general, is based on its economic performance. The regime might attempt to compensate with an appeal to nationalist sentiment through a hardening of its policy on Taiwan, perhaps to the point of trying to seize it by force.

Such a course could bring China into direct conflict with the United States, and a Sino-American war could do the kind of damage to the global economy that it suffered in the two world wars. Both countries have nuclear armaments and a war in which they used these weapons would have horrific consequences. Even short of that, a war could bring trans-Pacific trade to a halt, shake the world's markets, devastate global manufacturing, and jeopardize the monetary order on which international commerce depends. As removed as they are from the main flows of global trade and investment, Africans, too, who sell raw materials to China to feed its industrial machine, would feel the effects.

Fortunately, the economic costs of war make the Chinese government reluctant to wage one.[22] The governments of India and Russia are similarly reluctant, and for the same reason: their countries, like China, benefit from the global economy. Indian and Russian leaders' prospects for remaining in power, like those of their Chinese counterparts, rest on the delivery of economic growth, with which war would interfere. They, too, must reckon with the possibility of the disastrous use of nuclear weapons in a conflict involving their own forces.

Yet another restraint common to all three reduces the likelihood of war: the international role of the United States. American foreign policy, and the armed forces that back it up, do more to protect the global economy than simply safeguarding the maritime highways for global trade.

American military power deters Russia and China. During the Cold War the United States said clearly and frequently that it would repel any Soviet act of aggression. In the post–Cold War era the American government does not use such language about Russia and China, but the continuing deployment of American military forces in Europe and East Asia and the close American ties with countries in those regions convey its readiness to fulfill that promise even while not expressing it as explicitly as in the past. During the Cold War the United States was the sheriff on the job; in the post–Cold War era it is the retired sheriff who still lives in town and keeps his gun well oiled.

The American forces in these two regions also reassure the countries there that a sudden, dangerous shift in the military balance will not take place, thereby fostering the confidence necessary for trade and investment.[23] The American military presence in Europe reassures the Europeans that if Russia adopts a Soviet-style policy toward them the United States will be on hand to help them resist, but also reassures post-Communist Russia that Germany, which invaded its territory twice in the last century, will remain safely anchored in an American-led alliance and thus pose no threat. Similarly, in Asia the United States reassures the countries there that they will not have to face China alone while simultaneously reassuring the Chinese that Japan, as an American ally, will not pursue an independent, let alone an aggressive, foreign policy, as it did at China's expense in the 1930s and 1940s.

Beyond deterrence and reassurance, the United States provides the peace-reinforcing service of mediation. American diplomats have worked, with some success, to limit the conflict between India and Pakistan, and to dissuade Taiwan from political steps that could precipitate a war with China. In the conflict between the mainland and Taiwan, America has practiced a combination of deterrence, reassurance, and mediation, keeping the mainland from attacking while preventing the island from declaring independence.

Because of these American policies, and because of the effects of global economic integration, armed conflict on the scale of the two world wars, or war involving one of the major countries, are, for the foreseeable future, a remote prospect. The prospect for lesser wars, however, is not remote. Such wars have the potential to limit, if less severely than major conflicts, cross-border trade and investment. The future of the global economy depends on them as well.

The World's Policeman

Roofs can collapse. They can also leak, making life difficult, although not intolerable, for the inhabitants of the houses they cover. So it is with the global economy. Like a deadly tornado, a major war could rip away the roof that shelters it, as the two world wars did. Fortunately, the countries capable of launching such a war have strong incentives not to do so. Lesser powers, however, have stronger motives for policies that can result in war and their policies have the potential to create leaks in the protective roof, causing disruption to international commerce. Here, too, American power shields international trade and investment. The United States has assumed the duties of plumber and roofer, bearing the lion's share of the responsibility for confronting and containing those who are actively committed to policies injurious to the globalized international economy.

North Korea and Iran harbor aspirations the pursuit of which could punch holes in the global economy's roof. Both are governed by regimes professing an aggressive ideology of the kind that harkens back to the fascism and communism of the twentieth century: North Korea's is a combination of Marxism-Leninism, the cult of personality of the ruling family, and violent nationalism; Iran's is Islamic fundamentalism. Both regimes seek to expand their control—North Korea's over the entire Korean peninsula, Iran's throughout the Middle East. Each has shown itself willing to use force to this end.[24]

Neither has any commitment to the integrated global economy—North Korea stands entirely outside it—and aversion to war plays no part in the thinking of the leaders of either country; on the contrary. Neither has formidable armed forces, although each devotes much of its resources to military purposes and both have worked assiduously to equip themselves with nuclear weapons: North Korea has actually detonated a nuclear device.

It is their respective locations that make each of them a threat to the global economy as, for example, the Congo is not. North Korea is situated between China and South Korea, which has Asia's fourth-largest economy, and is within missile range of the country with the third-largest economy in the world, Japan. A war on the Korean peninsula would almost certainly do significant damage to South Korea and would shake confidence and disrupt commerce throughout East Asia. In Iran's neighborhood, the Persian Gulf, is located much of the world's readily accessible deposits of oil. A war there that seriously interrupted the shipment of oil to the world's industrial powers would cripple the global economy.

The United States has undertaken to prevent war in each place through deterrence. It has stationed 35,000 troops in South Korea to demonstrate its commitment to thwarting a North Korean attack and has deployed naval and air forces in the Persian Gulf to deter Iran. American military power has helped to keep both North Korea and Iran from launching the direct attacks on their neighbors that their ruling ideologies justify, indeed encourage. It has not, however, prevented the two from practicing a different kind of aggression: terrorism.

Terrorists commit violent acts designed to shock and frighten in order to publicize their goals, to demoralize their opponents, and to turn the public against the government if, as sometimes occurs, the government responds harshly and indiscriminately. The North Korean regime has organized the assassination of South Korean officials. The Iranian government has murdered political opponents and citizens and coreligionists of the state it seeks to destroy: Israel. The terrorist act that made the biggest worldwide impression, however, and that enlisted the United States as the leader of a global campaign against terrorism, was the work of others. The attacks of September 11, 2001, on New York City and Washington, D.C., were sponsored by the group known as al Qaeda.

Al Qaeda's announced goal, the creation of a "caliphate" governing all Muslims, is scarcely realistic and its operatives, while present in a number of countries, for the most part lack the strength to challenge, let alone overturn, most established governments, even the weaker ones of the Middle East. Islamic terrorism does not pose a threat on the same scale as did fascism and communism. Terrorism is the weapon of the weak, an ancient tactic that has virtually never achieved the professed goals of its practitioners.[25]

Yet contemporary terrorism, whether state-sponsored, as in the cases of North Korea and Iran, or carried out by stateless networks such as al Qaeda, does threaten the global economy. A successful attack can shake the confidence necessary for economic activity. Estimates of the direct costs of the September 11 assaults range upward of $100 billion, and the indirect costs may have been far higher. The direct costs might have been even greater if the terrorists had been capable of using chemical weapons[26] or nuclear materials. An independent group probably cannot assemble a nuclear explosive by itself[27] (although it could conceivably get one from a sympathetic government, such as North Korea's or Iran's), but employing more easily obtainable radioactive material—a "dirty bomb"—has the potential to create widespread, market-subverting panic.

A terrorist attack would do maximal damage to economic production, trade, and investment around the world if it succeeded in disabling oil production facilities in the Persian Gulf. Terrorists have already unsuccessfully attacked them.[28] The United States has assumed major responsibility for protecting them as well.

The world runs on oil. Most land, sea, and air transport uses it. The concentration of much of the world's accessible oil in the Persian Gulf creates two vulnerabilities for the global economy: it must be shipped over long distances to the places where it is used, including through narrow passages such as the Strait of Hormuz in the Gulf and the Strait of Malacca in the western Pacific; and its region of origin is a politically volatile place.

One day the world may not need Gulf oil. Advances in the technologies of exploration and recovery have made available previously inaccessible oil in more stable parts of the world, including North America, and previously untapped reserves of natural gas, which can sometimes replace oil. Technology also promises to provide—although it is uncertain when—sources of energy other than fossil fuels. For the foreseeable future, however, the world will depend on oil, all the more so as consumption increases in China and India.[29] It will need a steady flow of oil from the Persian Gulf to distant countries, which means depending on the United States.

The American navy protects the oil tankers that traverse the world's oceans and is prepared to resist efforts to interrupt their progress at vulnerable points in their passage. Past interruptions, such as the politically caused reductions in supply of 1973 and 1979—the first the result of an Arab embargo, the second of the Iranian Revolution—raised the price of oil and triggered economic recessions around the world.[30] The United States has also assumed responsibility for protecting Persian Gulf regimes that, however distasteful their governing principles to those who hold Western political values, nonetheless can be trusted to make the oil within their borders available to the rest of the world. When Saddam Hussein, the dictator of Iraq, invaded and occupied Kuwait and menaced neighboring Saudi Arabia in 1990 and 1991, the United States organized and led a military coalition that evicted his forces. The purpose of the campaign was as much to maintain in power the

Saudi monarchy, an American client presiding over the world's largest national supply of oil, as to restore to power the Kuwaiti royal family.[31] In the twenty-first century, to safeguard the world's supply of oil the United States bears the burden of protecting the monarchies of the Gulf—most of them small and weak, none of them a democracy, but almost all of them rich in oil reserves—against the country that seeks to dislodge their governments and control their oil, the Islamic Republic of Iran.

Protecting the Gulf oil states and the oil itself as it is shipped far and wide, practicing deterrence, reassurance, and mediation not only in the Gulf region but in Europe and Asia as well: these are all services that the United States furnishes to the globalized international economy, services that shield cross-border trade, investment, and migration from the disruptions that war brings. The roof over the twenty-first century's globalized economy has two other sources of support—the political legitimacy of globalization and the strength of war-aversion—but the United States is its central pillar. The world economy's future therefore depends heavily on how sturdy that pillar turns out to be.

The United States has been able to function as the world's police force because of its enormous power. Historically, other countries have banded together to resist sovereign states as formidable as twenty-first-century America; but such a coalition has shown no sign of forming in this case because others know that the United States does not threaten them. Indeed, other governments often appreciate the global services America provides, although they almost never say so publicly. While American global power does not confront a serious external challenge, however, it does face threats from within. The great danger to the American role as global policeman comes not from an international consensus against it but from a lack of a domestic consensus in favor of it.

One internal threat stems from the political fatigue arising from the American wars in Afghanistan and Iraq. Neither operation made more than a marginal contribution to supporting the global economy; but the discontent the two of them generated within the United States reduced the American public's tolerance for policies that do.

The services the country provides to the world have another shortcoming: they lack a galvanizing rationale. In fact, Americans do not even think of themselves as providing such services. The United States launched the relevant policies during the Cold War, in order to protect itself and its allies from international communism. When communism collapsed, the policies continued. While safeguarding global commerce, as they do, is an important aim, it is not one the American public finds as urgent, compelling, and worth sustaining at considerable expense as self-defense.

The global-economy-supporting policies survived for two decades after the Cold War ended in 1991 because the United States could readily afford them; but the era when that was the case is coming to an end. The retirement of the baby boom generation— consisting of the 78 million Americans born between 1946 and 1964—will dramatically increase the costs of the country's two most expensive social welfare programs, in which every citizen is entitled to participate: Social Security and Medicare. This will put pressure on other government programs, including those that underwrite the country's global presence. The choice between international and domestic obligations—between guns and butter—which is a political choice, will become increasingly acute.[32] In these circumstances it is likely that Americans will tend to favor domestic expenditures, which benefit them directly.[33] They cannot eat guns.

Whatever the outcome of the inevitable political struggle over government expenditures, the United States will not bring all of its far-flung military forces back to North America. It will remain a formidable—for decades, in all probability, the most formidable— international power. The resources available for foreign policy over the long term will be determined by the country's rate of economic growth, which is unpredictable: it could turn out to be high. Historically, American foreign policy has waxed and waned in response to international events, and these, too, are unforeseeable. Americans might, in the years ahead, come to see the world, and their interests in it, as requiring the kind of policies it was carrying out in the second decade of the twenty-first century no matter what the cost.[34]

Still, it is reasonable to expect that the United States will do less global policing in the future than it has in the past. That would make the roof that shelters the global economy less sturdy and perhaps leakier. A weaker, poorer, less internationally active America could have an indirect effect on cross-border economic activity by making the world a politically and militarily more turbulent place. Such a development would also affect global commerce more directly.

The Factory Manager

Markets need protection in order to function properly, and government supplies that protection. In the nineteenth century that was all that governments supplied. They provided a roof, nothing more. A term came into use to describe this relationship of government to the market: the night watchman state. The government acted as the watchman standing guard at the factory gate to prevent theft or sabotage after the workers had gone home.

In the twentieth century, governments began to do more. They entered the factory and assumed a measure of responsibility for its smooth operation. Government became the manager, overseeing production, and the repair crew, fixing parts of the economy when they broke down. For economic life, security is not the only public good.

The global economy has the same need of management and repair as the national economies that compose it. Indeed, one influential account of the Great Depression of the 1930s imputes its depth and longevity to the lack of any single country willing and able to provide these services internationally: Great Britain was no longer able and the United States was not yet willing to do so.[35]

After World War II the United States did undertake to provide some non-security services to the global economy. It did not do all the things on an international scale that national governments do for the economies within their borders because of the convention of sovereignty—the division of the world into independent countries in each of which its government has ultimate authority. Americans do not pay for the pensions and health care of others, and the United States cannot compel other countries to carry out particular policies for international trade and investment, in both cases thanks to the prerogatives of sovereignty. When domestic interests conflict with international goals, in almost every country almost all the time the domestic interests take precedence.

The predominance of sovereignty means that, for political reasons, the world gets less economic governance than it needs. The absence of world government complicates at best and thwarts entirely at worst effective responses to what is perhaps the most serious long-term problem the world faces—global warming[36]—and to what is certainly its most serious short-term economic challenge—preventing ruinous financial crises.[37]

Sovereignty has not, however, kept the United States from providing two important economic services—two international economic public goods—to other countries: America has offered a market for much of the world's exports; and it has furnished the world with its most widely used currency, the dollar. The future of the global economy therefore depends on whether, and to what extent, it can and will continue to do both.

Sellers need buyers. Countries seeking to export must have welcoming markets for their products. Since 1945 the United States has offered the biggest and most open one, which proved to be big enough and open enough to enable Western Europe to restart economic growth in the wake of World War II partly through exports to the United States. Because they were able to sell so much to Americans, the American market also helped to make the strategy of export-oriented growth that Japan, China, and other Asian countries pursued in the second half of the twentieth century a success. From 1996 to 2005, in fact, America was responsible for almost 45 percent of global growth in consumer spending.[38]

It might seem odd to call American consumers' purchase of goods they desire a "service" to the rest of the world. Consumption is, after all, a self-interested activity; participants in trade engage in it because they benefit, not to confer a favor on the seller. Moreover, it is individual Americans, not the government of the United States, who buy Japanese cars, Korean electronic equipment, and Chinese clothing, household goods, and toys.

Self-interested though it may have been, American consumption did contribute more by far to global economic growth than that of any other country from the 1940s through the first decade of the twenty-first century. Others were not only less wealthy and thus less capable of buying from abroad, they were also less willing to do so: virtually all of them were less welcoming to imports than was the United States. Here again, politics shaped economics. The decisions to open and keep open the American market were political ones, and had political as well as economic motives. They were intended to strengthen America's allies in the common battle against communism as well as enriching America's citizens.

Those decisions had major economic effects, increasing global production, but also important political consequences. Europe's recovery from the destruction of war and the higher economic growth of countries that emphasized exports rather than import-substitution contributed to the late-twentieth-century triumph of the market and of global economic integration. Without the access to its market that the United States provided, the economic history, and therefore the political history, of the twentieth century would have unfolded differently.

As with its contributions to international security, this American service is unlikely to be available on the same scale and with comparable reliability in the future. By the first decade of the new century, American consumption, and global economic growth, were being financed ever more extensively by borrowing. The financial crisis of 2008, in no small part the result of that credit binge, put an end to the pattern. Individual American consumers and households, having suffered large paper losses of wealth, began to rebuild their balance sheets, concentrating more on saving than buying.

The government stepped in with spending programs financed by borrowed money to replace the demand that private consumers were no longer supplying (as well as with tax cuts intended to encourage more consumption). Overall demand fell, however, leading to low growth and high unemployment. And the rising level of debt the government incurred to try to spur economic output, as well as for other reasons, threatened the second important economic service the United States furnished to other countries: the global role of the dollar.

The participants in the international conference to reconstruct the world's monetary order in 1944 at Bretton Woods, New Hampshire, decided not to revive the gold standard. Instead, they devised a system with the American currency at its center: all other countries set the value of their currencies in relation to the dollar, and the dollar itself was tied to gold at the price of $35 per ounce.

The United States put an end to these arrangements on August 15, 1971, when President Richard Nixon severed the dollar's link to gold. This permitted the depreciation of the dollar, something impossible under the Bretton Woods rules. The president acted for domestic political reasons. The dollar's elevated value had come to hurt American exporters and thus it reduced employment in the United States, which Nixon considered a political liability for his candidacy in the upcoming 1972 presidential election. Faced with a conflict between a domestic—that is a national—interest and an international obligation, the United States chose to exercise its sovereign prerogative to act for its own good rather than for the world's benefit.[39]

Nonetheless, the dollar retained a central role in the global economy after the demise of the Bretton Woods system. Countries held dollars as reserves, to back their own currencies and to use in international transactions. The price of many internationally traded goods and commodities—oil being the outstanding example—were denominated in dollars, and a large fraction of global commerce continued to be conducted in the American currency.[40]

The world used the dollar for the same reason that currencies originally came into use and national governments came to supply them: convenience. Without currencies, trade would be reduced to the clumsy, costly, time-consuming localized barter of one product or commodity for another, which is the way long-distance exchanges were often conducted before the beginning of globalization in the nineteenth century. Without a common international currency, cross-border trade would always require converting one national currency into another, an uncertain process when currency values fluctuate and an inconvenient one at any time since most national currencies can be used only in their country of origin.

The dollar's global status remained secure as long as the world remained confident that it would retain its value and be accepted everywhere.[41] (National currencies also, of course, have to be relatively stable in value and acceptable within the country's borders for people to be willing to hold them.) In the second decade of the twenty-first century, however, that confidence began to waver. The severe financial crisis of 2008 called into question the American capacity to manage the financial system on which the dollar rests. The inability of the American federal government to reduce its swelling budget deficits caused particular concern globally: it raised the possibility that, faced with large national debt (the cumulative total of annual deficits), the American government would print the dollars needed for debt service and repayment, causing inflation that would reduce the value of all the dollars held around the world.[42] In response to the country's financial policies, in August 2011 the rating agency Standard & Poor's downgraded the credit rating of the United States for the first time.

A shaky dollar should, in theory, make other currencies attractive candidates to assume its international responsibilities. In the second decade of the twenty-first century, however, no other currency qualified.[43] The euro, to which seventeen wealthy European countries belonged and that made up roughly a quarter of the world's reserve holdings, was embroiled in a crisis so grave that its very survival was in serious doubt. Political decisions would determine whether, and in what form, the euro survived,[44] as they would determine whether and when the Chinese currency, the renminbi, would join the dollar as a full-fledged global reserve.

The renminbi has the advantage of being issued by a country with a large and rapidly growing economy. The Chinese government has expressed interest in having its currency achieve the global status the dollar has enjoyed. As matters stand, however, citizens, businesses, and governments in other countries have little incentive to hold China's currency.

It is not freely convertible into other currencies. Even if it were, unlike the United States, China does not have deep, varied, and liquid capital markets in which foreigners can invest. And the renminbi's exchange rate remains under the control of the Chinese government, which means that the value of the currency, and thus the net worth of all who hold it, are subject to the whims and wishes of the ruling Communist Party. Here again, politics will govern the economic future. A political decision by the Party to reduce its own power over the Chinese economy is required to build the confidence necessary for the renminbi to function as has the dollar.[45]

If all national currencies have drawbacks as international mediums of exchange—and they do—it would seem sensible to establish a truly global currency. Keynes suggested this at the Bretton Woods Conference, where he was representing Great Britain, but nothing came of his suggestion.[46] A germ of a global currency does exist, in the form of Special Drawing Rights (SDRs). These consist of a basket of four currencies—the dollar, the yen, the euro, and the British pound[47]—and are issued by the International Monetary Fund (IMF). They make up, however, less than 5 percent of the world's total reserves, and governments holding 85 percent of the voting power in the IMF must agree on issuing them, something that is not always easy to achieve.

The difficulty in managing SDRs points to the central obstacle to the creation of a genuine global currency, which is rooted in politics as well as in the institution of sovereignty. A genuine global authority, a kind of global central bank, would have to supervise it, and the countries of the world are unlikely to surrender their sovereign powers over their own monetary policies in order to create one. The countries using the euro did surrender this sovereign power, but their experience in so doing has not been such as to encourage the Americans, Japanese, and Chinese or anyone else to follow their example.

Here again, politics shapes economics and sovereignty obstructs the provision of an international public good. What seems economically reasonable, even necessary, is politically impossible because nations and their governments reserve the right to act in ways that serve their own interests, even at the expense of global well-being. Nor, it should be added, can this be understood simply as an instance of shortsighted human selfishness prevailing over wise, disinterested action that will ultimately benefit all: if one desirable aspect of government is efficiency, including efficiency at supplying public goods, another and perhaps even more important feature is democracy. The policies of individual sovereign states, where governments are chosen through free elections and that protect economic, religious, and political liberty, do reflect the will of the people. It is not at all clear how a global government would or could function democratically, especially since it would necessarily encompass countries that are not themselves democracies.

If the United States proves unable to supply all of the protection and economic services that the global economy will need in the years ahead, if no other single country can replace the United States in this role, and if pooling national sovereignties to create a global government to furnish these heretofore American-provided international public goods is politically infeasible and in important respects undesirable as well, one other way of doing so still remains. It is the most promising alternative, or supplement, to the American role as the world's quasi-government. The member states of the international system, or at least some of them, might cooperate, while retaining sovereign independence, to do some or all of what the United States has done to sustain the integrated global economy.

The Future of International Cooperation

Sustained cooperation among independent countries, both the idea and practice of it, was born in the nineteenth century and came into its own in the twentieth. Once confined to occasional, temporary military alliances formed to fight specific wars and dissolved after their conclusion, cooperation has become routine. International organizations are the vehicles for cooperation and the post–World War II era is the great age of international organizations. Most that have ever existed were established only after 1945.

The proliferation of organizations in which cooperation on a wide range of issues takes place—or is intended to take place—suggests a logical progression in the provision of services to the global economy. Just as Great Britain gave way to the United States as the world's quasi-government in the twentieth century, so, in the twenty-first, American global leadership will yield to international cooperation for this purpose. The world will become a version of a cooperatively owned apartment building in the United States, in which each resident pays a fee for the maintenance of its common areas, including the roof.

Unfortunately, a smooth transition from an American night watchman and factory manager to a team of countries furnishing the same services is not likely. Once again, sovereignty stands in the way. International organizations and ad hoc multinational groupings, rather than requiring independent countries to give up their sovereign prerogatives, allow them to exercise those prerogatives, which can block effective action.

For one thing, the greater the number of countries that must agree on a course of action, the more difficult it will be ever to reach agreement. At the Bretton Woods Conference, Great Britain and the United States dominated the proceedings, and the United States was by far the stronger of the two. In the second decade of the twenty-first century, the equivalent of the two of them, the group with nominal responsibility for managing the global economy, was the Group of Twenty. It is far more difficult to coordinate twenty entities than to coordinate two.[48]

This is so because countries can and do disagree. In 2012, for example, as popular resistance to the long-ruling Assad regime in Syria threatened a region-wide conflict that could endanger access to Middle Eastern oil, the United States and its western European allies insisted that the regime's leaders give up power, while the Russians and the Chinese wanted Assad to remain in charge. Had they all been able to agree they might have generated the political pressure necessary for peaceful political change in Syria; but they could not agree.

Even when they do agree on goals, countries often differ on how to achieve them, thereby blocking effective multilateral action. All major countries agree that North Korea should not possess nuclear weapons. China could exert maximal pressure on the regime in Pyongyang to give up its nuclear program by cutting off the food and fuel it supplies, but despite the urgings of other countries, especially the United States, the Chinese government has declined to do so. It fears the collapse of the North Korean regime and refuses to implement policies that might bring this about, even at the cost of permitting North Korea a nuclear arsenal.

Finally, for a particular problem sovereign states may agree on both the desirable goals and the appropriate methods for reaching them but differ about which country will contribute what to the agreed solution. Disagreement about who will pay how much of the salaries of the night watchman and the factory manager of the global economy is a perennial obstacle to the supply of public goods that that economy's smooth functioning requires.

Since 1945 an international organization with universal membership has in theory had responsibility for global security, but the United Nations cannot act when its most influential member states, the five veto-wielding permanent members of the organization's Security Council, disagree, as they almost always did during the Cold War and often have since. The Soviet dictator Joseph Stalin, told that he ought to take into account the views of the Vatican, responded scornfully, "How many divisions does the Pope have?" The United Nations has exactly the same number as the Holy Father—zero—so even when the five permanent members all agree on a military operation, the member states must provide the manpower. In 1991 the U.N. authorized the eviction of Iraqi forces from Kuwait, which certainly made assembling a broad coalition for this purpose easier than it would have been otherwise; but it was the United States that took the lead in organizing the coalition and that supplied most of the troops that won the war.

In the post–Cold War era, ad hoc military coalitions have formed to conduct several military operations: in the Balkans in 1995 and 1998 under the auspices of the North Atlantic Treaty Organization (NATO); in Libya in 2011, with a UN Security Council resolution but also the approval of both NATO and the Arab League; and in 2003 in Iraq without the blessing of any international organization.[49] In each case, while a number of countries took part, the vast majority of the troops and most of the firepower they employed came from the United States. The others approved, and showed up, but didn't pay much.[50] These were less multinational military operations than American operations with multinational trimming. The others supplied the frosting: the cake was made in America. None offers a precedent for the genuinely multilateral management of threats to the global economy's protective roof.

The countries most often willing to join the United States have been the Europeans and the Japanese. This is not surprising: they are Cold War era allies and have decades-long histories of cooperation among themselves and with the Americans, with whom they share political values and economic interests. So pervasive had the sentiment of war-aversion become in the twenty-first century in these once-formidable military powers, however, and so accustomed had they become to leaving their own defense to the United States, that most of them had only modest military forces.[51] They could manage only minor participation in military operations. They avoided contributing a major share of the military forces to these operations by not having military forces to contribute.

If and as American power contracts, the world will have to rely on the strength of Western war-aversion, not the active military policies of other countries, to keep the peace: the prospects for replacing or supplanting the United States as the protector of the global economy with cooperation among other countries are poor. The prospects for the collective provision of the more strictly economic services that the United States has supplied are, fortunately, somewhat better.

In order to sustain global purchasing power at an economically healthy level while American consumption retrenches, other countries must consume more. The leading candidates to do so are Germany, Japan, and China. Historically each has saved and exported on a large scale, which American consumption and imports have helped to offset. They have saved more than they have spent domestically and sold more than they have purchased internationally for the same ultimate reason that Japan, Germany, and other European countries lack robust military forces: politics, specifically a series of policies adopted over a number of years that have favored exports and saving. To replace American consumption they will have to reverse or modify these policies.

It will be easier for savers to spend more at home and buy more from abroad to compensate for the retreat of American purchasing power than for war-averse countries to build up their armies, navies, and air forces to compensate for the retreat of American military power. Replacing spending does not involve the degree of international coordination that effective military operations do. Nor would independent decisions to pursue more expansive economic policies by China, Germany, and Japan alarm other countries, as would independently undertaken military expansion by any of the three. To the contrary, unilateral economic expansion would be taken as a sign of good international citizenship. Unilateral military expansion, outside an agreed-upon international framework, would be seen as a step toward damaging, not reinforcing, the roof that protects the global economy.

In addition, the citizens of the exporting and saving countries would be happy to consume more. Doing so would raise their standards of living. By contrast, they would not welcome the costs, sacrifices, and risks that a higher regional or global military profile would bring. Still, formidable political obstacles in all the relevant countries stand in the way of the economic policies needed to rebalance global consumption.[52]

As for the world's need for a global currency, here, too, it is feasible for other countries to help supply an economically necessary international public good. Already at least a third of all international reserves are held in currencies other than the dollar. If the European Union manages to stabilize its monetary affairs, and the Chinese government liberalizes its financial system—two big ifs, to be sure—the proportion of euros and renminbi in international reserve portfolios will grow, at the expense of the dollar. The world can accommodate several reserve currencies, and to the extent that confidence ebbs in the dominant one, the addition of others would serve to strengthen the global economy.[53]

To summarize, international cooperation as a way of supplying the protection the global economy needs seems a dubious prospect, but the multinational provision of more strictly economic services is more plausible, in no small part because it does not require active cooperation and coordination. A collection of countries cannot readily substitute for the single night watchman who protects the global economy, but can, in principle, do the job of the factory manager.

Of all international public goods, one stands out for its potential long-term significance. Success or failure in providing it may, over the long term, determine—*will* determine, according to some scientists—the fate of the planet and its human inhabitants. The United States alone, even on the most optimistic reading of its political future, cannot furnish it. This public good involves restraining the rise of the Earth's temperature. It can only be supplied through international cooperation, and in the second decade of the twenty-first century the prospects for such cooperation seemed decidedly poor.

The "greenhouse effect" is causing the Earth's temperature to rise. Heat-trapping gases accumulate in the planet's atmosphere and reflect heat back to its surface, making it warmer.[54] In recent decades the world's mean temperature has risen unusually rapidly. At the same time, the blanket of heat-trapping gases has thickened unusually rapidly. Scientists have no good explanation for what has come to be called global warming other than the increase in the concentration of greenhouse gases—most of it through human activity, above all (but not exclusively) the burning of fossil fuels. This, in turn, is the consequence of the expansion of fuel-consuming economic growth that global economic integration has helped make possible.

Up to a point the greenhouse effect confers a priceless benefit: it makes the planet warm enough for comfortable human habitation. The increasing emission of greenhouse gas threatens, however, to push the Earth's temperature to dangerous levels. Estimates of the effects of too-steep rises (the figure usually cited as the upper bound of a safe increase is 2 degrees centigrade) sound like latter-day versions of the biblical plagues visited on the Egyptians as described in the book of Exodus: massive floods, destructive storms, terrible droughts. At worst, the human-generated increase in the

Earth's temperature could cause the kind of destruction associated with major wars.[55]

The problem that global warming presents is in some ways a familiar one. The greenhouse effect is a form of air pollution. It differs from other forms, however, in that it cannot be effectively addressed by single countries, let alone smaller jurisdictions. All greenhouse gas emissions everywhere contribute to a rise in temperature of the entire planet, and thus affect all countries. Nor does the United States, the largest consumer of fossil fuel per capita, generate so much of the world's total emissions that by unilaterally reducing its own it could solve the problem. Restraining the rise in the Earth's temperature is a global public good for which action by a number of countries is indispensable.

Air pollution whose effects are felt mainly locally, or nationally, is controlled by government-imposed regulations. In the absence of a formal global government, limiting the emission of greenhouse gases depends on voluntarily cooperation. Efforts at achieving it have failed. The Kyoto Protocol, adopted in 1997, did not reduce the overall rate of greenhouse gas emissions; China and the United States, the two largest emitters did not agree to it. A follow-up conference in Copenhagen in 2009 failed entirely.

The obstacle to addressing global warming effectively through international cooperation is familiar: disagreement about cost-sharing. Capping the rise in the Earth's temperature will require using far less fossil fuel, but the use of the three main such fuels—coal, oil, and natural gas—pervades the global economy. Substitutes for them are less plentiful than they, and more expensive. Large-scale substitution would reduce global output in the short term, making people poorer.

The best way to reduce the use of fossil fuels is to raise their price through taxation. Higher prices lead immediately to conservation: people use less. In the long run, higher prices would encourage substitution through innovation. Alternative sources of energy would become more viable commercially, which would attract investment and produce technological progress in non-fossil fuels. The immediate impact of higher energy prices, however, would be to penalize everybody. Not surprisingly, energy taxes do not command broad popular support, especially where they are most needed, in the United States and China.

Deciding who will pay what to obtain this particular global public good—indeed, persuading anybody to pay anything for it—faces special difficulties. While the fact of global warming is well established, its precise consequences are uncertain. Just how fast the Earth's temperature will rise is unknown.[56] Climate scientists cannot say where, when, and at what magnitudes the storms, floods, and droughts they anticipate will occur. The ultimate social, economic, and political costs of global temperature increase therefore cannot be predicted, which makes it impossible to say how much sacrifice it would be worthwhile to make to avoid incurring those costs.

Whatever the consequences of global warming turn out to be, moreover, they will arrive in the future, perhaps the distant future. To reduce global warming, governments and those they govern must pay in the present to obtain benefits that most of them will not live to enjoy and that, because these benefits consist in avoiding costs, even their descendants will not notice.

Voluntary sacrifice is not unknown. Individuals and countries do make sacrifices, for example—sometimes far greater than controlling global warming would require—for the sake of a better future when they go to war. War, however, presents a clear and present danger, which creates a powerful incentive for action. Global warming, by contrast, presents a distant, uncertain peril and so does not trigger a comparable public commitment.[57] The countries of the world are more likely to cope with the consequences of global warming by adapting to them, which they can and presumably will do by means of individual domestic policies, than by international cooperation to prevent them.

In that case, the global economy's protective roof—even if war-aversion, the legitimacy of international economic integration,

American military power and some multilateral policies continue to support it—would do little to shield international economic activity from whatever the effects of global warming turn out to be.

• • •

In 1857 Richard Cobden, an English politician, declared that "Free trade is God's diplomacy, and there is no other certain way of uniting people in the bonds of peace."[58] He was expressing an expectation that the emergence of a genuinely globalized economy in the middle of the nineteenth century inspired: that globalization would abolish war. The more countries gained by trading with one another, the reasoning went, the more they would have to lose by fighting each other. Eventually, none of them would fight. Another Englishman, Norman Angell, published a widely read book in 1910 entitled *The Great Illusion* arguing that the economies of European countries had become so closely integrated with one another that war had become obsolete.

Alas, the expectation of a entirely peaceful future proved inaccurate for the twentieth century. In the twenty-first century, however, the world has moved in the direction that Cobden and Angell had predicted. Armed conflict continues to take place, but the largest, strongest countries are more reluctant to wage war on a large scale than ever before, in no small part because globalization gives them so much to lose by doing so. War is to the protective roof that shields the global economy what tornadoes are to the roofs of houses in their path: a mortal threat. In the twenty-first century those globalization-threatening storms have become rarer and milder, brightening the prospects for trade, investment, and immigration in the years ahead.

The hundred years between the end of the Napoleonic Wars in 1815 and the outbreak of World War I in 1914 were, with important exceptions, peaceful and prosperous in no small part because the roof over the global economy received support from Great Britain. In the twentieth century Britain could not continue this support and its loss of power contributed to the collapse of globalization between 1914 and 1945. Now the United States, which replaced Britain as the mainstay of globalization, faces challenges to its own capacity to provide the military, political, and economic public goods that the British once did. Fortunately for globalization's future, the United States has a stronger position in the twenty-first century than Britain did in the twentieth: it is more populous, produces a larger share of total global output, has a more powerful military in comparison with the armed forces of other countries, has a wider, more robust network of friends and allies, and does not, as did Britain, depend for its strength on a far-flung but fragile empire. America's globalization-supporting power will almost certainly decline in the decades ahead, but not nearly as sharply or rapidly as Britain's did.

In addition to the dimensions and durability of the American global role and the frequency and severity of wars, the future of globalization will depend on the scope of international cooperation to support it. Here the prospects are mixed: reasonably good for the economic services that support cross-border trade, investment, and immigration, but poorer for joint military tasks.

Cooperation to cope with what may ultimately prove to be the greatest danger to international well-being, global warming, is unlikely. Yet even here the prospects for the future are not entirely bleak, because of the United States. While the American government has been unwilling to join any international agreement to reduce its emissions of temperature-increasing greenhouse gases, private American energy companies have produced an innovation that is having precisely such an effect.

They have developed the process of hydraulic fracturing—"fracking"—of rock by the use of pressurized fluid, which provides access to large quantities of hitherto inaccessible natural gas. Because it has a milder environmental impact than, and can be substituted for, coal and oil, the more extensive the use of natural gas becomes, the lower the emission of global-warming-causing greenhouse gases will be. Despite the absence of effective international cooperation, therefore, the United States is helping to lessen the danger of climate change.

Even with the protective roof firmly in place and the effects of a warming planet far milder than many scientists predict, however, the global economy will still be subject to disruptive shocks. Compared to the shocks wars and financial crises administer, these will be modest; but they will also occur more frequently. Indeed, they will occur constantly. These shocks, the subjects of the next chapter, are a regular, integral feature of the contemporary international economy, the unavoidable consequences of globalization.

CHAPTER TWO

THE GATES

There are no gains without pains.

—Benjamin Franklin

. . . social dislocation, and consequently often social resistance, may
result when economies become more open. . . . The resulting shifts
in the structure of production impose costs on workers and business
owners in some industries and thus create a constituency that opposes
the process of economic integration. More broadly, increased economic interdependence may also engender opposition by stimulating
social or cultural change, or by being perceived as benefiting some
groups much more than others.

—Ben Bernanke[1]

Creative Destruction

Joseph Schumpeter had three ambitions in life: to be the world's best
horseman, its greatest lover, and its foremost economist. History does
not record his equestrian or amatory achievements, but he did become
one of the twentieth century's most influential economic thinkers. His
principal economic legacy is an oxymoronic phrase from which arises
the second important way in which politics will determine the future
of the global economy: creative destruction.

In his 1942 book *Capitalism, Socialism, and Democracy*, Schumpeter wrote that market capitalism "is by nature a form or method of economic change and not only never is but never can be stationary. . . . The fundamental impulse that sets and keeps the capitalist engine in motion comes from the new consumers' goods, the new methods of production or transportation, the new markets, the new forms of industrial organization that capitalist enterprise creates." Market activity "incessantly revolutionizes the economic structure *from within*, incessantly destroying the old one, incessantly creating a new one. This process of Creative Destruction is the essential fact about capitalism."[2]

It is the process of creative destruction that produces economic growth, and economic growth is the Holy Grail of economic activity. It makes individuals richer, governments more popular, and countries more powerful. Economic growth is the purpose and the achievement of, and thus the rationale and source of support for, global economic integration. It comes, however, at a price.

Growth occurs, as Schumpeter noted, through production by new people, or in new places, or in new ways, or of new things altogether—or through some or all of these. This creates more and better food, shelter, clothing, tools, and all the other things human beings need and want, but those invested in the old ways lose out. Hand in hand with creation goes the disruption of settled routines, the destruction of established enterprises, the dispossession of people whose jobs are done more efficiently elsewhere or no longer done at all. All this threatens others who are not immediately affected but upon whom economic growth may some day visit the same fate.

Creative destruction means the creation, but also the destruction, of jobs, firms, entire economic sectors, and the customs and neighborhoods that go with them. The repeal of the Corn Laws in Great Britain in 1846, which inaugurated the first era of globalization, gave British workers and city-dwellers cheaper food and American farmers higher profits; but the owners of the great grain-growing landed estates throughout the United Kingdom, and those who labored on these estates, were made worse off economically: many had to give up their properties or leave their homes for different jobs in other places. Londoners won; landowners and those they employed lost. The losses that creative destruction causes invariably lead to a political backlash, and the backlash against globalization will shape the global economy in the twenty-first century—as it did in the twentieth and nineteenth.

As market-driven economic growth generates winners and losers, the losers act to defend themselves by mounting political resistance to whatever they believe is injuring them, with almost the same regularity as the human immune system produces antibodies in response to the intrusion of bacteria and viruses. This backlash against markets' destruction is normal, natural, and inevitable. It varies in strength over time and from place to place.

The political response to global economic activity takes place at the national level. A national government controls its country's borders, which means that a government-administered fence runs, metaphorically (and sometimes literally), along those borders. It is punctuated by occasional gates through which goods, money, and people from abroad can enter.[3] Those who are or feel injured by cross-border flows, or anticipate being injured in the future, act politically to pull the gates closed. Those in favor of these flows enter the political arena for the opposite purpose: to push the gates open. The ensuing tug-of-war takes the form of political contests over trade, investment, and immigration, which dominate the domestic politics of the countries that take part in the globalized international economy.[4] Because democracies guarantee their citizens the right to organize to achieve political goals, the contests tend to be more intense in democratic than in undemocratic countries.

While it is in one sense normal, the political resistance to cross-border economic activity is in another way odd. Economic growth causes injury, to be sure, but for most countries most of the time the sources of growth, and of injury—the new workers, the relocation of production, the new products—do not come from abroad. They originate *inside* national borders. Closing the gates at the border cannot eliminate them: jobs and firms move more frequently within countries than from one to another. Moreover, by many accounts the major cause of dislocation and displacement, as well as of economic growth, is technological change, not the cross-border movement of goods, money, and people.[5] Why then does the political backlash almost everywhere have as its principal target perceived economic threats from abroad?

For one thing, it is much easier to control economic activity across than within borders. Countries seldom build fences within their own territories. Trying to block goods, money, and people from abroad is in this sense a case of looking for a lost key under the street lamp at night not because that is where it was lost but because that is where it is easiest to look. Furthermore, suppressing technological change is not only difficult, it is widely seen in the twenty-first century, after almost 250 years of such change, as futile and therefore foolish—a deluded fantasy akin to the legend of King Canute trying to hold back the tide.

Perhaps the most powerful reason for seeking to block inflows from abroad, however, stems from the significance of borders. They do more than merely define an administrative unit. They demarcate a nation—a community whose members feel a common destiny with and a common responsibility for one another. The sense of belonging to a national community—nationalism—was the most powerful political force of the nineteenth and twentieth centuries and remains potent in the twenty-first.

Economic injuries inflicted on the national community by outsiders seem less acceptable than the more extensive injuries that come from within. The losses from international activity are widely seen not as simply the results of the normal workings of free markets, which is what they generally are, but rather as the products of assaults, similar to military attacks. While cross-border trade, investment, and immigration all provoke resistance based on nationalist sentiment because they injure some part of the national community, the three differ in the types of injury they inflict.

Trade imposes economic costs. Workers in industries that compete with similar goods made or grown elsewhere (such as nineteenth-century British farmers) get lower wages or lose their jobs entirely. The proprietors of import-competing firms earn lower profits or lose their businesses altogether. The victims of trade thus have powerful, concrete, indeed quantifiable economic incentives to resist it. Those not directly injured often sympathize with the plight of their fellow citizens and support trade-restricting measures to help them.

The appeal of restricting trade is evident in the word for it: "protection." Outside the context of trade, the word has a positive connotation. Protection of the weak and vulnerable, of family, friends, and neighbors, is a good thing. It is often a religious, moral, or civic duty. Those seeking to open their countries' gates to trade, however, can also invoke a widely shared value. The term for what they seek to do is "liberalization," from *liber*, the Latin word for "free." Trade liberalization does promote human freedom, the freedom to buy and sell. It is the economic counterpart of the political term "liberation."

The cross-border movement of people causes economic injury as well, but its costs go beyond profit, wages, and joblessness. Immigration can threaten, or at least seem to threaten, to alter a country's social fabric—its language, its customs, its religious orientation, and even its legal system. It threatens, that is, a society's sense of its own collective identity, and that can generate a powerful backlash. The very things that make a nation what it is seem to be under assault. As for the resistance to investment from abroad, this stems from the conviction that foreign capital can gain an unhealthy degree of control over the affairs of the country where it is invested. Money from other countries, it is feared, puts at risk sovereignty itself, the major political goal of nationalism.

These three kinds of concerns—economic, cultural, and political—have fueled backlashes against cross-border flows since a genuinely integrated global economy first came into existence in the middle of the nineteenth century. Through the years, globalization has generated resistance of one kind or another among rich and poor countries alike. By the second decade of the twenty-first century, however, most of the opposition was to be found among the pioneers of globalization, the core members of the post-1945 integrated economic order, the trilateral countries of the West: the United States, Japan, and the nations of western Europe.

The Politics of Trade

Trade is the oldest cross-border economic activity: exchange over long distances has taken place for millennia. It is also the most visible: more of the world's people have owned, seen, or eaten something made or grown abroad than are personally acquainted with an immigrant or have direct experience with foreign investment. Moreover, trade has been a quintessentially political matter, an issue on which economics proposes but politics disposes.

The politics of trade varies, of course, from country to country, but virtually everywhere it involves the interplay of three features of economic and political life: the economic law of comparative advantage; the inevitably unequal economic impact of trade within the countries engaging in it; and a political tendency, found even—indeed especially—in democracies, toward minority rule.

The principle of comparative advantage, first formulated by the English economist David Ricardo in 1819, states that two countries that trade with each other will both benefit even if one has an advantage over the other in producing everything that they exchange. Each can make itself better off if the superior producer concentrates on the products in which its advantage is relatively greatest and buys from the other the things for which its advantage is comparatively smaller. The implication is clear and momentous: all trade everywhere is good because all countries benefit from it in all circumstances. Comparative advantage, so stated, is a law of economics in the same way that the law of gravity is a law of physics: it is always and everywhere true.[6]

Over two centuries economists' studies have vindicated Ricardo. Trade does make the countries engaging in it better off, which is the reason that the volume of world trade has expanded. It has not, however, expanded steadily, or without opposition. The resistance to unrestricted trade, the political efforts to keep countries' gates closed to products from outside their borders, has come from two sources: the unequal economic impact of trade within countries and the political consequences of this particular form of inequality.

The Stolper-Samuelson theorem, formulated by the American economists Wolfgang Stolper and Paul Samuelson in 1941, although not as well known as Ricardo's law of comparative advantage, does almost as much to explain the politics of trade, and in particular the omnipresent backlash against it. The theorem states that when two countries trade, the highest returns for each will accrue to the factor—ordinarily capital or labor—used intensively in the traded product. (The theorem is based on a model of trade devised by the Swedish economists Eli Heckscher and Bertil Ohlin in 1919, which holds that countries will tend to export products that make intensive use of the factor they possess in abundance.) Stolper-Samuelson provides the key to understanding the politics of trade because it shows that, while countries as a whole always gain from trade, as per Ricardo, the gains are invariably distributed unequally within those countries, and some people are bound to lose.[7]

Its unequal impact within countries pitches trade into the political arena, as the losers act to block the imports that have penalized them. Still, the winners from trade almost always outnumber the losers. Since they have the advantage of numbers they should, theoretically, be able to push the gates of their countries open to products from abroad. Often, however, they have been unable to do so. Often, in fact, they haven't even tried. Why is this so? And how can it happen in democracies, where, by definition, the majority rules?

It happens because in politics, particularly democratic politics, minorities can get their way at the expense of the majority when the minority's motivation is strong and the majority's is not, as is often the case with trade. Ordinarily, the gains from trade are diffuse while the losses are concentrated. The numerous beneficiaries of trade all make modest gains—a slightly lower price for an imported shirt than they would pay for a domestically made one, for example. The losers, by contrast, often lose a great deal: in this case the jobs of the domestic shirtmakers.[8] So while the gains exceed the losses overall, each winner gains so little that he or she has no incentive to act to preserve his or her gains. In fact, winners from international trade are typically unaware that they are making any gains at all. The losers, by contrast, because each loses so much, have a powerful motive to act politically—by organizing, lobbying, making campaign contributions, and voting—to prevent or reverse their losses.[9] The American comedian and film maker Woody Allen is credited with observing that "ninety percent of life is showing up." In political battles over trade the losers usually show up and the winners usually don't.[10] For that reason the losers, although outnumbered by them, carry more political weight than do the winners.[11]

Those striving to shut the gates to imports have advantages beyond the peculiar political arithmetic of trade. They can invoke national solidarity: they are protecting the livelihoods of people who belong to the same national community.[12] They need not necessarily get formal tariffs enacted to keep out foreign products. Governments erect non-tariff barriers to trade, such as quotas, health and safety regulations, and a managed currency.

The economics of trade—the fact that, because of comparative advantage, exchange always makes countries engaging in it richer—raises the question of why the gates to imports are ever shut. The politics of trade, on the other hand, which confers such a powerful advantage on those resisting the inflow of goods and services from abroad, not only answers that question but raises the opposite one: why are the gates ever open?

Trade takes place because Ricardo was right. It does make all countries and most people richer, and becoming richer is something that virtually everyone strongly desires. All trade, to put it another way, may be understood as an ongoing experiment to test Ricardo's theory; and the results of the experiment have validated the theory.

The original impulse to conduct the experiment arose from historical circumstances. In 1846, the shifting balance of political power in Britain prompted the repeal of the Corn Laws: the new middle class prevailed over the landowners.[13] Trade received another jolt of political support in the wake of World War II. The leaders of the United States were convinced that restrictions on trade in the 1930s had worsened the Great Depression and contributed to the political developments that had led to World War II. Determined to prevent a recurrence of those two disasters, they promoted the freeing of trade, using America's formidable economic power and political influence.

They also helped to establish formal, multilateral institutions that propped open the gates to imports. The General Agreement on Tariffs and Trade (GATT), which 128 countries ultimately joined, committed its adherents to lowering barriers to goods made abroad. The eight rounds of negotiation that took place between 1947 and 1995 had the same purpose. The built-in resistance to trade inspired these negotiations, whose sponsors assumed that without an ongoing process for opening the gates to trade the inevitable countervailing pressures would pull them shut.

The existence of multilateral negotiations pays tribute to the power of the resistance to trade in another way. These negotiations rest on the assumption that one country will not open its borders to imports from another unless the other opens its own borders as well. Multilateral negotiations are necessary because unilateral opening is impossible. The proposition is usually (although not always) politically accurate, but it is economically foolish: any country will gain economically by accepting exports from another *even of the other does not reciprocate.* In the parlance of trade negotiations, agreeing to admit a class of products from abroad is called a "concession" to others, even though the country making the concession is not conceding an advantage but rather obtaining a benefit.

The magazine that calls itself a newspaper, *The Economist*, which was founded in London in 1843 to promote the repeal of the Corn Laws, summarized the political logic of the twenty-first-century trade negotiations in this way: "Multilateral liberalization is a sort of jujitsu that uses exporters' determination to get into foreign markets to overwhelm domestic lobbies that would sooner keep home markets closed. The trade diplomat's incantation that to open his market is a 'concession' granted in exchange for an opening somewhere else is an economic nonsense spouted for domestic political purposes."[14]

After 1945, governments in the trilateral countries reinforced tolerance for trade, or at least reduced opposition to it, through increasingly generous programs for the losers from it—unemployment insurance and job retraining in particular. These programs were a way for the whole country to chip in to compensate (and rehabilitate) the victims of trade, just as countries do for the victims of war.

Perhaps most importantly, the politics of trade changed as trade increased. In every country increasing numbers of individuals, firms, and sectors of the economy exported what they made. Exporters have a stake in keeping the gates of their countries open to imports so that other countries will keep their own gates open as well. They favor openness to imports because they fear, for good reason, that protection will provoke retaliation against the products that they themselves sell. Exporters are therefore winners from trade and have the same kind of incentive to act politically to free it as the losers have to restrict it. While the vast majority of the winners from trade are consumers, who don't realize that they are gaining something, exporters are winners who do understand this very well and act accordingly.

In the twenty-first century the line between exporting and import-competing firms has eroded. Many companies have come to do both. They often rely on suppliers from different countries to make the component parts of their final products. An airplane made by Boeing, the flagship aircraft manufacturer of the United States, for example, draws on suppliers at more than 130 sites around the world.[15]

The events that created a third distinct period of global economic integration at the outset of the 1990s imparted renewed momentum to the expansion of trade. Countries that joined the global economy after discarding centrally planned economic systems or radically modifying economic strategies of import-substitution embraced the cross-border exchange they had previously shunned. Some actually did what the trilateral countries had been reluctant to do after 1945: reduce their own barriers to trade unilaterally. Between 1983 and 2003, 65 percent of all tariff reductions occurred in this way.[16] The volume and value of global trade soared. As the new century wore on, however, the momentum faltered, and the headwinds to trade became more powerful.

The multilateral trade negotiations begun at Doha, Qatar, in 2001 made little progress. Tariffs on manufactured products, the traditional subject of such negotiations, had already come down to very low levels almost everywhere[17] and it proved difficult to reach agreement on other tradeable items such as agricultural products and services. In agriculture, the political arithmetic of trade generated particularly strong opposition to liberalization.[18] More than a century and a half after they suffered a major defeat in Great Britain with the repeal of the Corn Laws, agricultural interests remained politically powerful in much of the rest of the world.

The Doha Round proved difficult to conclude as well because, with the expansion of the globalized international economy in the last decade of the twentieth century, more countries than in the previous eight rounds had to approve a final treaty, and, as noted earlier, the difficulty of agreeing on anything rises with the number of parties that must agree.

Trade negotiations around the world increasingly focused on bilateral arrangements,[19] often undertaken as much to cement political ties between countries as to enhance their economic well-being. Bilateral arrangements do not expand overall welfare at all if they merely divert trade from one place to another, rather than fostering exchange that would otherwise not have occurred. Proponents of bilateral trade treaties often claim that such accords can pave the way for broader agreements, serving as "building blocks" for, rather than "stumbling blocks" to, multilateral arrangements.[20]

The trilateral countries injected new issues into trade negotiations, which also bogged them down. They wanted to include standards for the treatment of labor and for environmental protection. All parties would have to meet these standards in order to receive the benefits of expanded trade. Such initiatives met with resistance from poorer countries, whose labor and environmental policies fell short of the proposed standards. Their policies fell short in no small part because these countries were poorer: historically, protection for workers and for the environment has increased as per capita income has risen.[21] The poorer countries regarded these efforts, with good reason, as indirect ways for North Americans and Europeans to shut their gates to products cheaper than those of domestic manufacturers made in places that happen to be less scrupulous about child labor and clean air and water.[22]

The great recession that began in 2007 further dampened whatever enthusiasm there was for forging new trade accords. Historically, hard economic times have strengthened the forces intent on pulling shut the gates to trade.

Finally, even as, for all these reasons, the formal efforts to push open the gates to trade around the world failed to gain traction, the forces seeking to pull them closed grew stronger. The expansion of the globalized international economy at the end of the Cold War generated a tailwind for the cross-border flow of goods. It enhanced the benefits and the prestige of cross-border trade. That same expansion, however, also strengthened the backlash against trade through the impact of the two largest new members of the globalized international economy, China and India.

The Asian Giants

The inclusion of China and India distinguishes the third era of the integrated international economy, which dates from the outset of the 1990s, from the second, which began in the wake of World War II. These countries' changes of economic direction changed the world. When China and India chose to abandon central planning and import-substitution respectively, embrace free markets, and open their gates far more widely to goods and money from abroad, this tipped the political balance in the world decisively in favor of globalization. Those choices also injected millions more producers and consumers into global markets and made possible more extensive specialization in those markets, which made the world richer.

As cross-border flows invariably do, those originating in China and India generated a backlash—in both cases against their exports—although in different ways. The pressure that Chinese-made products exert on workers and firms in the trilateral world is intense but familiar. The consequences for employment in the wealthiest countries of India's exports are novel, and potentially far more disruptive.

In 2004, as journalist James Kynge reports in his book *China Shakes the World*, manhole covers began disappearing in large numbers from cities all over the world. It turned out that thieves were stealing them and shipping them to China.[23] As the world's largest manufacturer, the country had developed an enormous need for scrap metal. China has acceded to the position Great Britain held in the nineteenth century: the "workshop of the world," the global leader in exporting a wide range of manufactured products: approximately three-quarters of the world's toys, for example, come from China.

Chinese exports have given rise to a new term: "the China price." It refers to the price at which something made in China can be sold abroad, which is usually lower than the price for the same thing made anywhere else.[24] China has consistently exported more than it has imported, with its balance of trade with the United States being particularly lopsided.

With its large population, China specializes in products that use low-skilled labor intensively. The effect on comparable sectors in the trilateral countries is predictable: their low-skilled workers have had to accept lower wages or have lost their jobs entirely. Firms specializing in low-skill-intensive products have made lower profits, or downsized, or moved their factories to China, or all three—or gone out of business altogether.

This general pattern did not begin with China's entry into the globalized international economy. Manufacturing moved from high- to low-wage countries throughout the second half of the twentieth century. Nor are such jobs going only to China. Other countries with abundant low-skilled labor entered the global economy at roughly the same time. But China's size, the literacy of its workers, and its vast, up-to-date, government-built infrastructure have made the sheer volume of its exports, and thus their impact on the global economy, far greater than those of any other country.

While Chinese manufacturing has made losers of low-skilled workers in the trilateral countries, it has brought economic benefits to others, including possessors of scarce commodities and those owning or managing businesses in a position to take advantage of globalization by, among other things, producing in and selling to China.[25] In general, the increase in the world's supply of labor, thanks in no small part to China's entry into the global economy, has reduced the ratio of capital to labor worldwide. With capital relatively less and labor relatively more abundant, the returns to capital in the trilateral countries have increased, while those to labor have declined.

In this way, the emergence of China as the workshop of the world has contributed to widening economic inequality in the trilateral countries and in particular in the United States,[26] a trend that, to be sure, has had other causes as well, most notably technological change. All this made China a prominent target of the inevitable political backlash against trade, a backlash strengthened by the widely held perception that the world's most populous country does not abide by the rules of the global economy.

"Cheaters never prosper," goes an old schoolyard taunt. China, however, seems to its critics to have cheated and prospered—indeed, to have prospered by cheating. The Chinese have breached the norms of good international economic conduct with their currency policy. The United States and many other countries allow their currencies to "float." The value fluctuates according to the international demand for the currency: when demand rises, the value of the currency rises; when it falls, so, too, does the value of the currency. Floating leads, in theory, to the automatic adjustment of a country's balance of trade. When its exports rise, the value of its currency increases, making those exports more expensive so that it sells less to other countries. At the same time, imports from abroad become cheaper and these increase. The trade surplus disappears.

This has not happened with China because the Chinese government has managed its currency, the renminbi, rather than allowing it to float freely. Beijing has "pegged" the renminbi to the dollar, routinely buying dollars to keep its own currency cheap in relationship to its American counterpart rather than allowing it to rise, as it would do without these purchases of dollars. The government's policy has made Chinese exports less expensive, and the volume of those exports greater, than they would be if the renminbi had been allowed to float.

No international law or treaty forbids currency management, but the practice does violate the norm of free trade. It has the same impact as a subsidy for domestically made goods and a tariff against foreign products: it amounts to "exchange-rate protectionism."[27] The Chinese currency policy has the same consequence for China as the mercantilist trade policies that predominated among European countries from the sixteenth to the nineteenth centuries: the accumulation of a trade surplus.[28] Unlike Europe's mercantilist regimes, China has not adopted this trade policy to enhance its military might; but like traditional mercantilism, which aimed to accumulate stocks of precious metals with which to purchase arms and soldiers, China has had political reasons for its mercantilist practices. Foremost among them has been the goal of preserving jobs in the exporting industries on its eastern coast, which the Communist regime apparently deems crucial for sustaining political stability and so maintaining its grip on power in China.[29] For Chinese trade policy, as for so many other features of the global economy, politics has determined economics.

Although it is the most visible method by which its economic policy harms people in other countries, China's currency policy is not the only one. Counterfeiting and the theft of intellectual property are common. They deprive the foreign companies whose products—from pharmaceuticals to software to movies to leather goods—are illegally copied or whose ideas and technologies are used without payment, of revenue they would receive in a country more respectful of commercial law. Corporate espionage, with Chinese firms (sometimes owned by the government) stealing proprietary information from Western ones, is not unknown.[30] Indeed, in February 2013 a report by a private security firm revealed that Chinese cyberhackers, working in a building in Shanghai owned by China's People's Liberation Army, had stolen valuable and confidential information from more than a hundred private American firms in a number of industries, including defense contractors. The hackers had also broken into the network of a company that helped run public utilities and power grids in North America.[31] The Chinese government also imposes standards for products that are designed to favor Chinese firms and skews the procedures by which lucrative government contracts are awarded in ways that discriminate against foreigners.[32]

While not the only country to have run persistent trade surpluses,[33] China's size, the volume of its exports, and the impact of those exports on the global economy combined with the political arithmetic of trade have, not surprisingly, triggered a particularly strong political backlash against it. In the trilateral world, Chinese trade policy has created an odd opposing coalition. It brings together workers and businessmen hurt by Chinese imports who seek protection against them, with others who favor free trade in principle and believe that under normal circumstances no industry anywhere should be protected, but are convinced that China's mercantilist policies are doing terrible damage to the global trading system and so favor retaliation to force the Chinese to change them.[34]

Other Chinese policies anger different constituencies in the trilateral world, which expands even further the potential political support for restricting trade with that country. As the largest emitter of greenhouse gases, China makes a major contribution to global warming, which particularly offends environmentally conscious Europeans. In response, French and Italian leaders have proposed carbon tariffs on imports, with the fees on incoming products set according to the amount of carbon used in making them. (Not coincidentally, such tariffs would help shield European-made products from Chinese competition.) An energy bill passed by the American House of Representatives in 2009 but not the United States Senate and so not enacted into law contained a comparable provision.[35]

China's internal political practices also offend sensibilities in the West. In the United States, for several years in the 1990s the Clinton administration attempted to link these practices with trade by making access to the American market for Chinese products conditional on the Chinese government respecting the political rights of its citizens. The government in Beijing refused to accept these conditions and the Americans abandoned the effort; but the Chinese regime's undemocratic ways, and its harsh treatment of dissidents, continues to generate anti-Chinese sentiment that could be mobilized politically in support of restrictions on Chinese imports.

An all-too-possible political and even military confrontation between China and the West, perhaps over Taiwan, also has this potential. Such an event would give rise in the trilateral world, especially in the United States, to punitive economic measures against China.

The widespread unhappiness with China's trade practices among its trade partners has led to a series of minor economic sanctions. The United States brought a number of complaints against China to the World Trade Organization,[36] imposed a three-year tariff on Chinese-made tires in 2009, and in 2012 put tariffs on Chinese solar panels and towers for wind turbines. (China in turn placed tariffs on American poultry and some American-made automobiles.) Although less vociferously and less frequently, the European Union has also expressed disapproval of Chinese trade policies, especially of what European officials considered illegal subsidies to high-tech companies competing with European ones.[37] The United States, the EU, and Japan lodged a complaint with the World Trade Organization against China's restrictions on the export of rare earth minerals.

Members of the American Congress have regularly introduced bills to penalize China's economy more severely—by imposing a surtax on all Chinese imports, for example, in response to their currency manipulation. The one proposed in 2005 called for a 27.5 percent levy on all Chinese goods. None became law, but they attracted significant support, suggesting the potential for a full-scale trade war with China.[38] During the 2012 American presidential campaign, in the dozens of televised political commercials aired by the two major candidates, President Barack Obama and Governor Mitt Romney, only one foreign country came in for mention. That country was China, which both candidates criticized for its unfair trade policies. Each promised to resist those policies more vigorously than his opponent.

Not all twenty-first-century economic trends and political developments have heightened tensions between China and its trading partners. Some have mitigated them. The value of the renminbi did rise in relation to the dollar, although not as far or as fast as American officials and economic commentators, in particular, thought fair. China's overall trade surplus did shrink, although this did not impress Americans because the bilateral balance with the United States remained lopsided.[39]

As wages rose in China,[40] companies began relocating factories to countries such as Vietnam, Cambodia, and Bangladesh, where workers earned less.[41] As Chinese wages continue to rise, that exodus will surely increase. Such jobs will not return to the trilateral countries, but the Chinese will increasingly share with other countries the perceived responsibility for their loss, which may dilute some of the West's resentment.

In the second decade of the twenty-first century manufacturing seemed, in fact, poised to enjoy a minor renaissance in the rich countries,[42] thanks in part to the remarkable ongoing innovations in information technology. As manufacturing goes digital, according to a survey in *The Economist*, products can "be made economically in much smaller numbers, more flexibly, and with much lower input of labour, thanks to new materials, completely new processes such as 3D printing, easy-to-use robots and new collaborative manufacturing services available online."[43] This "third industrial revolution" will take place, in its initial stages at least, mainly in the trilateral countries and not in China.

As with the previous stages of the Industrial Revolution, digital manufacturing will generate well-paying jobs in the countries that play host to it. Because it is capital-intensive, however, such jobs will not be numerous; automated, digital factories will employ many fewer people than the American and European automobile plants and steel mills of the first half of the twentieth century.

As for the prospect of Sino-American economic conflict, China's huge store of dollar assets gives it leverage, in theory, over the United States and so helps to deter an American-instigated trade war.[44] Selling these assets in large quantities would cause the dollar to plummet, doing serious damage to the American economy. The threat to do this is not entirely credible, however, because the massive sale of dollars (assuming buyers for all those assets could be found) would also damage China. It would make its exports more expensive and lower the value of the dollars it continued to hold.

Finally, the ever-growing Western investment in China, and the expanding volume of Western exports to China, give politically influential economic interests in the trilateral countries a stake in keeping the gates of their countries open to Chinese imports, lest China close its own gates to their products. Although they tend to be less public than the opponents, trade with China has politically active and powerful friends as well.

On issues of trade, China and the trilateral countries, especially the United States, have been compared to partners in a bad marriage. Serious issues divide them. They bicker constantly. Each of them threatens the other with the equivalent of divorce: a full-scale trade war. Yet they also need each other, and have enough invested in the relationship to refrain from taking steps that would sever it.

In the history of warfare World War I occupies a special niche: a war no one sought and yet seemed, in retrospect, unavoidable. In 1914 none of the belligerent parties, it seemed, wanted to fight.[45] But the causes of war were so numerous and powerful—the division of Europe into two opposing blocs, rising nationalism, arms races, domestic pressures—that its outbreak appeared in retrospect to be neither puzzling nor mysterious, but rather all but inevitable. So it is with the potential for a trade war between China and the trilateral countries. Neither China nor the countries with which it trades wants such a thing, from which all would suffer. As the experience of rampant protectionism in the 1930s demonstrates, trade wars have no winners. Yet the tensions that could provoke such a conflict are obvious, formidable, and will not soon disappear. The accusatory rhetoric and the tit-for-tat erection of minor trade barriers amount to a low-level economic cold war, and it is characteristic of cold wars that they have the potential to turn hot.

The greatest threat to the open trading system in the years ahead, however, may turn out not to come from China and its manufacturing prowess. It may come instead from the other huge new member of the globalized international economy, India. In manufacturing, India is an underachiever; but in the twenty-first century it became the main source of another kind of export, which has the potential to cause far more economic disruption than the toys, textiles, and telecommunications equipment that China makes. China is the nagging toothache of the world trading system: consistently painful, dangerous if it becomes infected, but otherwise not a serious threat to overall health. India, by contrast, is a less-noticed and slow-growing but possibly carcinogenic tumor. An appreciation of the threat it poses begins with the basic structure of modern economies.

All economic activity is divided into three parts: agriculture, industry, and services. The jobs in these three sectors are performed by, respectively, farmers in fields, workers in factories, and employees in offices. The initial stage of the Industrial Revolution, with its advances in transportation through the invention of the steamship and the railroad, made it possible for the first time to trade the outputs of the agricultural and industrial sectors regularly and on a large scale. This made farmers and industrial workers vulnerable to the losses that trade inflicts. White-collar service workers were safe—until the revolution in information technology in the late twentieth century.

The digital revolution made it possible to perform services—routine clerical operations but also some of the work that highly trained specialists such as lawyers, accountants, architects, and physicians do—in one place and deliver them in another on a large scale. As with trade in agricultural commodities and manufactured goods, what had once occurred episodically and on a small scale could now take place regularly, in large volume, and rapidly.[46] As something new under the sun, the remote provision of services required a new word, "offshoring"—sending work to be done in a different country. (A similar term, "outsourcing," refers to work for a firm that is performed outside that firm, although not necessarily abroad.)[47]

Many of these remotely provided services originate in India. That country's call centers, which handle inquiries from thousands of miles away about matters ranging from credit card bills to computer malfunctions, came to symbolize this new feature of the global economy. Three features of India's society and economy combined to make it the center of offshoring: a high competence in the English language; a cadre of people with sufficient education to perform the services—a small percentage of all Indians, to be sure, but a large number in absolute terms because India's population is so large; and very low average wages, even for the well educated, in comparison with other countries.[48] The logic of offshoring is familiar. It conforms to the standard pattern of trade, in which jobs go where they can be done most efficiently in economic terms—and wages are an important component of efficiency—whether the work involves growing wheat, assembling cell phones, or reading X-rays. India has an advantage in the provision of some tradable services and so exports them. It is yet another chapter in the long and ongoing history of creative destruction. In another sense, however, offshoring represents a revolutionary change: for the first time in history, services as well as grain and cell phones can be traded routinely and in bulk over long distances.

This development may have enormous consequences because many, many more people in the trilateral countries work in the service sector, which typically employs more than 70 percent of the workforce, than in agriculture or industry. Not all service jobs will be vulnerable to offshoring. Some services have to be delivered in person: haircuts, for example, cannot be remotely provided. But as information technology improves, as it surely will,[49] more and more jobs will become "impersonal" and therefore tradable. By the estimate of the noted economist and former vice chair of the Federal Reserve Alan Blinder, it may ultimately be feasible to perform as many as 30 to 40 million American service-sector jobs in other countries.[50]

The political backlash against trade in services could therefore be fierce. The resistance to cross-border exchange can be strong, because of the political arithmetic of trade, when only a small fraction of a country's jobs are at risk. How much more powerful will it be when the risk hovers over a much larger minority, conceivably even the majority, of all workers?

Furthermore, many of the white-collar workers who find their jobs in jeopardy will be far better educated, much more affluent, and considerably more sophisticated politically than the farmers and assembly-line workers whom trade has injured in the past. This will give the forces of protection the basis for far greater influence over trade policy than the losers from trade were able to wield in the twentieth century.[51] Many will belong to professions, which will provide them with a source of leverage in trying to close their countries' gates that farmers and factory workers do not have. Historically, one of the defining prerogatives of a profession is the power to decide who is qualified to do the work in question. Professionals can (and do) keep out foreign practitioners simply by pronouncing them unqualified.

Opponents of offshoring will, however, face a particular logistical obstacle. It will be far more difficult to block the transmission of services from abroad by electronic means than it is to stop, or impose tariffs on, wheat or cell phones at their ports of entry. Electronically delivered services can go over, under, around, and through a sovereign state's gates.

Yet another reason to expect the backlash against offshoring to be formidable is the fact that, in the nineteenth and twentieth centuries those who lost their jobs to trade could move from the farm to the factory and from the factory to the office. White-collar workers in the twenty-first century, by contrast, have no new sector of the economy to which to move. There is none. As the floodwaters of foreign competition rise, the potential victims will no longer have higher occupational ground to which to retreat.

Since its beginning in 1846 the international economy has experienced two broad, deep, and politically effective backlashes against trade. The first, from the 1870s through the end of the nineteenth century, came in response to the initial period of trade liberalization. Along with the United States, most of the countries of Europe, with Great Britain being the notable exception, put up barriers to imports. (The cost of transportation fell so rapidly that the overall value of trade did not decline.) The second came about as a reaction to the Great Depression. Countries resisted imports in the vain hope of sustaining employment within their own borders. The ongoing digital revolution, with the consequent offshoring of an ever-wider array of services, could conceivably usher in a third such period, one in which, at least in the trilateral countries, the forces seeking to pull shut their national gates to trade will achieve political ascendance.

Just how powerful the political backlash against offshoring will become will depend, of course, on how many service jobs migrate from the trilateral world to India and other low-wage countries. The total number of jobs lost might remain small, as it was through the first decade of the twenty-first century.[52] Wages will rise in Indian call centers just as they have in Chinese factories. That, plus shortages of the requisite skills in low-wage countries, will surely keep many service jobs from moving. Moreover, the United States, at least, has in the past run trade surpluses in business services. It is other countries, including India, that have created barriers to their trade.[53]

Some services will not move because they depend for their quality and effectiveness on proximity to others doing the same kind of work. Computer engineers, film makers, and purveyors of financial services all benefit from "clustering"—the concentration in one place of people with similar skills. That principle has given the world Silicon Valley, Hollywood, and Wall Street. Finally, as wages and incomes rise in service-exporting countries such as India, these countries will purchase more from abroad, including services from the countries to which they are also exporting services.[54] It is even possible that, as more service occupations become tradable, the trilateral countries will actually gain rather than lose jobs.[55]

Moreover, however many service jobs do emigrate, the law of comparative advantage will still hold. Whatever injuries it inflicts on some fraction of their populations, all countries will benefit economically overall from offshoring, as they have from trade in agricultural and manufacturing products. However many losers there are, the value of countries' overall gains will exceed their losses. For this reason, as with trade in agriculture and manufactures, offshoring will create a coalition favoring its continuation and expansion as well as one seeking to restrict it. The inevitable political tug-of-war over trade in services will not be one-sided.

Whatever its consequences for them, the trilateral countries will adjust to the impact of offshoring, just as they did to the losses to their agricultural and industrial sectors that international trade caused. If there are large job losses, however, that adjustment will be painful. As Blinder put it, "I believe the adjustment to offshoring will be of major magnitude, will last a long time, and will create millions of losers. Those are precisely the ingredients needed to create a big political issue. . . ."[56] If it instigates job losses on a very large scale, trade in services will generate a backlash powered not only by purely economic injury but also by a perceived threat to an entire way of life. That perception, as it happens, fuels the political resistance to the second constituent part of the process of globalization: immigration.

Human Traffic

Human beings are, among many other things, what economists call "factors of production"—part of what goes go into the making of goods or services. Indeed, humans are more important than the other two factors—land and capital—because without humans (and with all respect to beavers, bees, and ants, the master builders of the animal kingdom) economic activity cannot take place.[57]

Like capital but unlike land, humans are mobile. They change their residences and places of work, sometimes moving across sovereign borders. While people have been moving from one place to another from time immemorial, as with trade the Industrial Revolution's nineteenth-century innovations in transportation and communication substantially expanded the number of people who moved. They traveled across continents on railroads and crossed the oceans on steamships. Increased immigration was one of the hallmarks of the initial era of globalization and it is a feature of the current, third one as well.

In 2011, 215 million people lived outside their countries of birth, an increase of 50 percent over two decades.[58] The foreign-born made up nearly 13 percent of the population of the United States. In the countries of western Europe, not traditionally destinations for immigrants, typically 10 percent or more of the population consisted of immigrants and their children.[59]

Like trade, migration creates winners and losers and so, like trade, it generates a political backlash. The losers seek not to tax incoming immigrants the way protectionists seek to impose tariffs on imports but rather to keep them out altogether. Beginning in the nineteenth century and carrying through the twentieth and into the twenty-first, immigration, like trade, has provoked political conflict in the recipient countries. As with trade, that conflict revolves around economic gains and losses—but not exclusively around them.

The immigrants themselves are almost by definition winners. They move in order to better themselves economically, typically from poorer to richer countries.[60] If they do not do well economically, they often leave. (They sometimes return to their countries of origin when they do do well, to use the money and experience that they have gained abroad to start businesses or to retire comfortably in familiar surroundings.)

As with trade, immigrants enhance the welfare of the places to which they immigrate. They expand the labor pool and the number of consumers. They sometimes bring technical expertise and entrepreneurial drive: from Andrew Carnegie to the Chinese, Russian, and Indian founders of twenty-first-century high-tech companies in Silicon Valley,[61] the United States in particular has drawn major economic benefits from the enterprise and business acumen of people born elsewhere.

Workers who remain in countries that immigrants leave enjoy higher wages because the labor force shrinks.[62] Those countries might seem likely to suffer losses on balance to the extent that they lose gifted, energetic people,[63] and it is true that a "brain drain" can have a negative effect on economic performance. But emigration can also increase total wealth, particularly in very poor countries, when emigrants send back money—remittances—to family and friends they have left behind. The global total of remittances far exceeds the level of international economic assistance.[64] In addition, when immigrants achieve success in their new countries, they form networks that can help their countrymen who stay at home start and manage businesses there. Such networks have contributed, for example, to India's economic growth.[65]

Migration does create losers as well. Workers who compete with immigrants can see their wages drop, indeed can lose their jobs entirely. Immigration may prove to be a losing proposition economically for jurisdictions with heavy concentrations of immigrants, which have to spend more on social services for the newcomers than the immigrants generate in new economic activity. Most foreign-born residents of the United States live in six of the fifty states,[66] for example, and one of them, Arizona, passed a controversial law aimed at locating, and presumably expelling, those without the legal right to be in America.

Still, the gains it brings are large and consistent enough that immigration qualifies as the greatest underutilized resource for the promotion of global economic growth.[67] A 2005 World Bank study concluded that a 3 percent per year increase in immigration from poor to rich countries would deliver $300 billion annually in benefits to the low-wage countries and be worth $51 billion to the countries to which they emigrated.[68] By some admittedly very rough calculations, lifting all restrictions on immigration worldwide could yield a total gain of $40 trillion. That would double global economic output.[69]

A substantial increase in immigration could therefore have a powerful impact on the future of the global economy. It could increase the efficiency with which labor is utilized worldwide. In so doing, it could lift the world's output as dramatically as did the decisions of China, India, and other countries to participate in international economic activity toward the end of the twentieth century. Despite the enormous economic potential of permitting much greater international movement of workers, however, and despite the supreme importance of what this could enhance—economic growth—the rich countries are not likely to open their gates to massive inflows of workers from poorer countries.

The reason goes beyond economic considerations and is captured by an observation about his country's experience with immigration by the Swiss playwright Max Frisch: "We hired workers and human beings came instead."[70] Human beings are more than factors of production. They are not simply part of a country's economy, although they are certainly that. They are also the building blocks of its society, the bearers and shapers of its customs, rules, traditions, and institutions. While economic concerns can generate political conflict over immigration,[71] the stiffest political resistance stems not from economic grievances but from the fear that the large-scale influx of foreigners will change the social fabric in unwelcome ways. Immigration provokes angry opposition from natives when it makes them feel that they are in danger of losing their social bearings and of being transported against their will to a strange new world.[72]

Just as nationalism fuels the backlash against trade by triggering support for resisting a practice by which foreigners take jobs from fellow countrymen, so it underwrites opposition to immigration. A sense of national identity lies at the heart of nationalism, and opponents of immigration often feel that the influx of foreigners is eroding that identity, depriving the society of something precious and essential, in almost the way that invading armies seek to do. Or, if immigration is not erasing the local identity, natives worry, it is establishing an alternative, rival one that will trigger the kind of conflict that has plagued multiethnic political entities the world over. Someone moving from Massachusetts to Texas can deprive a Texan of his job but does not threaten his culture, as a Mexican moving to Texas can appear to do. For this reason immigration, more than trade, incites active resistance from people who suffer no direct economic injury from it, indeed even from people to whom it brings economic benefits.[73]

The strength of the backlash against immigrants varies among the countries where they are numerous. The oil-rich monarchies of the Persian Gulf have many foreign workers. In some, they actually constitute a majority of the population. This does not cause open political conflict because in these autocratically ruled states open political conflict on any issue is prohibited and suppressed. The guest workers have no political rights and in most cases can be deported at the whim of the authorities. In sharp contrast, Israel welcomes, absorbs, and gives full citizenship to all Jewish immigrants and many non-Jews as well, although an influx of economic and political refugees from sub-Saharan Africa has caused concern.[74] In Australia, New Zealand, and Canada, all former British colonies initially settled by emigrants from the British Isles (many of them convicts in the Australian case), ongoing immigration does not, on the whole, provoke strong political reaction. The absence of a backlash is due in part, no doubt, to the fact that these countries generally regulate the inflow of migrants, giving preference to those with economically useful skills.

The future of the global economy depends far less on what

happens in the Gulf, in Israel, and in Australia, New Zealand, and Canada, however, than it does on the economics and policies of two places where the backlash against immigration is strongest—western Europe and the United States.

European countries need immigrants for economic reasons. Their low birth rates, which fall below the replacement rate of 2.2 live births per female all across the continent, are turning them into aging societies with shrinking workforces and, ultimately, declining populations.[75] To sustain economic growth, Europe needs to import what it is not producing: people. Yet immigration gives the Europeans the worst of both worlds: fewer immigrants than they need economically but more than they can tolerate politically.

They do not make productive use of the immigrants they have admitted. The jobs that people came from Asia, the Middle East, and the Caribbean to do in the 1960s in Europe's textile factories, steel mills, and automobile plants have disappeared. It was assumed at the time, without giving the matter much thought, that the jobs were permanent and the immigrants, who would one day return home, were temporary. The reverse proved to be true. Unfortunately, many of those who came to do the disappearing jobs, and their offspring, have not acquired the skills to fill the positions that the evolution of the continent's economy has made available. A startling statistic cited by Christopher Caldwell in his book *Reflections on the Revolution in Europe* makes the point: while the number of foreign residents in Germany rose from 3 million to 7.5 million between 1971 and 2000, the number of foreigners employed in the workforce remained static.[76]

Nor have all of Europe's immigrants become integrated into the societies to which they have come. To the contrary, some have segregated themselves from their native neighbors and do not identify with the countries in which they are living.[77] Governments inadvertently encouraged this through policies of "multiculturalism," which put a low value on learning the local language, adopting the local customs, and absorbing the local values. The impulse to live apart also came from within the communities of immigrants, especially those of the Islamic faith.[78]

The social patterns of European Muslims realized one of the fears that immigration arouses: the growth of an alien and hostile culture within the familiar one. In Denmark, for example, Muslim residents encouraged a worldwide Islamic campaign against that country because a Danish newspaper published cartoons they found offensive. Europe's Muslim immigrants presented, in addition, a more familiar problem: crime, including terrorism. A few such immigrants and their children were responsible for planning or actually carrying out acts of terror in Great Britain, France, Italy, Germany, Spain, and The Netherlands.[79]

To be sure, not every European Muslim kept him- or herself separate from the wider society, and only a small minority became terrorists.[80] Enough did, however, to cause a political backlash. The political cleavages over immigration in European countries tended to run vertically, not horizontally. They divided, that is, not so much the left from the right as the political elites from much of the rest of society.[81]

A book published in Germany in 2010 vividly illustrated the differences in attitudes toward immigration between elites and the public as a whole. The book was entitled *Deutschland schafft sich ab*— Germany Is Abolishing Itself—and was written by Thilo Sarrazin, a governor of the German central bank. The book argued that immigrants were doing serious damage to Germany, and advocated restrictions on immigration. Its publication provoked two telling reactions, representing the two different views on immigration. The public bought the book, making it the best-selling volume by a German author in a decade, with over a million copies sold in a matter of a few months. The political establishment responded differently: Sarrazin was fired from his position at the central bank for having breached a taboo by giving voice to unacceptable ideas.[82]

Mainstream political parties, conscious of Europe's brutal twentieth-century treatment of minorities, have, like the German central bank, often considered opposition to immigration and to immigrants outside the bounds of acceptable policy, although with growing public discontent that began to change. European voters wishing a change in immigration policy therefore had to turn to less well-established, less respectable parties, whose electoral strength increased.[83]

With poor countries with high birth rates and large numbers of unemployed young people nearby—in North Africa, for example— the number of non-Europeans seeking entry to Europe will surely increase. Resistance to admitting them is also likely to increase, at least in the short term. Already the Schengen Accords, which permit free movement of people within the European Union (but not from outside it) have become unpopular.[84] In the ongoing political contest over immigration across Europe, those seeking to pull the gates to immigrants shut will likely gain in strength, with those trying to push them open becoming politically weaker. Just how the Europeans will deal with the unassimilated immigrants already among them is a question to which no government, in the second decade of the twenty-first century, has found a good answer. Resistance to immigration will affect the European, and therefore the global, economy in two ways: by keeping the countries of the continent from offsetting the impact on their workforces of population decline by importing people from abroad; and by heightening domestic social tensions, which, if they become severe enough, will drag down economic performance.

On immigration America differs from Europe, a difference symbolized by the Statue of Liberty. The great bronze sculpture that stands in New York Harbor was originally a monument to geopolitics, a traditional European concern. The statue was a gift to the United States from France in recognition of the friendship between the two countries that was established during the American War of Independence against France's enemy of the time, Great Britain. When placed on a small island off the southern tip of Manhattan, however, the point of entry for so many people coming to the

United States from Europe, and with the sonnet "The New Colossus" by Emma Lazarus engraved on its base, including the words "Give me your tired, your poor/Your huddled masses yearning to breathe free," the statue came to stand for immigration, a more important and more highly valued feature of American history.

The United States has attracted many more immigrants than Europe,[85] for far longer, and has done much better at assimilating them[86]—that is, inducing them to abandon their previous loyalties and customs and to become Americans.[87] Still, the American history of immigration has not lacked conflict. Earlier arrivals to America's shores and their offspring have resented, feared, and discriminated against those who came later. In east coast cities in the late nineteenth and early twentieth centuries it was common for advertisements for employment to include the words "No Irish need apply," evidence of economic competition as well as cultural prejudice. By the mid-1920s, the country had all but cut off the inflow of foreign-born workers.[88] In the twenty-first century the expense of coping with immigrants caused resentment where taxpayers had to bear a disproportionate share of it, as in Arizona.

The fear that immigrants will change the national culture has arisen in North America as well as in Europe. The late, distinguished political scientist Samuel P. Huntington published a book in 2004 entitled *Who Are We?*[89] that expressed the fear that the Hispanic immigrants of the late twentieth and early twenty-first centuries would not assimilate as previous waves of newcomers from Europe had done, with dire consequences for the country.

The twenty-first-century political backlash against immigration in the United States thus has historical precedents and familiar features, but it also has a novel characteristic. It has drawn much of its energy from the fact that many of the people coming to the United States from Mexico and Central America entered the country illegally, by sneaking across its southern border. In the second decade of the new century, as many as 12 million people fit this description.[90]

They provoked resentment because they had, in effect, stolen something valuable, something to which they were not legally entitled, something that millions of people outside the Western Hemisphere had patiently pursued by legal means: residence in the United States. The illegals (those sympathetic to them used the more neutral term "undocumented") had jumped to the head of the line instead of waiting their turn. In a country in which fairness is important, that variety of unfairness rankled. As with trade everywhere and with immigration in Europe, immigration policy in the United States became the subject of political conflict. One side sought not so much to pull the gates shut as to police them more effectively in order to keep people from slipping through them illegally. The other side favored legislation giving legal status to those who had entered the country unlawfully. As with the European conflicts over immigration, the one in the United States did not follow the familiar political pattern.

The division over illegal immigrants in the United States runs not between the two major parties but within each. Within the Democratic Party, Hispanic groups and professional politicians have sought to confer legal status and eventually citizenship on the illegals out of ethnic solidarity in the first case and the belief that the beneficiaries will vote for Democrats in the second. Labor unions, on the other hand, an important part of the Democratic coalition, resist such generosity because immigrants are willing to work for low pay and in so doing depress the wages of union members.

Many rank-and-file Republicans oppose legislation granting legal status because they do not want to reward law-breaking. Many businessmen in industries such as meat-processing and construction, by contrast, who also support the Republican Party, employ such immigrants to lower their costs and raise their profits. These divisions led, in the early years of the twenty-first century, to a political stalemate. The American government proved unable to deal legislatively with the millions of people in the country illegally.[91]

While the political backlash against immigration will never abate entirely in the United States, it will be less powerful and less bitter than in Europe. Americans, after all, are accustomed to immigration. Immigrants built the country. They have strengthened and enriched it in the past and there is good reason to believe they will continue to do so. The evidence suggests that, rather than forming separate enclaves as some Muslims in western Europe do, Hispanics in the United States are assimilating in much the same way that previous immigrants did.[92] As for the other non-economic factor driving American resistance to the cross-border flow of people, unlawful entry into the country, the volume of illegal immigrants decreased at the end of the first decade of the twenty-first century, by some accounts stopping entirely.[93]

The recession that began in 2007 reduced the number of jobs available. Illegal immigrants to the United States, like their legal counterparts, enter the country in order to work. When jobs are unavailable, they stay home or, in the case of many already there, return home. Here the United States differs from Europe, where welfare benefits are both more generous and more readily available to immigrants. (Illegal immigrants in the United States receive none.) Immigrants offend native Europeans because, among other reasons, they do not work; they offend Americans because they do.

Increasing the incentives for ultimately reaching a compromise to revise the immigration laws in the United States is the agreement among all political factions that the national interest requires modifying them to attract and retain more highly educated and entrepreneurially energetic people from abroad. Immigrants of that description, virtually all agree, bring conspicuous economic benefits.[94]

The backlash against immigration in Europe will thus be stronger and politically more consequential than the one in the United States as the twenty-first century proceeds. Non-economic fears and grievances will fuel the European resistance. This will be the case, as well, for the backlash in the trilateral countries against the third major feature of the process of globalization, the cross-border movement of money.

The Smell of Money

The flow of money for investment across sovereign borders takes three distinct forms: debt, including bank loans, bonds, and other financial instruments; portfolio investment—shares in companies; and foreign direct investment, which gives a foreigner or foreign entity title to physical assets such as factories and mines. Of these, the first has the potential to do the most economic damage. In fact, it helped to cause the most severe decreases in production and losses of wealth the globalized international economy has suffered in its third, post-1990, era.[95] Stock purchases and direct foreign investment, however, have provoked the most conspicuous political backlashes. Where money is concerned, what is least damaging economically has proven most controversial politically.

In fact, it is hard to see how foreign money invested in private companies, either by buying shares in them or building physical facilities, does any economic harm at all. Investment, after all, is the key to economic growth, which is, as noted, almost everywhere the highest goal of economic policy, indeed of public policy in general. Investment comes out of savings, and saving requires sacrifice: money saved is by definition money that is not spent on consumption. When they invest, families, firms, and countries forgo satisfaction in the present for the sake of a better future. Foreign investment makes use of other people's savings and so allows a country to have its cake and eat it, too, by enjoying both present consumption and future benefits. Foreign trade can destroy local jobs. Foreign investment creates them. It is the countries from which the capital comes that have cause for complaint—that the money is not being invested in producing jobs at home.

In general, moreover, people do not look carefully into the origins of the money they receive, let alone reject it on the basis of an unsavory provenance. An ancient Roman saying expresses this timeless human tendency: *pecunia non olet*—money doesn't stink. Why is foreign investment an exception?

As with immigration, the reason for the political opposition to foreign investment goes beyond purely economic considerations. Investment confers property rights and with the right to property comes control of it. Foreign control of a country's economic assets can seem to violate the essence of sovereignty. It can appear, like immigration, to be a kind of invasion, depriving citizens of something fundamental and precious—mastery of their own country—with foreigners directing its political and economic affairs. Foreign investment provokes a backlash when it is seen as akin to a hostile takeover of a private company, or, to employ another metaphor, as an economic Trojan horse that allows potentially hostile interests to take command of strategically vital economic assets.

The perception of foreign investment as a vehicle for illicit political control gained wide currency in the twentieth century because it was integral to one of that era's most influential ideologies, Marxism-Leninism. Marx considered all private property an instrument of class oppression, and the Communist parties that governed in his name abolished it. Lenin, the founder of the Soviet Union, added an international dimension. He asserted that foreign investment, which he called "finance capital," led to imperial expansion and that the ineffable impulse for expansion would inevitably set the imperial powers at war with one another. That was his explanation for the outbreak of World War I.

Contrary to Lenin's expectation, capitalist countries proved capable of prospering without imperial possessions and of coexisting peacefully; but imperial expansion, when it occurred, did bring foreign investment in its wake and did sometimes enrich the investors at the expense of the local people. The gains from agriculture and the extraction of raw materials in European empires in Asia and Africa, for example, often accrued to foreigners, not to natives.

For that reason, when the last European empires ended after World War II the new local rulers assumed power with an aversion to investment from abroad. Communist governments banned all private investment, wherever it originated, and those pursuing strategies of import-substitution often acted to block the import of foreign capital as well as foreign goods.

In the last decade of the twentieth century, however, the economics and the politics of cross-border capital flows changed. The discrediting of central planning and of the strategy of growth through import-substitution dissolved the stigma attached to foreign investment that had been part of both. Far from being shunned as an agent of foreign exploitation, it came to be seen as an effective instrument for achieving the supremely desired goal of economic growth. China, for example, established special "enterprise zones" with hospitable rules for foreign capital.

At the same time, the global movement of capital changed direction. In the nineteenth century it had flowed, so to speak, downhill, from wealthy to less wealthy places: Great Britain, the major overseas investor, was the world's richest country. After 1945 it circulated horizontally: the trilateral countries invested in each other. In the era that began around 1990, however, capital began to flow "uphill," from poorer to richer places, especially from China, a country with hundreds of millions of very poor people, to the United States. This third pattern took hold because, for a variety of reasons, these new capital exporters achieved surpluses in trade with the rest of the world and chose to invest some of what they earned in Europe and North America. On several occasions their proposed investments triggered a hostile political reaction, because the investing countries were neither democratic nor unambiguously friendly and because the investments came not from private interests but from governments.

In 2005 the state-controlled China National Offshore Oil Corporation attempted to purchase the American oil company Unocal. In 2006, Dubai Ports World, a government-owned corporation located in the United Arab Emirates, tried to buy the Peninsular and Orient Steam Navigating Company, a London-based firm that managed several ports in the United States. On both occasions a public outcry forced cancellation of the purchase.[96] In 2009 the Anglo-Australian mining firm Rio Tinto withdrew from a deal to sell a minority share to a Chinese company.[97] In 2012 the committee on Intelligence of the United States House of Representatives recommended that American firms not make purchases from two large Chinese telecommunications companies, Huawei and ZTE, and barred those companies from acquiring American ones.[98] Concern about foreign control of strategically important assets underlay each incident.

Chinese investment arouses particular anxiety because China is large, increasingly powerful, and potentially a threat to its neighbors and a rival to the Western powers. Chinese companies, even when nominally privately owned, often have close relations with the government. Their foreign investments, it is feared, may therefore aim as much at achieving political goals as at earning profits. Through the ownership of foreign assets Chinese companies could conceivably acquire sensitive, militarily valuable technology, or engage in espionage or even subversion.[99]

The rise of China has coincided with, and indeed contributed to, the growing importance of an institution that blurs the line between governmental and private investment. That institution is the sovereign wealth fund, a large pool of government-owned or government-controlled money invested outside the home country.[100] The assets of these funds were expected to total as much as $12 trillion by 2015. In 2010 seven countries had funds with assets exceeding $100 billion: the United Arab Emirates, Norway, Singapore, Russia, Kuwait, Hong Kong, and China. (Saudi Arabia's international holdings bear a strong resemblance to these funds.) Of these only Norway had a democratic political system and belonged to the Organization for Economic Cooperation and Development, the association of wealthy countries. Among all of them, the trilateral countries would consider only Norway (and perhaps Singapore) to be unambiguously friendly and above any suspicion of using its investments for political purposes. In 2011, Britain had invested $454 billion in the United States, compared with only $2.3 billion by China.[101] But China was growing far more rapidly than Britain, the British investment came from private firms, not state-owned enterprises, and in any event, it had been well over a century since Americans had regarded Britain as a potentially hostile power.

Increasing investments by sovereign wealth funds swollen by the proceeds from trade surpluses and the sale of energy thus have the demonstrated capacity to trigger political reactions similar to the ones that trade and immigration provoke. In response to the controversies of the first decade of the twenty-first century, the recipient countries tightened their oversight of investment from abroad. In the wake of the Dubai Ports affair, the United States passed the Foreign Investment and National Security Act of 2007, which revised the framework and the procedures of the federal government's Committee on Foreign Investment in the United States.[102] Germany, France, Italy, Australia, and Canada all took similar steps.[103]

In Stanley Kubrick's 1964 film, *Dr. Strangelove*, one of the darkest and wittiest of all comedies, an American Air Force general, Jack D. Ripper, launches an unauthorized nuclear attack on the Soviet Union because he is convinced that the fluoridation of America's drinking water is an insidious Communist plot to weaken the country by poisoning its citizens and ultimately delivering it to Communist control. It is possible to imagine a backlash against large-scale foreign investment in the trilateral countries from Russia, China, and the Middle Eastern oil exporters arising from the fear that foreign money is having something like that effect politically, giving unfriendly foreigners control of vital economic assets and thus eroding sovereign independence—although even the strongest such reaction would surely not generate anything like the response that General Ripper launched.

It is possible to imagine a nationalism-fueled political backlash leading to widespread "financial protectionism"—barriers to investment from abroad comparable to those erected to reduce the influx of trade and immigration.[104] It is possible that the backlash against foreign investment will have as powerful an impact on the future of the global economy as the resistance to the offshoring of service jobs and to Muslim immigrants in Europe. All this is possible, but it is not at all likely. The cross-border flow of money will in all probability turn out to be far less contentious, and inspire far less opposition, than the movement of goods, services, and people.

Sovereign wealth funds and state-owned enterprises will have strong incentives to steer clear of controversy-producing investments, especially majority ownership in politically sensitive firms and industries. They will prefer avoiding trouble to courting it. Like private investors, they will generally seek high economic returns rather than decisive political influence.[105] Many will observe all or part of the international code of conduct known as the Santiago Principles, whose purpose is to reassure recipient countries by promoting transparency and accountability in the investments of sovereign wealth funds.[106] For their part, the trilateral countries will need investment and will not generate so much of it internally that they will feel affluent enough to spurn it from countries whose domestic and foreign policies do not fully measure up to their own standards. On the contrary, Chinese investment in distressed sectors of the automobile industry in the American Midwest—the country's "rust belt"—has received a warm welcome.[107]

Incidents such as the ones involving Dubai Ports and the China National Oil Company will surely flare up from time to time but, in truth, where concerns about the dangers of economic infiltration and subversion through foreign investment are concerned, even very modest versions of the fictional General Ripper's alarm about fluoridation are overblown.

• • •

In his State of the Union address on February 12, 2013, Barack Obama endorsed the Transatlantic Trade and Investment Partnership (TTIP). The initiative was designed to expand commerce between the United States and Europe by further lowering the already-low tariffs on both sides of the Atlantic, harmonizing often-conflicting regulations, and reducing trade-distorting subsidies to particular industries, especially to agriculture. The initiative demonstrated that, in the face of the twenty-first-century political pressures to restrict trade, the countervailing forces, pressing to keep the gates open, will remain formidable.

The president and his European counterparts embraced the TTIP because they understood the truth of Ricardo's proposition: trade enhances the welfare of all countries that take part in it. It is a major engine of economic growth and, at a time of sluggish to negligible growth in the United States and the European Union, governments in both places were attracted to a sure-fire way to boost it.

Its sponsors also had a geopolitical motive for the initiative. Mindful of China's growing strength, they were seeking to create a Western economic bloc to counterbalance rising Chinese power. They aimed, as well, to protect the open trading system that they had built after 1945. China's economic practices, notably its currency manipulation and its theft of intellectual property, pose a threat to that order. The Western countries hoped that the economic entity that they aspired to create would be powerful enough to exert leverage on China to conform to their own standards and practices. The most effective antidote to the major threat to trade, Western governments had agreed, is more trade.

The initiative showed, finally, that for the international economy the future will resemble the past in a way that favors the continuation of a high volume of cross-border commerce. In both previous eras of globalization, political initiatives—the repeal of the Corn Laws in 1846, the establishment of the Bretton Woods monetary system and the free-trade-promoting General Agreement on Tariffs and Trade (GATT) near the end of and after World War II—had made possible an expanding flow of international economic activity by counteracting the normal, natural, indeed inevitable political resistance to it. While its ultimate fate remains uncertain, and it faces many political obstacles, the TTIP is powerful evidence that pro-globalization political forces will be active in the twenty-first century as well. Whether or not it is ultimately enacted, the fact that the TTIP has been proposed at all, and widely endorsed, demonstrates that the ongoing and unavoidable tug-of-war over whether and how far to permit the entry of goods, people, and money from abroad will not be one-sided.

While no country will throw open its gates to unlimited immigration, most are likely to keep those gates open to trade and investment. Trade will, as Ricardo showed, make all countries engaged in it richer. So will portfolio and direct investment from one country to another. The cross-border flow of money in the form of debt, however, is a different matter.

CHAPTER THREE

THE RIVER

Money is more fluid than water and less steady than air.
—HEINRICH HEINE

Finance is the machine that governs the economy, but it is unstable and dangerous. The managers of banks and other financial outfits cannot be trusted to counter the euphoria of investors, yet governments feel compelled to throw money at a bust. The case for regulation, in a nutshell, is that financiers make mistakes and everyone else has to pay for them.
—EDWARD CARR[1]

. . . the big issues of financial instability, trade and global imbalances are . . . global problems demanding new levels of global co-operation.
—GORDON BROWN[2]

Money and Its Discontents

For any economy, money is the ultimate mixed blessing. It is, on the one hand, indispensable. Without it, economic activity on any but the smallest scale is impossible. It has a good claim to being the most important innovation in the entire history of economic life, for it serves three crucial purposes. It is a unit of account and a medium of exchange, without which only face-to-face barter can take place. It is also a store of value, without which economic activity geared to the future, notably investment, cannot occur. An economy without money is like a computer without an operating system: severely limited in what it can do and in the advantages it offers. On the other hand, money can inflict immense, catastrophic damage on an economy. The future of the global economy depends on whether, when, and how money's dangerous properties make themselves felt.

In its dual and opposite effects money resembles a river. The world's rivers provide much of the water that all living creatures need to survive. They support the crops that sustain life. In the past they furnished a surface over which long-distance transport was cheaper, easier, and swifter than it was over land. The world's earliest civilizations grew up on the banks of rivers. Benign, indeed generous though their impact on daily life ordinarily is, however, rivers occasionally flood. Their waters surge over their banks and destroy the crops and the cities they have nurtured. So it is with money, because of two of its inherent properties.

Money consists of small coins, pieces of paper, or, increasingly, intangible digital signals; it is therefore far more portable than the other two travelers across borders in a globalized international economy—products and people. Unlike them, the volume of money can also, especially in its intangible form, be rapidly and almost limitlessly expanded. In addition to its portability, money has a psychological aspect. At the heart of all economic transactions is belief: the term for the fuel of a financial system—credit—comes from the Latin word *credere*, to believe. Vendors of products or services accept money in payment because they believe that others will accept it as payment for products or services they themselves wish to purchase. Lenders advance money to borrowers in the belief that the loans will be repaid. Investors put money in assets in the belief that the assets' value will rise.

The combination of portability and psychology makes money

volatile. It can move suddenly, unexpectedly, and in large volume, like a river when it floods. When that happens, money can have the same impact on the economy in which it is used that a major flood has on the territory it covers. In fact, the term for a large gusher of money that can wreak destruction comes from the vocabulary of hydrology. It is called a bubble.

Bubbles form when investors bid up the price of an asset, believing that it will continue to rise in price. The belief is self-fulfilling: when people believe the price of a stock or a painting or corn futures will rise and are willing to invest in it, the price does rise. The fact that others believe this is a good reason to invest: as the price climbs, investors become wealthier, at least on paper.[3] The volatility of money means, however, that bubbles can burst as well as inflate. The price of an asset can fall very rapidly. When investors decide that it is destined to fall (and especially when it actually is falling), they sell, and this belief, too, is self-fulfilling. Selling actually produces the decline in price.

All this can happen rapidly. Anything can cause investors to lose their belief—their confidence—in the future value of an asset and abandon it.[4] Once they do, and whatever triggered the change in psychology, it becomes rational for others to follow because the price does fall, and the longer an investor waits to sell a declining asset, the greater will be the loss he or she will suffer. Investors behave like a herd of gazelles on the African savanna. They move together. When one senses danger and bolts, the rest follow, whether or not the danger was real. They are right to bolt: it is dangerous to be the last antelope at a watering hole, just as it is dangerous, or at least a formula for losing money, to be the last person owning an asset when others are frantically selling it.

The combination of money and free markets makes bubbles possible, and so they have formed and burst throughout history.[5] Perhaps the best-known bubble prior to the Industrial Revolution is the mania for tulips in the Netherlands in 1636, in which Dutch citizens made and lost fortunes speculating in the bulbs of the popular flower. Although familiar in economic history, bubbles do not occur with the frequency of the inevitable and perpetual political backlashes against trade and immigration. But they can do far more damage to the economies that spawn them than does the regular political resistance to the cross-border movements of goods and people. The damage can approach the impact of the collapse, through a major war, of the political roof that shields the global economy. The frequency and the size of financial bubbles will therefore shape the global economy's future.

Bubbles can inflict massive damage because of their connection to banks. Like the money they receive and lend, banks are indispensable for modern economies. They channel funds that people have saved to places where these can be put to productive use. They also contribute to the growth of bubbles. Borrowing money from them to invest in an asset is attractive because it multiplies the investor's gain when the price rises; but it also multiplies the loss when the price falls.[6] If a person invests $10 of his own money and borrows $90 to purchase a $100 asset, for example, and the price of the asset rises to $110, the investor has doubled his or her own personal investment. If, on the other hand, the price falls to $90, the investor has lost everything. A 10 percent movement in the price of an asset, that is, has an impact on the investor's stake equal to 100 percent. Borrowing can thus inflate a bubble more rapidly, and make it larger, driving the price much higher and so causing more economic destruction when it collapses than would otherwise be the case.

Banks not only help to inflate bubbles; in important respects they resemble them. They are structured in ways that make them vulnerable to the psychology that causes bubbles to burst. Modern banks hold "fractional reserves:" that is, the resources they have on hand at any one time ordinarily amount to only a fraction of what they can be required to pay out. They also operate with a temporal mismatch between their assets (the loans they have made) and their liabilities (the deposits they have taken). Depositors can demand the money they have put into a bank immediately: the bank, by contrast, usually cannot quickly get back the money it has loaned out.

As with the herd-like behavior of investors in a bubble, banks' depositors have been known to act on fears that also become self-fulfilling. If they worry that their money is unsafe and withdraw it, and other depositors follow suit, the deposits do become unsafe since the bank can only reimburse some of the depositors at any one time and generally cannot get more funds rapidly by calling in the loans it has made. A run on a bank follows the same pattern as the bursting of a bubble. As the saying has it, "If you see a line in front of your bank, get in it."

Bank failures penalize shareholders and depositors in the bank, of course, but they can have much farther reaching negative economic consequences. This is so, in the first place, because financial institutions tend to be interconnected: the failure of some drags down others. The widespread failure of such institutions can, in turn, drag down the entire economy because of the financial system's central role in it.

That system does for the economy as a whole what the heart does for the human body: it circulates what the component parts need to survive and flourish—blood in the case of humans, money in the form of credit in the case of the economy. Heart failure shuts down the rest of the body. Bank failure, for the same reason, can shut down the rest of the economy.[7] It was the failure of national banking systems in the United States and Europe at the beginning of the 1930s that caused the Great Depression,[8] the greatest blow to the global economy since its nineteenth-century beginnings other than the two world wars.

Because its malfunctioning can do so much damage, the financial industry almost everywhere has been subject, since the 1930s, to regulations designed to prevent catastrophic failure. The industry also has, in effect, its own social safety net. In the United States, for example, the federal government insures individual bank deposits up to $250,000 for the purpose of reassuring depositors so that they will not engage in herd-like withdrawals that could cause the banks to collapse. When the major financial institutions and the financial system as a whole seem shaky, governments step in to rescue them. This is what happened in 2008 in the United States and Europe.

This ongoing regulation and occasional salvation by governments makes finance an economic activity—because it is the consequence of many individual decisions made for the sake of profit—that is also, like trade and immigration, deeply affected by politics. In this way it resembles the course of a river—a work of nature that is also at least partly controlled by human intervention through dams, dikes, levees, and weather forecasts that warn of floods and enable those affected to take appropriate precautions. The failure of human restraints on a river can produce, in the worst case, a natural disaster such as the one that struck the city of New Orleans in 2005, when man-made levees on the Mississippi River were overwhelmed by Hurricane Katrina. Similarly, the failure of the political restraints on finance can produce economic devastation, as happened with the near-meltdown of the American financial system in September 2008 and the deep recession that followed.

Bubbles can appear and burst when confined to a single country. But their frequency and severity increases when finance becomes global, with money flowing across borders,[9] as it has during the era of globalization that began in the early 1990s. More countries joined the global economy, and the volume of cross-border capital flows expanded rapidly, increasing by an average of 11 percent per year between the beginning of the 1990s and the middle of the next decade.[10]

As a result, more money became available to invest everywhere, and some of it went into investments that ran up the value of assets in foreign countries. Also as a result, finance became more volatile—sudden flights became more likely—because investors are more skittish about investments in places with unfamiliar political

and economic systems. In general, the farther from home the location of an investment or a loan is, the more fragile confidence in it
will be.

The increased volume of money and the enhanced propensity for sudden flight from foreign assets combined to create, in
East Asia, the first major international financial crisis of globalization's third era. Western banks made large loans to Thailand, South
Korea, and other countries in the 1990s, then pulled them back
when the local Asian investments began to seem risky,[11] causing
substantial losses. Two other features of this crisis, both stemming
from its international dimension, magnified the economic damage
it inflicted. The Western loans had come mainly in dollars, which
the Asian banks had then converted to the local currency before
lending to local borrowers. In order to repay the Western loans the
Asian governments had to devalue their own currencies,[12] which
increased the cost of their imports and made their firms and people
poorer.[13] In addition, the crisis spread first among Asian countries
and then beyond Asia to Russia and Brazil through a process known
as contagion.[14] Western banks, suffering losses in Asia, sold assets
elsewhere to replenish their own resources. And seeing investments
go bad in some non-trilateral countries, Western banks and investors began to fear for the value of the assets they held in other
such countries and rushed to sell them. Like gazelles at one watering hole seeing another herd at a nearby oasis bolt, they, too, took
flight.

The international scope of capital flows, enlarging the pool of
capital available for investment all over the world, contributed substantially to the largest and most damaging bubble of the post-1990
period. It was, in fact, the largest financial bubble in history and
its collapse inflicted more damage on the global economy than any
economic event since the Great Depression. This bubble, centered
on housing in the United States, offers the most vivid possible il-
lustration of the perils of international finance and the importance

of political considerations in triggering, preventing, and mitigating the damage it can do.

A Drinking Binge, a Heart Attack, and the Flu

The great American housing bubble expanded from the middle of the 1990s to the middle of the first decade of the twenty-first century. Between 1997 and 2006 housing prices in the United States rose by 124 percent.[15] As long as they were rising, investors in real estate made money and those who failed to invest missed that opportunity. Prices stopped rising and began to falter in 2005. The slide continued, and accelerated, over the next three years. By the end of 2008 the average price of a house or apartment was fully 30 percent lower than it had been three years earlier.

Like all asset bubbles, the rise and fall of this one resembled a drinking binge, in which someone drinks more and more and feels better and better, mirroring the euphoria that marks the rush into a particular asset by investors. Eventually, the drinker collapses, passes out, and wakes up with a severe hangover, the equivalent of the enormous loss of wealth that the bursting of the housing bubble caused. Like drinking binges, bubbles end painfully.

This particular bubble, however, did more than inflict painful losses on individual American home buyers and real estate investors, extensive though those losses were.[16] Its collapse posed a mortal threat to the American, and ultimately to the global, economy because it threatened to paralyze America's and other countries' financial systems. Given the economic centrality of financial systems, this was the equivalent of a life-threatening heart attack.

The collapse of the housing bubble dramatically constricted the flow of credit within the United States because so many important financial institutions had invested so much, directly or indirectly, in housing. Some large firms had borrowed so much that the failure of their investments swallowed up their capital and they went out of business: they could no more make loans or investments than the dead can run a marathon. In March 2008, the investment bank Bear Stearns found itself effectively bankrupt and the federal government forced its sale to the JPMorgan Chase bank at a very low price. Seven months later, on September 15, the even larger and older investment bank Lehman Brothers ran through its capital, but rather than being taken over by a solvent institution it was allowed to perish.

The Lehman collapse triggered a financial panic. The bank had undertaken so many transactions with so many other institutions that the consequences of its failure were felt throughout the United States and around the world:[17] all of its many counterparties—the financial institutions with which it did business—suffered losses. Moreover, the demise of an old, powerful, respected firm spread anxiety and uncertainty by raising a troubling question: if Lehman could go under, was any firm safe?[18] Under these circumstances, the institutions that normally would have supplied life-giving capital to the American economy closed their lending windows. They had no confidence that any loan would ever be repaid.

In the days after the Lehman collapse, as the channels for distributing credit froze, the American economy suffered a near-death experience. Fortunately, it did not die. The financial system received a massive injection of capital from the government, like a defibrilator applied to a malfunctioning heart or a car getting a jump start to its battery. Credit began to flow again, albeit haltingly. But the combination of the bursting of the housing bubble and the severe financial crisis produced yet a third serious economic malady: a recession,[19] which can be compared to a siege of influenza.

Like outbreaks of the flu, economic downturns, with production dropping and unemployment rising, periodically afflict free-market economies. No country can escape recession forever, just as almost no one lives out a normal life span without coming down with the flu. Like bouts of the flu, recessions vary in severity. The recession brought on by the crash of housing prices and dramatically aggravated by the resulting financial crisis was by virtually every measure the worst since the Depression.

The growth of the great American real estate bubble had a number of causes.[20] Some were strictly economic. Real estate is a large sector of the American economy, offering many opportunities for investment. While the bubble was inflating, interest rates remained very low, making it attractive to borrow money for such investments, and individuals and institutions went deeply into debt. Standards for issuing loans fell. Banks made more and more of what were called "subprime" housing loans, to people whose credit ratings would not previously have qualified them to borrow. The shakiest of these came to be known as NINJA loans, given to people with no income, no job, and no assets. Such loans increased the size and the fragility of the bubble, as did two innovations in finance.

One of them involved bundling home mortgages together as securities, which could then be sold and traded.[21] Mortgage-backed securities attracted investors who would not otherwise have put money into the housing market. The other product of financial engineering that attracted money into real estate was a form of insurance on mortgages known as credit default swaps, which were sold not only to mortgage-holders but also as investments to other individuals and institutions, and could also be traded.[22] It was thought that these innovations would make the housing market safer by spreading the risks housing loans created. In fact, they had the opposite effect.[23]

Finally, the logic of bubbles drove prices up and roped investors in. As long as real estate prices were rising, even dubious loans were safe since a home buyer who could not pay the mortgage costs could sell the property at a higher price than the one at which he or she had bought it, pay off the loan, and walk away with a profit. Because house prices in the United States had tended to rise for seven decades, it was widely—and, in retrospect, erroneously—expected that they would keep rising.

The bubble was not, however, a purely economic creation. If

money rushed into real estate assets for economic reasons, politics held the door open. Public policy in the United States had long encourged the construction and purchase of housing. The government provided a tax deduction for borrowing to buy a house, applied pressure on lending institutions to make loans to people of modest means for home purchases, and created two housing-related "government-sponsored entities:" the Federal National Mortgage Association, known as Fannie Mae, and the Federal Home Loan Mortgage Corporation (Freddie Mac), which acted as brokers and owners of mortgages. Their ties to the government enabled them to borrow money at below-market rates.[24]

The growth of the bubble stirred far less concern than, in hindsight, it should have for a reason also related to politics: a view of economic life that gained wide currency, including among officials responsible for regulating the American economy in globalization's third era. According to this view, markets can be counted on to function efficiently without any interference from public authorities. Participants in markets—investors, above all—invariably behave rationally and, because their own money is at stake, prudently. This makes markets self-regulating and self-correcting. In keeping with this outlook, some regulations of the financial system were removed, others were not enforced, and the authorities regarded the growth of unregulated financial institutions—the "shadow banking system"[25]—with equanimity. Like the conviction that housing prices would always rise, the belief that all this was benign turned out to be incorrect.[26]

The attraction of real estate as an investment, the low interest rates and lax lending standards, the financial engineering that multiplied and broadened the channels for real estate investing, the official support for housing, and the belief in the inerrancy of free markets that combined to create a huge inverted pyramid of debt resting on American real estate[27] all originated in the United States. The great real estate bubble was made in America—but not only there. It was also very much the product of globalization. The global economy helped to inflate the bubble, and the global economy suffered when the bubble burst.[28]

The sharp increase in international economic integration in globalization's third era helped to inflate the housing bubble through the billion or so workers, most with modest skills, who joined the world's labor force in that period. Especially in China, many went to work in factories making consumer products in large quantities for export at low prices. In the United States, the tidal wave of imports from these factories, while injuring domestic workers in industries that competed with them, helped to restrain the overall price level. Absent signs of inflation, the prevention of which is ordinarily its highest priority, America's Federal Reserve Board kept interest rates low, making it inexpensive to borrow money for housing.

The flood of Chinese and other imports helped to inflate the bubble in another way. The Chinese government re-exported to the United States much of the money Americans spent to buy their goods, often by purchasing American government securities. Expanding the supply of capital lowered its price—that is, the interest rate.[29] Without the large inflow of capital to the United States, American interest rates would surely have risen higher than they did, perhaps high enough to keep investment in housing within prudent limits. Besides exerting downward pressure on the cost of capital, some of the foreign funds coming into the United States went directly into housing-related assets—bonds issued by Fannie Mae and Freddie Mac, for example, which were regarded as entirely safe and yielded an attractively high rate of return because of their presumed safety.[30]

Finally, other countries followed America's lead (sometimes at the urging of American officials) in deregulating their own financial systems and dismantling barriers to the cross-border flow of money. By expanding the total supply of capital available for investment everywhere, this, too, helped to drive American housing prices upward.

Like its causes, the negative consequences of America's financial heart attack and economic influenza were global in scope. Economic distress spread outward from the United States through two different channels: to Europe through the transatlantic networks of global finance; and across the Pacific via the trade relations between America and Asia.

Europe's financial systems suffered, in varying degrees, the same kind of shock that brought the American system to the brink of collapse. European banks had weaknesses similar to those of their American counterparts. Some of them, including in Switzerland and Germany, in other ways economically very conservative countries, had assumed stratospheric levels of leverage—the ratio between their investments and the capital they kept on hand. In several countries banks had helped to finance real estate bubbles comparable to the American one.[31] Many had purchased securities tied to housing in the United States, something they would have been unlikely to do with traditional American mortgages. They had also purchased the debt of the two American government-sponsored entities, which was considered as safe as American government bonds.[32]

Moreover, European banks had become more and more deeply enmeshed both with American financial institutions and with one another. Trouble in one part of what had become a transatlantic financial system quickly spread to all parts of it in the wake of the Lehman collapse. A few European banks, Northern Rock of Great Britain being the most notable example, had failed even before September 15, 2008. Afterward, banking crises similar to the one that struck the United States broke out across the continent.[33]

Asian countries avoided the American and European financial disasters. Their banks had followed, on the whole, more conservative and prudent borrowing and lending policies. One major reason for their relative conservatism was the sobering example of the Asian financial crises of the late 1990s, which had involved the sudden withdrawal of Western loans, falling exchange rates increasing the costs of repayment, and severe recessions. The Asian crisis in fact contributed to the American housing bubble. Traumatized by the stampedes out of their currencies, the victims of that crisis—and China, which, lacking a convertible currency, had not suffered their fate but nonetheless feared exposure, at some point, to the same kind of panic—decided to accumulate a large supply of hard currency for the purpose of self-protection. This was a major reason for the trade policies that brought the Asians, especially China, the surpluses that they then recycled to the United States.

The Asian countries' prudent financial behavior did not spare them entirely from the impact of the America-centered economic disaster. Like bystanders at a car crash, they were hit by some of the flying debris. They depended heavily on exports,[34] a large share of which went to the trilateral countries, especially the United States. When these countries fell into recession, the demand for Asian exports dropped sharply, which spread the recession to Asia. Western consumers became poorer and began saving rather than spending. Asian workers employed in making the shoes and toys and electronic equipment that Westerners were no longer buying lost their jobs.[35] With the recession, the global demand for commodities as well as for manufactured products, and the incomes of the countries that depended on selling commodities, in particular oil, to the rest of the world also dropped sharply.

Like the causes and the effects of the financial and economic disasters that crested in late 2008, the response to them had a global dimension. The countries affected recognized the scope of the challenge by replacing the Group of Eight, which had consisted of the largest trilateral countries and Russia plus a representative of the European Union and had met annually since 1974 to discuss international economic matters, with the Group of Twenty, which included representatives from Asia, Africa, and Latin America as well as North America, western Europe, and Japan.[36]

The Group of Twenty held an emergency summit meeting in Washington in November 2008, two meetings in 2010 and 2011, and agreed to meet annually thereafter. The meetings' communiqués pledged solidarity in responding to the difficult economic circumstances the participants all faced. For the most part, the governments carried out parallel rather than coordinated policies. Still, their responses to both the financial heart attack and the economic influenza had much in common because all drew upon the lessons of financial and economic crises of the past, which prescribed political action in the form of government intervention to treat economic maladies.

To address the financial crisis they relied on the wisdom of the nineteenth-century English writer Walter Bagehot, an early editor of *The Economist* magazine. In his 1873 book *Lombard Street*, Bagehot argued that to stem a banking panic, to which free-market economies were susceptible in the nineteenth century as in the twenty-first, the government should step in as the "lender of last resort" and make sufficient resources available to banks to reverse the psychology of flight that threatened to destroy them.[37]

Accordingly, the American government adopted unprecedentedly strong measures to douse the flames of financial panic. Its central bank, the Federal Reserve, flooded the economy with money by lowering interest rates to near zero and by a policy of creating money known as "quantitative easing." The Fed opened its discount window not only to commercial banks, as in the past, but also to other financial institutions and even to foreign banks.[38]

When the vast and previously unimpeachably safe American money market funds came under pressure, the government guaranteed them, too. These funds played a crucial role in daily economic life: major firms relied on them for short-term operating funds. So concerned was the government about assuring the continuing flow of such funds that it provided some itself, purchasing, for the first time, the "commercial paper"—the short-term notes—of American companies.[39]

It went further, taking control of several large financial companies, not all of them banks, including Fannie Mae, Freddie Mac, and the giant insurance company AIG. The American Congress appropriated $700 billion for a Troubled Asset Relief Program, whose initial purpose was to buy the bad loans that were weighing down the banks' balance sheets and so discouraging lending. The government even decided to inject the capital directly into the banks, compelling the largest banks to accept it in return for shares of stock, thereby partly nationalizing the country's banking system.[40] These measures gave the government a larger role in, and greater control over, the American financial system and the American economy than ever before in peacetime.

European governments took similar steps. They, too, flooded their economies with money. They, too, took control of large failing institutions. The British government, like its American counterpart, engaged in "quantitative easing," forced a merger between two of its major financial institutions, and put capital, in the amount of $87 billion, into its largest banks.[41] In the same month as the Lehman crash the governments of Germany and the Benelux countries bailed out parts of their banking systems and ultimately France, Spain, Ireland, and Switzerland followed suit.[42]

All these policies were undertaken by national governments, demonstrating that, in coping with a global economic failure, effective power continued to reside at the national level. At the worst moment of the financial crisis, however, with financial systems paralyzed by the Lehman bankruptcy, national governments did act jointly. On October 8, 2008, central bankers in the United States, Great Britain, the European Union, Sweden, Switzerland, and Canada simultaneously cut their interest rates by 0.50 percent, and China cut its rate by 0.27 percent.[43]

These extraordinary measures did, to use yet another medical metaphor, stop the bleeding. The transatlantic financial system did not immediately return to robust health, but it did not collapse. The blizzard of money that governments showered on their banks and bank-like institutions turned what could have been a fatal seizure into a frightening, destructive, but not catastrophic near-death experience. The decisive character of politics for the global economy could hardly have been more persuasively demonstrated. Political intervention prevented economic calamity.[44]

Politically determined intervention also mitigated, although it did not prevent, the deep recession that followed the financial crisis.[45] Here, too, governments took their cues from an English economic sage of the past, John Maynard Keynes. In 1936, Keynes published *The General Theory of Employment, Interest, and Money*, which is in part a critique of economic policy during the Great Depression. He argued that when economic activity falls sharply governments should not simply stand idly by and wait for the economy to right itself, which was the accepted theory and standard practice in the 1930s. Rather, they should borrow and spend money to create demand that would lead to higher production and employment.[46] Subsequent economists, notably the American Nobel laureate Milton Friedman, contended that what made the Depression so severe was the decision of central banks to restrict when they should have expanded the supply of money in their countries.

In 2008 and thereafter the world's governments did both. Those with stricken banking systems had already loosened monetary policy to cope with their credit crises. In addition, almost every government reduced taxes and borrowed and spent money expressly for the purpose of increasing demand. In early 2009 the American Congress authorized $780 billion in "stimulus" spending (one-third of which consisted of tax cuts.) The comparable European initiatives generally felt short of the American one as a proportion of total economic output; but most European countries did create such programs and their total spending expanded because the recession triggered outlays from their generous social welfare programs. (Subsequently, the Europeans and the British opted for policies of greater austerity than had the United States, in part because of the debt they had accumulated in fighting it.)

The countries of Asia, largely unburdened by beleaguered financial systems but caught, nonetheless, in the global economic downturn, concentrated on anti-recession measures and generally spent more, as a percentage of national output, than did their Western counterparts. China acted early and forcibly to stimulate its economy, spending an estimated $585 billion.[47]

As important as what governments did to fight the severe economic flu that attacked their countries was what they chose not to do. They did not, as governments had done in the 1930s, erect tariff barriers or make sharp unilateral reductions in the value of their currencies. Cross-border flows of goods, money, and people did decline at the end of 2008 and thereafter, but this was because of the drop in overall economic activity, not because of concerted government policies to bring it about.[48] During recessions, commerce, investment, and population movement within countries all decline. They therefore decline between and among countries as well.

As they slowly recovered from the great financial shock of 2008 and its aftermath, and adopted measures they hoped would accelerate the recovery, the world's governments faced a different but, in the long term, no less important task. That task was the prevention of further such shocks.

An Ounce of Prevention

Given the disaster wrought by the American housing bubble, preventing another such event was, in its wake, an urgent matter. Moreover, one result of the crisis of 2008 made any subsequent episode of inflated asset values even more dangerous for the global economy. In the United States and other trilateral countries, as small banks fell by the wayside, the financial sector consolidated itself. It came to be dominated by a smaller number of very large interconnected institutions, whose failure could easily bring about what came close to happening in the fall of 2008: the collapse of the entire system.

These institutions have been called "too big to fail," which means that governments cannot allow them to fail, which will, in turn, encourage them to engage in potentially highly lucrative but at the same time very risky behavior. The term for circumstances that make financial crises more likely in this way is "moral hazard," and the financial crisis of 2008 and governments' responses increased it.

Moral hazard is present when the gains from economic activities are privatized but the losses are socialized: that is, when individuals and firms keep the money they make but the government compensates them for what they lose. It is then rational to take great risks. When the risks pay off they bring great rewards; when they don't, no loss is incurred. To put it differently, moral hazard takes the risk out of economic activity. It is capitalism without bankruptcy, which has been compared to Christianity without hell. It encourages bad behavior by removing the penalty for it.[49]

In the years leading up to the housing bubble, the American government, in particular, took steps that fostered moral hazard. When a series of financial problems occurred—the Asian financial crises in 1997, for example, the failure of the giant American hedge fund Long-Term Capital Management in 1998, and the sharp decline in high-tech stocks in 2000 and 2001—the Federal Reserve Board, under the leadership of its then-chairman Alan Greenspan, lowered interest rates to cushion the effects of these shocks on investors. The practice became known as "the Greenspan put"—a term that bespoke confidence that the Greenspan Federal Reserve could be counted on to protect investors when markets fell. Such confidence contributed to the inflation of the housing bubble.[50]

The rescue of financial institutions after the bursting of that bubble broadcast the same message. True, the extraordinary measures governments took to stop the banking panic did not spare millions of people from calamitous losses. Nor did it spare the stockholders of the major financial institutions, or indeed some of these institutions themselves, which went out of business altogether—Lehman being the most prominent but not the only example. But when, in the wake of Lehman's demise, governments stepped in to save the largest surviving financial institutions, they set a precedent that could eventually encourage precisely the behavior that had made the rescues necessary. A major legacy of the events of 2008 was therefore the need to reform the world's financial systems so as to reduce, as far as possible, the chances of repeating them.

The American and European governments moved to restructure their financial systems in order to guard against the recurrence of dangerous bubbles. They proposed a series of reforms: increasing the amount of capital financial firms are required to keep in reserve; bringing all bank-like firms under government regulations and limiting the size of such firms;[51] regulating the new financial instruments that had contributed to the real estate bubble; establishing new regulatory bodies to oversee financial activity and to manage the failure of systemically important institutions; and preventing any single financial institution from functioning as both a deposit-taking commercial bank and an investment bank engaged in trading.

All these proposed reforms were sensible, but virtually all encountered political opposition from the financial industry, which claimed, perhaps accurately, that circumscribing its activities would reduce overall economic growth. The industry was also motivated by the concern, which was certainly well founded, that the reforms would reduce its own profits. Despite this opposition, some regulatory reform did occur, but as barriers to the inflation of dangerous bubbles, they suffered from a common shortcoming, rooted in the familiar mismatch between politics and economics.[52]

Because effective political authority exists only at the national level and not on an international scale, binding financial reforms can only be made on a country-by-country basis; and the reforms in different countries differed from one another.[53] This gave the largest financial firms, which already operated in many jurisdictions around the world, the opportunity for "regulatory arbitrage"—concentrating their operations where the regulations did least to restrict them and where they could therefore take the biggest risks in order to earn the highest profits.[54]

Because they are in competition with other countries to attract financial businesses, which bring with them jobs and tax revenues, governments have an incentive to establish regulatory regimes that are attractive to such businesses. The businesses tend to gravitate to regimes that are more permissive than is optimal for preventing financial crises.[55] To eliminate this incentive would require having a single set of financial rules for all countries and a mechanism to enforce them.[56] To be maximally effective, that is, financial regulation would have to be global in scope. That would require a genuine global government, but establishing one is not a goal that even the worst economic times since the Depression have made appealing to the world's sovereign states.[57]

Another way to reduce the frequency and the size of financial bubbles is to limit the amount of money available to inflate them. Gushers of money from abroad contributed to the Asian financial crisis of the late 1990s and to the American housing bubble, inspiring proposals for restricting the cross-border flow of capital—inevitably, as with financial regulation, on a national basis. Capital controls were common in the international economy's second period of global integration, between 1945 and 1990, when capital was treated like a prescription drug: life-giving in appropriate doses but potentially harmful in excessive quantity. Despite the push for the liberalization of capital flows after 1990, controls remained in place in many countries outside the trilateral world.

Unlike the barriers to trade, capital controls do not attract the near-unanimous disapproval of professional economists. There is no equivalent for the international flow of capital of David Ricardo's principle of comparative advantage, according to which politically inspired interference with trade always lowers total welfare. Because floods of money can wreak such destruction, politically imposed obstacles to capital can make countries richer than they would otherwise be—by preventing them from becoming poorer.

As safeguards against the recurrence of destructive financial bubbles, however, capital controls, like financial regulations, have shortcomings. If some countries have stricter controls than others, this may simply divert dangerously large flows of money elsewhere, to more permissive places, rather than preventing them altogether.[58] Here again, the absence of truly global regulations makes a difference.

Moreover, controls can reduce economic growth. The weight of the evidence suggests that, on balance, enhanced capital flows make the countries receiving them better off.[59] For that reason, and despite the dangers involved, countries are likely in the future, as they have in the past, to compete for rather than obstruct foreign capital, just as they will compete to have financial companies operate within their borders.

Furthermore, controls on capital, like restraints on the import of services from offshore, present problems of implementation. In the age of instant global communication, when money consists of electronic impulses that can be sent around the world with the click of a computer mouse, clamping down on the circulation of capital will not be easy—when it is feasible at all.[60]

Bubbles can and do form anywhere, but a major reason the great real estate bubble appeared in the United States is that the United States received a huge inflow of foreign capital as a result of a large global financial imbalance. America ran big current account deficits, saving less than it invested and consuming more than it produced. Other countries ran major surpluses and used them, in part, to finance the American deficits. At one point the United States absorbed fully 70 percent of the surplus savings of the rest of the world.[61] Some of that money fed the housing bubble, indirectly by keeping American interest rates low and directly through investments in real-estate-related assets.

Without a rebalancing among its surplus and deficit countries, the world risks not only more bubbles but also a major economic shock if lenders should take fright at the large and chronic American deficits and refuse to fund them,[62] or if the American government should cope with its huge total debt by wantonly printing money. If, on the other hand, the United States reduces its borrowing but other countries fail to expand their consumption, the world will suffer from a shortage of demand and the global economy will grow slowly, or not at all. Global rebalancing, with deficit countries (meaning, above all, the United States) consuming less and surplus countries consuming more, is therefore needed to guard against disastrous financial shocks. Achieving it is, once again, ultimately a political task, and not an easy one.

For the world's biggest debtor, the United States, lowering dependence on foreign oil[63] and cutting its federal budget deficit are crucial.[64] The economic imperative to do both is widely understood, but the American political system has had difficulty in achieving either, and for a simple reason: both inflict economic pain. In the first case consumers pay more; in the second, the beneficiaries of government programs get less. Neither group—and many Americans, of course, belong to both—looks favorably on such measures, so through the first decade of the twenty-first century politicians could not, or in any event would not, court unpopularity by proposing, let alone imposing, higher fuel costs and lower benefits.[65] (Increased domestic energy production in the United States, the result of technical advances in the extraction of oil and natural gas, shows some promise of reducing the American dependence on foreign energy.)

It would seem easier for surplus countries to contribute to global rebalancing, since this involves having their citizens engage in more of what the Americans do in excess and what is the ultimate goal of economic activity: consumption. While to do its part the American government would have to act as Scrooge, the governments of the surplus countries would need to assume the more popular role of Santa Claus. But reducing surpluses turns out to be as difficult, in its way, as cutting back on deficits because it involves more than simply spending money. It entails altering long-standing policies, modifying attitudes with deep cultural and historical roots, and overcoming powerful political forces.

When the economic crisis of 2008 struck, the three largest non-oil-exporting surplus countries, Japan, Germany, and China, had for decades been pursuing national strategies of growth based on exports. Their industries, their financial systems, their economic policies, their workers' and managers' ingrained habits and expertise were all geared to making things to sell abroad. Changing them to encourage more imports and higher levels of domestic consumption could not be accomplished quickly or easily.[66] Moreover, the political will to change was weak in all three countries because their export-led economic strategies had produced impressive economic growth, and countries, like people, are disposed to change what fails, not what succeeds.

Each of the three major surplus countries has specific domestic reasons, rooted in politics, for keeping to the economic path that has generated surpluses. Japanese society is aging. With few children to support them and a social safety net less generous than in Europe, the Japanese people consider it necessary to save, whatever the needs of the global economy.[67] German society is aging as well, and Germans have another kind of reservation about saving less and consuming more: both contradict deeply held values. Even more than Japan's, theirs is a culture of thrift. They abhor debt, making less use of credit cards than any other people with a comparable standard of living. Abandoning the deeply ingrained preference for frugality and hard work in favor of consumption and leisure would be distinctly un-German.

Similar reservations about buying things are not in evidence in China, and with hundreds of millions of potential consumers, that country has wide scope for consuming more. The country's still-widespread poverty contributes to its surpluses because poor people do not buy imported goods.[68] Further enhancing the surplus is the fact that China consumes a relatively small slice of its own total output and invests a very large share. And the Chinese save a great deal because their social safety net is modest. The system of social protection established during the Maoist era has been largely dismantled and will take time to replace.[69]

China's political system plays a role here as well. Exporting industries exert influence on the government to pursue policies favorable to them, including (but not limited to) a weak exchange rate. Thus, Chinese politics, along with Japanese demography and German values, reinforce the difficulty of rebalancing the global economy to reduce the chances of further serious financial crises.

Considerations of international economic policy as well as domestic politics drove the Asian countries to accumulate their surpluses. They were amassing "rainy day funds" of hard currency to protect themselves against sudden and substantial demands for it of the kind that had triggered the Asian financial crisis of the late 1990s. Yet another method of rebalancing the global economy, therefore, is to eliminate the felt need for such protection. That could be accomplished by reforming the international monetary system. During the era of the gold standard, which roughly coincided with the first period of global economic integration from the mid-nineteenth century to the outbreak of World War I, and then when the Bretton Woods system was in force, from 1944 to 1971, rules governed international monetary flows that inhibited the accumulation of the kinds of imbalances that piled up in the early twenty-first century.

An effort to reinstate those or comparable rules, although in important ways economically desirable, would encounter formidable political difficulties. Too many governments would have to agree on them. Moreover, surplus and deficit countries would be at odds, with each insisting that the other bear the costs of adjustment. During and immediately after World War II the United States, the world's largest creditor, resisted the efforts by John Maynard Keynes, representing the indebted British government, to promote policies, institutions, and rules by which surplus countries would have to contribute to rebalancing.[70] By the twenty-first century the shoe was on the other foot: American officials, representing the world's largest debtor, were importuning their counterparts in China and Germany to do their fair share to rebalance the global economy.

Monetary reform for this purpose remains a pipe dream; but serious monetary reform for other purposes did take place in one part of the trilateral world at the outset of the twenty-first century. In the boldest and most consequential innovation in monetary affairs since Bretton Woods, seventeen members of the European Union gave up their national currencies and formed a common one. Unfortunately, their currency union, the euro, produced, in the second decade of the new century, a crisis as serious, in its own way, as the near-meltdown of the American financial system in 2008. That crisis will have a powerful impact on the future of the global economy.

Euro Troubles

The history of the euro illustrates the truth of the maxim "Be careful what you wish for; you might get it." Its formation was an important stage in the fulfillment of a grand vision of European unity that emerged from the wreckage of World War II. The euro was expected to continue the six-decade-long project of bringing the countries of Europe closer together politically while making them more prosperous economically. Instead, it has had the opposite effect on both counts. Even more than with the great American-centered financial crisis of 2008, the causes of the economic problems to which the euro has given rise, the solutions to those problems, and the difficulties in carrying out those solutions all have their roots in politics.

To be sure, the establishment of the euro had an economic rationale. By merging many currencies into one it eliminated the uncertainty among its members, in their economic dealings with one another, that stems from exchange-rate volatility; and greater certainty did expand the volume of intra-European trade and investment, although not, perhaps, as much as the euro's founders had expected.[71] The creation of a single currency complemented the construction of a single market for goods, capital, and labor in the European Union. It also diminished Europe's reliance on the dollar, the management of which, in European eyes, did not always serve Europe's interests. This was not surprising: the American government naturally gave priority, in its economic as in its other policies, to promoting the interests of the people who elected it, not to those of the members of the European Union.

The governments that established the euro had political goals for it as well, however. With its own currency, and the enhanced measure of political unity a common currency was expected to bring, Europe would, they foresaw, be able to play a bigger role on the world stage. In geopolitical terms it would count for more. As with the issue of immigration, European attitudes toward enhancing the continent's geopolitical weight varied according to social location: it had only faint resonance, at best, among the publics, but it mattered a great deal to the political elites, who were responsible for envisioning, designing, and creating the euro.

The immediate impetus for a common currency also had a political component. The negotiations leading up to its authorization, in 1992, took place in the shadow of the collapse of European communism and the reunification of Germany. Although never explicitly described in this way by the participating governments, the common currency was intended to bind the suddenly larger and more powerful Germany into a pan-European framework, continuing the dual efforts to contain German power and reintegrate the Germans into Europe that had begun after the defeat of the Third Reich in 1945.

The powerful political momentum behind the euro's creation is surely one reason that what were widely recognized as flaws in its design were not corrected before it was launched. Those flaws had the same disastrous consequence as a poorly constructed levee that breaks when a river crests.

The euro deprived the countries that joined it of independent monetary policies, and monetary policy, as it happens, is particularly useful in coping with two common economic problems. One is economic downturns. When a sovereign country with its own money experiences a slump, it lowers interest rates to revive growth. Members of the euro, which has a single interest rate for all its members, cannot do this. Of course, regions in a single country cannot do it either. None of the fifty states of the United States can conduct its own monetary policy. But when Ohio's economy declines, Ohioans can move freely and easily to states where economic conditions are more robust. In addition, the federal governments directs money from employed and therefore taxpaying citizens in other states to unemployed Ohioans through federal unemployment insurance.

Because of the availability of those methods of relieving economic distress the United States is what economists call an "optimal currency area;" and an optimal currency area invariably coincides with sovereign borders. It requires an effective government, something the euro did not receive from its founders.[72] That omission was and remains its greatest flaw.

An independent monetary policy is also handy for dealing with current account deficits. A country in deficit that has its own currency can devalue the currency, which will increase its exports while decreasing its imports and thus reduce the imbalance. Without the capacity to devalue, which members of the euro relinquished, a country can fund deficits by borrowing, but borrowing only postpones the need for adjustment, which occurs, as it did under the gold standard, by reducing spending at home and by lowering wages—making exports cheaper and giving domestic workers less money to buy imports. Adjustment occurs, that is, by lowering, at least temporarily, a country's standard of living, the political difficulties of which in increasingly democratic countries rendered the gold standard unworkable.[73] It was the reliance on borrowing of countries with deficits in the eurozone that led to the crisis of the euro.

While the dangers involved in giving up national currencies were well known long before the currency was launched,[74] its founders believed—or hoped—that its members could avoid the problems for which an independent national currency is the preferred solution. In particular, they sought to avoid large deficits by requiring that no country enter the currency with a total debt higher than 60 percent of its GDP and that none run a deficit of more than 3 percent of GDP in any year.

The second requirement proved toothless. Greece falsified its economic data to meet it, as Greek officials later admitted.[75] Shortly after the common currency came into existence, both Germany and France, its two largest and most influential countries, exceeded the deficit limit, rendering it unenforceable. It was also expected that the different countries would, over time, become more alike economically, with none lagging far behind the others in economic productivity, so that trade between and among them would not get very far out of balance. This, too, did not come to pass.

On the contrary, in the euro's first decade the northern and southern members diverged in economic performance.[76] The exports of the north, especially Germany, became increasingly competitive. As for the southern countries, while their citizens may have enjoyed life more than did their northern counterparts, as the term often used to refer to them—"Club Med"—implies, they proved better at importing from abroad than in making things people in other countries wanted to buy. The result was something all too familiar in economic history: a bubble.

To fund their deficits the southern European countries sold bonds, and those bonds followed the trajectory of a bubble. At first, the southerners found willing purchasers at low interest rates: European banks, in particular, were eager to buy them because membership in the euro, they assumed, guaranteed creditworthiness. Then the flow of easy money on generous terms stopped.[77] The bond bubble burst. The interest payments required to sell them rose sharply.[78] This happened first with Greece, whose huge gap between government spending and government revenues made its prospects for repaying its loans seem dubious. The bond market's doubts spread to Portugal, to Spain, where a burst real estate bubble caused government revenues to plunge and government social welfare payments to soar, to Ireland—neither a southern European country nor one with a profligate government, like that of Greece, but one whose government had assumed the obligations of the country's enormous banking system during the financial crisis of 2008—and to Italy. In 2013 the Greek problems led to the prospective failure of banks on the tiny island of Cyprus, also a member of the euro, institutions that had purchased Greek bonds that, as a result of the rescue package, had plummeted in value.

This posed a mortal danger to European and ultimately the global financial systems. If indebted countries could not pay what they owed, banks all over Europe that owned their bonds might collapse,[79] with default in one country leading, by contagion, to soaring interest rates and defaults in others. Such a sequence of events would surely trigger a broad financial panic and a deep economic downturn similar to (and conceivably even worse than) what the world had experienced in 2008 and thereafter.[80]

The members of the euro responded by supplying funds to— bailing out—the distressed countries to keep them from defaulting. Greece, Portugal, Spain, and Ireland all received emergency loans. A permanent bailout fund, called the European Stability Mechanism, was set up. The European Central Bank, which had been established to manage the euro, became active, buying the bonds of national governments and offering easy credit to private banks to keep them solvent.[81]

These measures were aimed at enhancing investors' confidence in the creditworthiness of the debtor countries so that these countries could sell their bonds at lower, more affordable interest rates. This is the role that national governments, in their capacities as "lender of last resort," play to stem banking panics within countries by restoring the confidence of the banks' depositors. In the European case, however, the measures did not initially succeed. The interest rates the debtor countries had to pay to sell their bonds remained at economically punitive levels. The rescue packages were too small, and were devised and implemented too slowly, to revive confidence.

While the American government was able to muster resources on a very large scale very quickly in response to the financial crisis of 2008, the eurozone, not having a genuine government, was unable to do so. There was no effective lender of last resort. Once again, the mismatch in scope between economic activity and political authority was decisive. The rescue measures were too little, too late, for political reasons: there was no single source of authority that could mobilize, by itself, financing on a scale sufficient to impress the markets; too many governments with, inevitably, too many differing—even opposing—interests had to agree on any measures, no matter how modest;[82] and the country best positioned to lead Europe out of the crisis did not do so.

Although it is the largest and richest member of the eurozone, Germany hesitated to take the lead in addressing its difficulties. In the decades since its crushing defeat in World War II, it had concentrated on being a good citizen of Europe, not on being either the continent's or the EU's leader. It had taken political or economic initiatives only in partnership with others, usually France. Still, nothing could be done in dealing with the crisis without Germany's assent, and the German government, led by the federal chancellor, Angela Merkel, became the most important participant in the rescue efforts; but its participation had the perverse and unintended effect of making the eurozone less united politically without leaving it more stable economically.

The Germans insisted on placing conditions on the emergency loans the distressed countries received—which is, after all, what lenders usually do. Those conditions had the effect of imposing economic austerity on the borrowers. For this the Germans had good economic reasons. The debtor countries did have to learn to live within their means, and the absence of such conditions would have created a moral hazard: if the money were given unconditionally, the borrowers would have no incentive to make the economically painful changes required to get themselves out of debt.

The German government also had political motives for imposing these conditions. Mrs. Merkel, like the leaders of all democracies, had to answer to the German public, which was unenthusiastic about supporting the southern countries at all and would have rebelled against pain-free loans. The Germans had already paid a great deal after 1990—far more than they had initially understood would be required—to absorb the former East Germany. They had been promised that exchanging their own currency, the Deutsche Mark, for the euro would not involve paying for other countries' profligacy, which was exactly what the crisis of the common currency was forcing them to do. And having accepted reduced or stagnant wages and a deferred retirement age to keep their own country economically competitive, they resented being asked to subsidize people who had gotten into economic trouble because they themselves had refused to make such sacrifices.[83]

Still, justified though the austerity measures may have been on the grounds of moral hazard, and necessary though they undoubtedly were to achieve the grudging German political support for the bailouts, they could not, by themselves, resolve the debtors' problems. To balance their accounts, the southern Europeans would have to export more, which meant that Germany, in particular, would have to import more. Such a rebalancing could be achieved in one—or both—of two ways. The indebted countries could become more competitive by lowering wage costs—that is, by lowering their standards of living. This was not a popular approach in southern Europe, to say the least. Alternatively, or in addition, the German economy could become less competitive, perhaps through a higher inflation rate. But the German government refused to consider this way of solving the underlying problem. It insisted, in effect, that all eurozone countries become like Germany and run surpluses. But since by definition all current account balances together must equal zero, unless the eurozone as a whole somehow manages the unlikely feat of compiling a large and continuing surplus with the rest of the world, this is impossible.[84]

Moreover, the German-sponsored austerity measures had the perverse effect of worsening the debt crisis in southern Europe while producing a political backlash against the terms of the loans, the chief proponent of those terms—Germany—and the euro itself. In Greece and Spain particularly, lower government spending and less economic activity caused the government's revenues to fall, unemployment (and therefore unemployment benefits) to rise—exceeding 20 percent in 2012[85]—and the gap between the government's income and its expenditures to widen.[86] This made the bonds to finance the deficits even less attractive, and more difficult to sell. It threatened to ensnare these countries in an economically ruinous "debt trap," in which the national debt grows faster than national income.

For their part, as they became poorer, the southern Europeans became angry, blaming the northern Europeans, and especially the Germans, for their plight. The common currency, which was supposed to draw its members closer together politically, was instead driving them ever further apart. This made for an historical irony but also, potentially, for an economic disaster, because the salvation of the euro—the end of the crisis and the prevention of further ones—lay in greater political unity among the members of the eurozone.

The troubled history of the euro demonstrates what many observers knew before it was established: a currency union needs a political union. To function effectively, a currency requires effective governance, which can only come from an effective political authority. Such an authority could issues bonds with the guaranteed backing of all the euro members, including Germany: that would increase confidence in, and thus lower the costs of issuing, the bonds of the eurozone's weaker economies. A political authority could regulate banks, insure their deposits, and serve as the lender of last resort for them. It could impose measures to make the southern economies more competitive, including regulating their governments' spending and deregulating their labor markets. It could raise taxes to support its operations and implement its policies. In short, it could do for the eurozone and the euro what the government of the United States does for the American economy and the dollar.

Recognizing this, during the course of the euro crisis the member governments committed themselves, at least rhetorically, to deeper political integration. In October 2012, for example, they declared their intention to move toward a full banking union. The German government, in particular, insisted on political integration,[87] and not surprisingly: without some influence over the economic policies of the countries it was paying to bail out, after all, Germany would experience taxation without representation.

While movement toward political union has a powerful logic, even in the best of circumstances it will take time. It will require treaty revisions, constitutional changes, parliamentary votes, and perhaps nationwide referenda across Europe. All this can only proceed at a snail's pace. Financial crises, by contrast, unfold more rapidly. Dealing with the debt crisis by forging a pan-European political union therefore resembles revising the fire code while the building is burning: worthy and constructive, no doubt, but not an answer to the immediate problem.

Nor is there any guarantee that the political unity and effective eurozone-wide political authority necessary to make the euro work properly will ever be achieved. The southern Europeans have reason to resist it. They would lose the power to choose their own economic policies. They would have to accept the discipline from Brussels and Berlin that they have been unwilling or unable to impose on themselves; and what has already been imposed has proven very unpopular.

A cynical variation on the "golden rule" holds that he who has the gold makes the rules. Within the eurozone the northern Euro-peans have the gold and they would, in a political union, be able to impose the economic policies they prefer on the south. In exchange, however, they would have to support the southerners economically, running the risk that the "Club Med" countries would become per-manent drains on northern treasures, as southern Italy and Sicily have been on the north of that country and as the formerly Commu-nist eastern Germany has been on its western part. That price might prove too high.[88] The south favors money without conditions; the north favors conditions without money. Neither will produce a po-litical union.

Hanging over the future of political union in the eurozone, fi-nally, are questions of democratic governance and political identity. Could the citizens of the countries belonging to it exercise ultimate control over its political authorities and so preserve democracy in Europe? And would the Germans, the Spaniards, the Greeks, and the others come to regard themselves as citizens of Europe as a whole rather than (or in addition to) citizens of their own countries, and thus confer legitimacy on, and feel a measure of allegiance to, the political union? The answers are unclear.

The eurozone has two alternatives to ultimate political union. One is the breakup of the euro, either in part, with the exit of one or more of the weaker members, or entirely. Any country leaving the euro would regain the ability to issue its own national currency, which it would then be free to devalue. Although not painless, de-valuation has historically proven to be a politically more tolerable method of reducing a current account deficit than lowering wages.

Breaking up the euro would impose costs on all its members, and perhaps on other countries as well. The cost is unknown and probably unknowable in advance, but it could be stratospheric. The weaker euro members would probably be forced to default on their loans. Many of their own banks would fail, which would set in mo-tion a chain reaction of financial failure the scope of which could be vast. A global recession as deep as—perhaps even deeper than—

the one associated with the near-fatal heart attack suffered by the American financial system in 2008 might ensue.[89] Countries might drop out not only of the common currency but of the European Union itself. The entire six-decade project of European economic and political integration could be put at risk.

Keeping the euro together has proven economically expensive and politically contentious, but allowing it to fracture might well be much worse. For that reason its members have done what has been necessary to prevent or at least postpone its partial or complete demise, and may continue to do so. This is the other alternative to the breakup of Europe's common currency.[90]

Whatever course the euro crisis takes, however—political union, breakup, or muddling along—one consequence is all but certain and will have a major impact on the future of the global economy. For the next decade and beyond, Europe, once the vital center of the globalized international economy and still an important part of it, is destined to grow slowly, if at all. It is "destined" rather than merely likely to do so because the crisis of the euro is not the only thing that will depress its growth rate.

The Decline of the West

Economic growth began in Europe with the Industrial Revolution. Europe was the engine of economic growth in globalization's initial era in the nineteenth century and one of its three centers of dynamism, along with North America and Japan, in the second one. That will no longer be true as the third era proceeds.

Economic growth in Europe will slow, and perhaps even stall, because of the effects of the two financial crises of the century's early years—which will weigh on the American economy as well—but also for two other reasons: the continent's demographic pattern, which the United States does not share, and the relationship between technology and economic progress, which does affect America.

As would be expected in the aftermath of a major heart attack and a severe bout of influenza, the period of convalescence for the economies most seriously affected by the financial crises of the twenty-first century was protracted.[91] The financial systems on both sides of the Atlantic, the vital organs of the economies in which they are embedded, recovered slowly from the damage they suffered. The rescue operations their governments mounted and the collapse in tax revenues caused by declines in output saddled them with large debts; paying them off will divert resources from both consumption and investment—the causes of present and future growth respectively.[92] Heavy public debt burdens raise the prospect of government-induced inflation to ease them, but inflation, while good for debtors, is bad for economic growth.

In the second quarter of 2013 the European economy produced, for the first time in a long time, some good news. The gross domestic product of the eurozone grew at an annualized rate of 1.2 percent,[93] although unemployment remained high, especially in the southern countries. The growth, modest though it was, was a harbinger.

With basically healthy people, the effects of a heart attack and a flu eventually wear off, and so will the effects of the financial crises and recessions that the trilateral world has suffered. But even when they do, these economies will labor under other, more enduring, constraints. Europe, Japan, and, to a lesser extent, the United States are all undergoing a great, historic, demographic transition.[94] In all of them, birth rates and death rates have both fallen, making their populations, on average, steadily older.[95] This will slow economic growth in three ways.

First, as people get older, most have less energy for everything, including work, they tend to be less creative, producing fewer new ideas and technologies, and they become less prone to take the risks necessary to start new businesses.[96] Free-market economies need hard work, fresh ideas, and new businesses in order to flourish.

Second, in an aging society the ratio of non-workers to workers increases. This makes the social welfare benefits that retirees are entitled to claim a bigger economic burden to society at large because more people can claim them and, in relative terms, fewer people are working to generate the tax revenues to pay for them. In the twentieth century the European economies suffered extensive damage from aggression: in the twenty-first century the principal economic threat comes from generosity. Money spent on social welfare for older citizens is money that cannot be spent on growth-inducing investment, and the savings needed to fund investment will decline as societies age.

In one way Europe and Japan have an advantage over the United States on this score because America's health care costs are so much higher than theirs. In another way, however, the United States has the advantage. Because of a higher birth rate than theirs[97] and large-scale immigration, the American population will grow in the years ahead, while populations in the rest of the trilateral world, and the absolute size of the workforces, will actually shrink.[98] The total number of workers will correspondingly decline, and that is the third way that the demographic transition will limit economic growth. Still, while the American workforce will grow, the economic performance of the United States, as of the other trilateral countries, will suffer from another major handicap, this one inherent in the dynamics of economic growth.

Adding workers is an element of the extensive method of economic growth, in which higher output stems from increasing inputs—land, labor, and capital. Intensive growth, by contrast, expands output by making more efficient use of a country's repertory of inputs. The term for greater efficiency is productivity, and productivity, economists have shown, is a key to economic advance.

Although productivity can be measured, just how, exactly, greater productivity comes about remains imperfectly understood. It is well understood, however, that new technology makes an important contribution to it; and in this respect the trilateral countries labor under a handicap. They already use the most advanced technology. They invented it. In order to increase growth they have to devise, develop, and incorporate new and improved techniques and machines. That is an uncertain process, the pace of which varies for reasons that are not known. That pace cannot easily be accelerated, and in any event is almost always gradual. There is some evidence, moreover, that the rate of productive technological innovation has slowed in recent decades, although there is no widely accepted account of why this has happened or even unanimity that it has happened at all.[99]

The rich countries must move forward economically by, in effect, building the road on which they must travel. Poorer countries, those outside the trilateral regions, can move faster because, trailing behind, they can use the road that the rich have already built.[100] That is, poorer countries can incorporate the already-invented technology to achieve economic growth. Incorporation is cheaper, easier, and a more reliable source of growth than is invention. That is why poorer countries have the potential to grow faster than richer ones. Here, relative backwardness counts as an advantage. The propensity of the poor to catch up with the rich in per capita output is well known among economists, who call it "convergence." All other things being equal, over time the per capita outputs of different countries tend to converge.

Convergence is a tendency, not an iron law of economic history. It is not automatic: all other things are not always equal. Indeed, from the beginning of the Industrial Revolution until well into the twentieth century, the opposite trend—divergence in per capita output between the rich and the poor—dominated global economic life. The poorer countries lacked the institutions needed to capitalize on the advances of the rich,[101] and so the gap between them widened. The worldwide embrace of free markets in the latter part of the twentieth century represents a turning point in economic history because so many large, relatively poor countries did ultimately adopt the requisite institutions. As a result, their rates of economic growth increased; convergence shifted into high gear.

In the third era of global economic integration, the poorer countries have achieved higher growth rates than their trilateral counterparts, and that trend can be expected to continue, both because of the difficulties the trilateral economies will face and because of the ongoing process of convergence. Non-Western countries have the potential to grow much faster than Western ones in the years ahead, but how fast they actually do grow will depend on the extent to which, having provided themselves with the necessary free-market institutions, they proceed to adopt and carry out the policies that enable them to maximize their economic performances.

•　•　•

Among V. I. Lenin's many unfortunate contributions to politics was the phrase "the worse the better." Apparently borrowed from the nineteenth-century revolutionary writer Nikolai Chernyshevsky, the phrase expressed the belief that the worse conditions became for the people of Russia, the more likely they would be to exert themselves on behalf of the revolution to which Lenin had dedi- cated his life. Not only did these words bespeak a callous attitude to the people Lenin and his colleagues proposed to lead into a glorious future, as an actual prediction, they proved false. The Bolsheviks came to power through tsarist military failure, not the government- induced immiseration of the Russian people. Germany defeated the Russian army in World War I, opening the way for Lenin's party to seize power. "Worse is better" is, however, relevant to the future of the twenty-first-century global economy. It is an accurate assess- ment of financial crises and thus a reason for optimism that, for the foreseeable future, a repetition of the great financial crisis of 2008, which constitutes the greatest danger to globalization, can be avoided.

Bubbles whose bursting can cause immense damage, such as the American housing bubble, stem from conditions that do not change: the inherent volatility of money, the structure of free markets, and human nature itself, with its inherent desire for gain. The potential for financial disaster is therefore ever-present. If bubbles cannot be eliminated altogether, however, their size and frequency can be limited, in two ways.

Governments can impose rules for this purpose, and in the wake of 2008 they attempted to do so. The United States enacted a series of regulations designed to make finance safer, in legislation named for its principal Democratic sponsors, former Connecticut senator Christopher Dodd and former Massachusetts representative Barney Frank.[102] But rules cannot be designed or enforced to prevent every possible undesirable contingency, and serious twenty-first-century threats to global finance remain: the major American financial institutions are larger than ever, for example, and banks remain potentially vulnerable because they depend so heavily on debt rather than capital.[103]

Rules governing finance resemble speed limits: they can be imposed but are easily violated. Highway safety depends ultimately on the good sense of drivers. So it is with finance, where stability rests ultimately on the conduct of investors. And here, worse *is* better.

Crises are avoided when investors, rightly fearful of the risks of recklessness in making their investments, act with prudence. As human history demonstrates, prudence is all too often in short supply. But unhappy experience within recent memory, such as the 2008 financial crisis, helps to promote it.

Investors' behavior, to put it differently, is driven by both greed and fear. A proper balance between the two yields prudent conduct. In the years leading up to 2008, fear was lacking. The near-meltdown of the American financial system in that year restored it. Because the financial crisis was so deep, the memories of it, and the useful fear they engender, are likely to last for a long time, reducing the chances of another such episode.

If the world does manage to minimize the shocks from finance in the years ahead, this will reduce the threat to the principal goal of globalization: economic growth. Avoiding such a shock, however, will not in and of itself *produce* growth. The world's rate of economic advance will depend heavily on something else: the capacity of the largest and most important countries outside the trilateral re-gions—the BRICs: Brazil, Russia, India, and China—to fulfill their large economic potential. Along with the sturdiness of the roof that protects international economic activity, the strength of the inevi-table backlash against cross-border flows—especially goods from China and services from India—and the frequency and severity of the financial crises created by the nature of money and free markets interacting with the large river of capital that gushes across national borders, the economic futures of these countries will determine the future of the global economy. Like the other three, the economic performances of the BRICs will depend on politics.

CHAPTER FOUR

THE BRICS

The reversal towards an earlier norm has already started. Emerging and developing countries now account, for the first time in the modern era, for about half of total world output.

—SAMUEL BRITTAN[1]

... high growth and low growth cannot be explained by strictly economic factors alone. Leadership, politics, governance structures, and the effectiveness of government have crucial parts to play in the drama.

—MICHAEL SPENCE[2]

The capacity of politics to get in the way of economic growth has dominated most of the economic history of most of the world.

—JOHN KAY[3]

The Building Blocks of the Future

On June 16, 2009, in Yekaterinburg, Russia, a new international organization met for the first time. The initial BRICs summit brought together the leaders of the countries the first letters of whose names formed the organization's title: Brazil, Russia, India, and China. The group had an unusual origin. Most international organizations are

created by the initiative of governments to serve a particular pur-
pose or set of purposes. This was true, for example, of the North
Atlantic Treaty Organization—NATO—formed in 1949, and of the
European Union—the EU—which emerged from the European
Community in 1993.

The idea of the BRICs as a distinct grouping, by contrast, came
from a paper published in 2001 by Jim O'Neill of the Economics Department of the investment bank Goldman Sachs entitled
"Building Better Global Economic BRICs."[4] It argued that these
four countries were destined to become global leaders in economic
growth. The term caught on and began to appear in discussions of
international politics and economics. It spread so widely and became
so popular that the governments of the countries O'Neill had desig-
nated decided to turn it into an ongoing organization that agreed to
meet annually.[5] It is a rare example of life imitating research.

The term "BRICs" caught on because it denotes something new
and important: the rise to economic global economic prominence,
for the first time since the beginnings of genuine international economic integration in the mid-nineteenth century, of countries outside the trilateral regions. In the first two decades after 1990 all four
of the BRICs achieved growth rates impressive in and of themselves
and higher than those of the trilateral countries.[6] They have the
potential to continue to do very well in the years ahead, and if they
do, they and the countries like them—those that are poorer than the
Western countries, that participate fully in the global economy, and
are often called "developing countries" or "emerging markets"—will
become the engines of worldwide economic growth.[7] The term has
particular resonance because of its homonym: "bricks." These countries, if they fulfill their potential, will serve as the foundation, the
building blocks, of the global economy in the twenty-first century.

Slower growth in the trilateral world is one reason for this.
More important is the capacity, because of the dynamics of convergence[8]—that is, "catch-up"—for high growth in the ranks of the

developing countries.[9] It is they that will supply the majority of the world's new workers and consumers in the years ahead,[10] which will give the world more and better goods and services at lower prices. They will also, especially as their levels of education rise, generate inventions and innovations that will enhance productivity, and thus economic growth, everywhere.

In the nineteenth century the incorporation of the United States, Germany, and Japan into the global economy enhanced global output. After 1945 the addition of southern Europe and countries in East and Southeast Asia did so again. In the twenty-first century the participation of the developing countries has had and will continue to have this effect. There are, however, many such countries. Why single out the four BRICs?

Of all the developing countries the BRICs are the most important. They are the largest and most powerful countries in four crucial regions of the planet: Brazil in Latin America, Russia in eastern Eurasia, India in South Asia, and China in East Asia. Together their populations total 3 billion people.[11]

They have broadly similar recent economic histories. Each stood partly or entirely outside the globalized international economic order after World War II. Each had a "road-to-Damascus" moment when it saw the error of its economic ways and converted to free markets and globalization. Like a person who improves his or her health by switching to a more nutritious diet and beginning to exercise regularly, each was rewarded for its conversion by accelerated economic growth. The aggregate GDP of the four quadrupled between 2001 and 2011. In 2012 it stood at about $13 trillion and Jim O'Neill predicted that that figure would double in the ensuing decade.[12] All of them except Russia suffered less from the global recession of the first decade of the twenty-first century than did the trilateral countries, although growth in each began to slow thereafter.[13] By 2013 their growth rates had fallen below the levels attained before 2008; but they remained higher than those of the trilateral countries, and because of convergence the potential for future growth remained considerably higher in the BRIC countries than in the trilateral world.

To be sure, the BRICs differ from one another in important ways—in size of population, for example, with China and India dwarfing Brazil and Russia (and every other country on the planet as well.)[14] Their recent economic histories, while similar, are not identical. During most of the second half of the twentieth century, Russia and China had communist economic systems in which the government owned all major property and dictated all major economic decisions. These two countries had to start from scratch in building the institutions and cultivating the habits, skills, and practices that a free-market economy and integration into the global economic order require. Brazil and India, by contrast, pursued import-substituting socialist economic policies, with a lesser although still substantial economic role for the government. They had smaller, easier adjustments to make. Finally, Brazil and Russia have raw materials in sufficient abundance to export them. Russia's natural resources in fact have a decisive impact on its politics and economics. China and India, by contrast, have to import what the other two export, especially oil.

Nor, despite their annual summit meetings, have the BRIC countries found common interests to pursue jointly. They have talked about forming a common bank for economic development but have taken no steps to create one. The yearly meetings of their leaders have produced general declarations but nothing more.

The BRICs will almost certainly continue to grow faster than the trilateral economies, but just how much faster will depend, more than anything else, on a particular feature of their politics. For the future of the BRICs, politics, through its impact on governance, will shape economics. In the novels of the twentieth-century writer Raymond Chandler that feature the detective Philip Marlowe, there is often a character, usually a woman, whose past comes back to haunt her, threatening the new life she is trying to build. Similarly, for all four of the BRICs the crucial political feature is something that was an asset for the purpose of economic growth in the past but looms as a liability in the future.

The asset-turned-liability varies from country to country. For Brazil it is the political tradition known as populism. For Russia it is the distorting impact on public policy of the country's large reserves of energy. For India and China it is their respective political systems: democratic in the first case, authoritarian in the second. The economic future of all four BRICs, and therefore the future of global economy in which all will play an important part, depends heavily on how effectively each can discard, overcome, or modify a once beneficial but now dysfunctional political legacy of the recent past.

Brazil: The Perils of Populism

"Brazil is the country of the future," goes an old saying, "and always will be." In the twentieth century the country had a reputation for having the world's best coffee, its most beautiful beaches at Ipanema and Copacabana, its most creative and alluring dances— film's greatest dancing couple, Fred Astaire and Ginger Rogers, made their screen debut in *Flying Down to Rio* in 1933, introducing to the world "the Carioca"—and for unfulfilled economic potential.

That potential is vast. Brazil is the world's fifth-largest country in both area and population. It has large stretches of arable land some of which is so fertile that it yields three crops per year, substantial natural resources, the world's largest freshwater supply, an extensive Atlantic coastline with several good ports, and borders with every other South American country except Chile.[15]

In the twentieth century the approach to governance found throughout Latin America and known as populism, while producing growth for a time, ultimately held the country back economically. In the 1990s an economic shock led to a change of course in economic policy and Brazil at last began to fulfill its potential, achieving growth steady enough and high enough to qualify it for membership in the BRICs. Sustaining that growth will require keeping the forces of populism at bay.

The precise form populism took varied from one Latin American country to another but in Brazil, as almost everywhere else, it had three main elements: a strategy for economic growth, a large economic role for the government, and a particular political style.

Brazil's populists followed the strategy of import-substituting industrialization.[16] The government imposed tariffs on imports in order to protect local industries—steel, aluminum, automobiles, and shipbuilding among others. It provided subsidies to these industries, controlled the country's exchange rate, and allocated foreign exchange to strengthen them. In some cases it assumed direct responsibility for ownership and management.[17]

Under populism the government not only sought to promote a local industrial base, it also, in keeping with the populist commitment to enhance the people's welfare, provided financial benefits to many Brazilians. It established a generous pension system. By owning and managing firms in important sectors of the economy, it created jobs and paid high wages to the employees of these firms as well as to the bureaucrats in the ever-expanding departments of the government itself.[18] All this made public spending consistently high.

As for politics, populism emphasized the national leader at the expense of institutions. Populist leaders asserted, and drew their claims to govern from, a direct connection with the people. In fact, in Brazil they relied for political support not on all of the people but mainly on the workers and lower middle classes of the cities. The country's twentieth-century leaders did not always hold power by virtue of free elections.[19]

Brazilian populism's economic record in the years after World War II was eminently respectable. Between 1947 and 1962 the size of the country's industrial sector more than tripled and its average yearly growth rate exceeded 6 percent.[20] Overall, from 1950 to

1975 the country grew at 7 percent per year. Over the next twenty-five years, however, per capita income hardly grew at all.[21]

A major reason for this uneven performance was Brazil's continuing and sometimes ruinously high inflation, the result of its populist economic policies. The loans and subsidies to state-owned enterprises, the growing payrolls of government workers, and the generous programs of government-provided benefits were expensive. They produced large deficits, which the government funded by borrowing—thereby creating steep levels of debt—or by printing money.

In consequence, the price level rose. In the 1950s inflation averaged 17.3 percent per year, in the 1960s 44.7 percent, in the 1970s 34 percent, and in the 1980s 428 percent. It reached almost 1,400 percent yearly between 1990 and 1994 before it was finally brought under control.[22] Inflation discouraged saving and investment and provoked capital flight. At its worst, Brazil approached the condition known as "hyperinflation," in which money loses its value and people are reduced to conducting economic transactions through barter. From the 1970s through the mid-1990s it had four separate currencies. It became the land not only of coffee, beaches, and the samba, but also of soaring prices.

The shock that led to Brazil's change of economic direction came from a foreign exchange crisis. To operate its increasingly industrialized economy the country had to import oil.[23] The two oil shocks of the 1970s sharply raised the price of these imports. The cost of total imports rose from $5.2 billion in 1973 to $12.6 billion the next year.[24] The government borrowed heavily to pay the bill. Its external debt, $6.2 billion in 1973, had increased to $31.6 billion by 1978, an annual increase of 38 percent.

Unable to service its debt, Brazil had to enter into negotiations with the major international commercial banks and the International Monetary Fund (IMF) to restructure its obligations and obtain additional funding. The funds came with conditions and the conditions set in motion a decade-long series of economic reforms, as a consequence of which the country jettisoned many of the populist practices that had accumulated over half a century.

In return for loans and the use of its good offices to help restructure its debt, the IMF required that Brazil conduct a more austere fiscal policy, which meant reducing or abolishing some of the subsidies and other benefits the Brazilian government provided. In addition, the government began to transfer state-owned enterprises to private hands.[25] At the same time it lowered the barriers it had erected to international economic activity. After 1994 the volume of direct foreign investment increased substantially.[26] As for trade, between 1990 and 1994 average tariffs declined from 34.2 percent to 14.2 percent,[27] and in 1991 the country entered into a free-trade agreement known as Mercosur with Argentina, Paraguay, and Uruguay.

Along with its external deficit, the most urgent problem facing the Brazilian government was rampant inflation, which took more than a decade to subdue. While the country did achieve a positive trade balance after 1982, the methods by which it did so, in particular the devaluation of the Brazilian currency, had the effect of raising prices across the economy.[28] Inflation soared in the ten years after the debt crisis. For much of the 1980s and in the early years of the 1990s, the Brazilian government was preoccupied with trying to stop the upward surge of prices. A number of stabilization measures were implemented, but to no avail. Finally, with the economy teetering on the brink of hyperinflation, the minister of finance, Fernando Henrique Cardoso, introduced the *real* plan—so called because it created the *Unidade Real de Valor*, the Unit of Real Value—between December 1993 (a year in which the annual inflation rate reached 2,708 percent) and July 1994. Cardoso's plan did succeed in breaking the inflationary spiral.

The success of the *real* plan boosted the popularity of its chief architect and Cardoso was twice elected Brazil's president, in 1994 and 1998. During his term of office part of the structure of economic populism was dismantled, and his successor set the seal on Brazil's new, globalization-friendly economic course.

Luiz Inácio Lula da Silva had the trappings of a populist politician. He grew up in poverty, had little education, and rose to become an important labor leader. Before finally winning in 2002 he had run unsuccessfully for the presidency three times, always as an advocate of a broad economic role for the government. He appealed to the groups that benefited from populist economic policies, especially union members. Yet contrary to both the hopes of many of his supporters and the fears of the international financial community, Lula adhered to the economic policies of his predecessor. In doing so he ratified them as acceptable across the full range of Brazilian political opinion. The gradual opening of the Brazilian economy to the rest of the world continued and inflation remained under control. A mark of Brazil's economic success came in 2011 when its currency, long one of the world's weakest because of chronic inflation, had become, in the eyes of some economists, overvalued—that is, too strong.[29]

Even with the reforms, Brazil grew more slowly than Russia (during the following decade), India, and China. From 1995 to 2006 the real growth rate averaged only 2.25 percent annually. Between 2003 and 2006, when developing countries grew at an average annual rate of 7.3 percent, Brazil's rate was 3.3 percent.[30] Growth picked up in Lula's second term, rising to 6.6 percent in 2007 and 5.1 percent in 2008. The country weathered the great global recession of 2007–2009 comparatively well and achieved 7.5 percent growth in 2010, although the figure slipped to 2.7 percent in 2011 and 1.5 percent in 2012, partly as a result of the decline in the global demand for the commodities that the country exports.[31]

Brazil's growth trailed that of the other BRICs because, having done relatively well from the 1940s through the 1970s and not having inflicted as much damage on its economy as the Russians and Chinese had with their centrally planned systems, it could not make as large gains as they could simply by discontinuing counterproductive practices. Nor did Brazil have reservoirs of underemployed villagers as large as China's and India's to transfer from rural to more productive urban work and thus boost growth. Moreover, the country's economy suffered from the East Asian financial crisis of the late 1990s, which spread to Russia and from there to Brazil. As in the early 1980s, an international financial rescue had to be arranged, the conditions for which dampened economic activity.[32]

Brazil grew less rapidly than it might have even after the Cardoso reforms for another reason, which stands as the chief obstacle to sustained high growth in the future: a large residue of populism remains. The country has retained many of the commitments to public expenditure that had accumulated over the course of the twentieth century and the fulfillment of which made inflation a chronic problem. The government is still obligated to pay generous social welfare benefits: pensions, for example, account for a strikingly high 13 percent of GDP.[33] It continues to be responsible for the wages of the many employees of its own bureaucracies and the workers in enterprises that public authorities still own and operate, and these wages tend to rise rapidly.[34]

The structure of Brazil's political system expands the government's obligations. Political parties are numerous and weak. The platform of the typical elected official promises to bring government benefits to those who vote for him or her (Brazil is not, of course, the only country in which this is true), and legislative activity consists to a very large extent of efforts, often successful, to do just that.[35]

The Brazilian constitution adds pressure to spend money. It gives the country a federal structure, with 27 states and more than 5,500 municipalities. Each of them offers an arena for doling out patronage and favors. To compound the problem, the federal government is constitutionally required to remit 21.5 percent of the revenues it collects to the states and 22.5 percent to the municipalities,[36] enhancing the capacity of state and local officials to be generous to their constituents. The constitution itself is a populist document of sorts. Adopted in 1988, it mandates government responsibility for a range of social welfare benefits including "education, health, work, leisure, security, social security, protection of motherhood and childhood assistance to the destitute."[37]

Moreover, Brazil is a country marked by an unusually high degree of economic inequality. Many Brazilians are poor.[38] Lula supplemented the growth-promoting policies he inherited with income-support programs for the poor, which affected more than 40 million people in a country of 190 million. While poverty has fallen, and these programs have made a contribution to this development, they are nonetheless expensive.[39]

Because of these demands on the public treasury, budget deficits have persisted.[40] In the wake of the successful stabilization of prices in the 1990s, the Brazilian government has funded the deficits more extensively than in the past through taxation. This has helped to curb inflation, but high taxes and high public spending crowd out private investment, which is a major force behind economic growth.[41]

Furthermore, Brazil's public spending does less than it might to foster growth because populism channels government money to things that do not promote it. The pension benefits, pork-barrel projects, generous public sector wages, and income supplement programs support, on the whole, private spending.[42] For growth, however, Brazil also needs public investment—in roads, ports, power plants, and above all in education.[43] The shortcomings of its system of education in particular cloud the country's long-term economic future.

That future depends on the outcome of the country's ongoing political struggle over economic policy. On one side of this struggle, pressing for ever-greater public expenditure, stand the forces of populism, with their deep historical roots, their powerful constituencies, and in some cases—efforts to reduce poverty, for example—their strong moral claims. Opposing them are those favoring fiscal prudence and productive public investment, who have global economic history, including the last two decades of Brazilian economic history, on their side but shallower political support throughout the country.[44]

In determining Brazil's twenty-first-century economic destiny, to these conflicting forces will be added another important development. The country will have access to large offshore reserves of the world's most valuable mineral: oil. Indeed, it is almost certain to become a major oil exporter.[45] Oil revenues will of course add to Brazil's national income, and if used wisely can also augment its rate of long-term economic growth. But oil revenues are not always used wisely. Oil can have, for a country rich in it, harmful as well as beneficial consequences, as the experience of Brazil's fellow BRIC, Russia, all too vividly demonstrates.

Russia: The Resource Curse

On December 10, 2011, more than 50,000 people gathered in Moscow for a protest demonstration. Two weeks later as many as 120,000 people demonstrated in the same city. On February 4, 2012, an estimated 150,000 people turned out there. These demonstrations broke with the Russian tradition. In the Soviet period, which ended in 1991, public protests of any kind were immediately and forcefully quashed, with the participants jailed, or worse. In the first two post-Soviet decades demonstrations were rare, officially discouraged, and never very large.

The causes that drew so many Muscovites, most of them more affluent than the average Russian, into the streets were political. The demonstrators were protesting a rigged parliamentary election and an unfree election for the presidency in which the victory of the prime minister and former president Vladimir Putin was foreordained.

Although political in motivation, the demonstrations had important economic implications. The undemocratic regime whose conduct and, by implication, whose very existence were the subjects of the protests rested on more than coercion—although it certainly employed force to remain in power. The Putin government had an economic basis as well. During its rule the Russian economy had grown fast enough for the country to merit inclusion in the ranks of the BRICs and for the regime to earn public acceptance and even popularity. That growth had come from the revenues it received from the sale of the country's oil and natural gas.

While making possible economic growth in the present, however, Russia's energy resources have also, in a number of ways, reduced the country's prospects for future growth, not least by keeping in power a government that combined authoritarian political measures with a failure to build the economic and political foundation necessary for a steadily rising GDP. In this way energy is for Russia a liability as well an asset, a curse as well as a blessing. The country's economic future—its capacity to fulfill its potential for growth—depends on how it copes with its energy curse.

When Russia's post-Soviet history began, with the end of Communist Party rule and the transition from a centrally planned to a free-market economy, the country's biggest economic problem was not its energy reserves. It was, rather, the total absence of free-market institutions. Russia lacked, among other things, private property, the rule of law, and a financial system for allocating capital. As it embarked on its career as a free-market economy after seven decades of Communist rule, the country was in the position of a person who is giving a piano recital while at the same time learning to play the instrument.

It did not have the luxury of learning in a benign economic environment. Because the Soviet government had printed money recklessly during its final months, and because a number of the constituent republics of the Soviet Union had declared themselves autonomous and had begun issuing currency on their own, the new Russian government inherited roaring inflation.[46]

In addition, the new Russia suffered a large "trade shock" with the collapse of the economic ties among the fifteen new countries that had once formed the Soviet Union and the end of most of the economic connections with what had, until 1989, been the Communist-governed countries of Eastern Europe. Finally, Russia's overall output fell, by some estimates, by 40 to 50 percent[47] as the Soviet-era factories making products no one would buy had to close. As a result, unemployment rose.

Yet amid this economic turmoil the country did make major strides in constructing a working market economy. The government of Boris Yeltsin, the first post-Soviet president, freed most prices, which were thereafter set by supply and demand rather than by planners' dictates. The shortages that central planning had created disappeared. The government also broke the power of what had been the Soviet military-industrial complex. The armed forces, and defense spending, diminished dramatically. The new Russian government liberalized trade. The Soviet economy had been a highly protected one. Post-Soviet Russia opened itself to the world. The government also transferred property from the state, which had owned virtually all of it under communism, to private control. This was a gigantic undertaking that proved to be neither smooth nor entirely transparent, and the results were far from equitable. But privatization did give Russia the indispensable institution of any free-market economy, private property.[48]

In 1998, Russia stumbled into a financial crisis that arose from the large gap, amounting to 8 to 9 percent of GDP, between what the government spent and the revenue it collected. To fill the gap it sold bonds to Russians and to foreigners, enticing them by offering ever-higher rates of interest. By the summer of that year the government was having great difficulty in both paying the interest on the outstanding bonds and in selling new ones. On August 17 it defaulted on $70 billion of domestic debt and devalued the ruble by 75 percent, inflicting heavy losses on its foreign creditors.[49]

This effective declaration of bankruptcy, however, helped create the conditions for a sharp upward economic turn. The crisis of August 1998 led to the equivalent for Russia of the *real* plan in Brazil.

The shock of the crisis prompted the government to end its chronic deficits by substantially reducing expenditures. This eliminated the underlying cause of the inflation from which Russia was suffering, and the rate of price increases dropped sharply.[50]

Vladimir Putin succeeded Boris Yeltsin as Russia's president on December 31, 1999, and the structure of the economy over which he presided was, from the point of view of maximizing economic growth, imperfect at best. It was riddled with what economists call "rent-seeking," rents being defined as profits in excess of what the normal workings of the market would bring that are generally secured by the use of political power and influence. In both the Yeltsin and Putin eras economic privileges, above all control over valuable natural resources, were given away or sold at below-market prices to politically favored individuals and groups who were almost invariably cronies or political allies of the president and who proceeded to get rich from them.

Russia also came to be pervaded by corruption.[51] By the estimate of a Russian think tank, as of 2005 bribes accounted for fully 20 percent of the country's GDP. According to another Russian assessment, the value of bribes paid annually in the country rose from $33 billion when Putin came to power to more than $400 billion at the end of his second presidential term in 2008.[52]

In no small part because so much of Russia's wealth went into rents and bribes, little of it went to build the infrastructure—the roads, bridges, ports, and schools—that form the foundation of productive economic activity.[53] Nor did private investment, as a share of overall GDP, increase during Putin's first presidency.[54]

The Putin government also assaulted the crucial institution of private property, without which no market economy can function properly. In 2003 and 2004 the regime jailed Mikhail Khodorkovsky, the owner of Yukos, a large oil company, on questionable charges viewed by many as trumped-up and politically motivated. Yukos ended up in bankruptcy with most of its assets in the hands of the state-owned oil company Rosneft. What amounted essentially to an arbitrary confiscation of Yukos called into question the security of property rights in post-Soviet Russia.[55]

Yet in Putin's first two terms the Russian economy performed well—well enough to qualify the country for a place among the BRICs.[56] In sharp contrast to the initial post-Soviet years, in the decade between the Russian financial crisis in 1998 and the American one in 2008, Russia's economy grew by 7 percent per year, with real income increasing by a factor of 2.5 and real wages tripling.[57] A middle class with income to spend on consumer goods emerged in the major cities, especially Moscow. Unlike in the 1990s, government workers received their wages and retired people their pensions, both of which increased. The country accumulated the world's third-largest store of hard-currency reserves, after those of China and Japan, totaling almost $600 billion, only a decade after it had, in effect, run out of them.[58]

How was this possible? A legend from Russia's imperial past provides a partial precedent. The legend has it that in order to deceive the Empress Catherine II into believing that her newly conquered territories in the Crimean Peninsula were thriving, the imperial minister Grigory Potemkin had hollow façades of villages constructed along the banks of the Dnieper River, which became known as "Potemkin villages." Similarly, in the twenty-first century's opening decade Russia had a kind of "Potemkin economy"—not because Putin had deliberately engineered the appearance of prosperity but in the sense that the revenues from the country's large energy reserves camouflaged the economy's underlying weaknesses.

The price of oil, and Russia's revenues from its sale, remained low during Boris Yeltsin's term in office, but Vladimir Putin benefited from a dramatic rise in that price. In 1998 a barrel of oil sold for $15. By 2000 the price had climbed to $32, and after three years of stability it began, in 2004, a very steep ascent, exceeding $100 by the time Putin exchanged the presidency for the prime minister's office in 2008 and reaching a peak of almost $150 per barrel in August of that year.[59] This precipitous rise, combined with an increase in the country's oil production in the early years of the first decade of the new century, sent Russia's GDP soaring.[60]

In 2005, energy, including natural gas as well as oil,[61] accounted for 30 percent of that GDP and 60 percent of Russia's exports. The total value of energy exports, which was $29 billion in 1990, climbed to $76 billion in 1999 and $350 billion in 2007.[62] Half the country's economic growth came not from anything Russians made or did but simply from the rise in the price of oil.[63] By one estimate, a $10-per-barrel rise in the price of oil boosted Russia's GDP by about 2 percent.[64]

The benefits of oil, and especially the benefits in Russia for the Putin regime, whose members siphoned off a large share of the revenue it brought for themselves and whose popularity soared with the oil-funded economic boom,[65] are obvious. But energy reserves have economic drawbacks as well. They can do for economies what steroids do for athletes, enhancing performance in the short term but having deleterious effects in the long run. Indeed, energy riches can produce pathologies common enough that a term for those that suffer from them has come into common usage: "petro-states."[66] Studies have shown that petro-states have sometimes actually grown more slowly than have countries without energy resources.[67] The presence of large energy reserves can retard long-term economic growth in four ways, all of them relevant to Russia.

Petro-states often suffer from what economists call the "Dutch Disease," named after the effect on The Netherlands of the discovery of deposits of natural gas off its coast in 1959. Demand for the gas pushed up the value of the Dutch currency, which led to an expansion of the country's imports but injured industries that competed with these imports as well as those that depended on exports, whose products became more expensive.[68] In the first decade of the new century Russia displayed the symptoms of the Dutch Disease. Import-competing domestic industrial output grew less rapidly than the imports with which they competed, suggesting that the energy-driven elevation of the ruble's exchange rate was hurting Russian industry.[69]

Oil wealth also tends to increase the size of the government, which diverts money from more productive uses. Oil revenues support a bloated bureaucracy and a variety of not-necessarily-productive government programs. When the revenues decline with reductions in the price of energy, bureaucrats and programs still demand funding. This can lead to large budget deficits, or inflation, or both—neither conducive to economic progress. True to form, the Russian government expanded during the Putin era; in his first two terms approximately 363,000 new bureaucrats were hired.[70]

Perhaps most damagingly, because the energy sector by itself supplies the revenues that the government needs, oil wealth relieves the pressure to carry out policies that promote the development of a robust and broad-based economy. Petro-states often lag in building the infrastructure and the institutions—legal and financial systems, for example—that support growth and in providing the education needed to prepare people for productive employment. These countries can get rich without working and so do not learn to work.[71] They resemble "trust-fund babies"—the children of very wealthy parents—who, because they anticipate inheriting all the money they will need, do not master the basic skills necessary to earn a living. Their trust funds may ensure a comfortable life, at least for a while, but if their money runs out, they have great difficulty in fending for themselves. Post-Soviet Russia fits this description.

Energy wealth can inhibit economic growth in yet another, indirect but important, way: by discouraging the development of democracy. The windfall from oil creates a formidable temptation for rulers to hold on to power indefinitely in order to keep a large share of the wealth for themselves. That is what happened in Russia.[72] During his initial presidency Putin made Russia less democratic, restricting liberties and limiting the Russian public's control over its government. Oil wealth gives autocratic rulers not only the incentive but also the means to retain power. They can, in effect, bribe the populace with generous welfare benefits in exchange for political passivity. Where they cannot purchase acquiescence, they can fund effective instruments of repression. That is how the oil-exporting Arab countries of the Persian Gulf are governed[73] and how Russia has been ruled during the Putin era.

The absence of democracy in energy-rich countries, including Russia, inhibits growth because the rulers have little incentive to take steps, or spend money, to promote it. They get rich from the proceeds from the sale of the country's energy; and besides, economic growth might foster political activity that would threaten their monopoly of power. Those outside the ruling circle do have such an incentive, but without channels of political participation they lack the power to press the rulers to undertake growth-promoting policies.[74]

Russia runs the risk of having its oil wealth turn the country into a giant, Slavic, Eurasian Saudi Arabia, with a self-selected elite growing rich on the proceeds from the sale of its energy and using what is left over to maintain political control by bribing and repressing the public. In that case, and unlike the other BRICs, Russia would make no appreciable contribution to twenty-first-century global economic growth.

Such a fate is not foreordained. Russia need not become a full-fledged petro-state. It has an industrial base, a populace well educated by global standards, with virtually universal literacy and a tradition of excellence in science and mathematics.[75] It has a fortunate location for a country embedded in the integrated global economy: it borders on what are in economic terms the four most important regions in the world: Europe, East Asia, the Middle East, and—across the Bering Strait—North America.

Moreover, Russia cannot fully become Saudi Arabia because it does not have enough oil. The ratio of reserves to population is much lower for Russia than it is, for example, for the oil sheikhdoms of the Persian Gulf.[76] Even continued high energy prices—and these are not guaranteed—will not by themselves make it possible for Russians to achieve a Western standard of living without having to work for it.[77]

It is therefore possible that Russia will experience the worst of both worlds: energy revenues high enough to generate widespread corruption and prevent robust growth, but not high enough to sustain the standard of living to which Russians aspire. Russia could become not Saudi Arabia but Nigeria. This would make the country's economic future all the more difficult because of its demographic prospects. Its population is shrinking. The combination of low birth rates and high mortality rates reduces the number of Russians by 700,000 per year. On this pace the Russian population will fall from 144 million to 121 million in 2030 and, if the trends continue, to 99 million and perhaps as low as 77 million in 2050—in which case it would have fewer than one-quarter as many people as the United States.[78]

Energy aside, in order to grow economically Russia will have to produce more output with fewer workers, which requires precisely the institutions and practices that energy wealth discourages. So the Russian people—and the rest of the world, which would benefit from BRIC-like Russian economic growth in the decades ahead—have a powerful interest in seeing the country throw off the energy curse that hangs over it.

That could happen through a decline in the global price of energy because of new discoveries of fossil fuel, new and different sources of energy, and the widespread diffusion of the techniques of conservation combined with a reduction in Russian energy production. Some of these things had already begun in the second decade of the twenty-first century.[79] In such a case Russia would suffer immediate economic losses, but if falling energy prices spurred the measures needed for long-term economic growth, the country would ultimately gain from their decline. Falling energy income might put Russia on a more promising economic course by removing the basis for the political support the Putin regime has enjoyed, leading to the replacement of that regime with one more democratically oriented and more committed to growth-promoting policies.[80]

Or, the Russian people might put an end to the regime even without a sharp drop in energy revenues, through a political movement that mounts the kinds of demonstrations that occurred in Moscow at the end of 2011 and the outset of 2012. That is how democracy came to Communist Eastern Europe in 1989, and to other countries around the world in previous years. Democracy is generally good for economic growth, and it would surely be good for Russia's economic future. Still, democracy by itself does not guarantee optimal economic performance, as the experience of another BRIC country, India, demonstrates.

India: The Dysfunctions of Democracy

On July 31, 2012, India set an undesirable world record. It experienced the largest blackout in history. Some 670 million people lost power—nearly 10 percent of the inhabitants of the entire planet. The event damaged the country's economy, with tens of millions of the affected people unable to work.[81] It was a national embarrassment. But perhaps its most damning feature was the fact that, for India, it was not an unusual occurrence. Power failures, although never before on such a large scale, are a fact of everyday life there.[82] Reliably uninterrupted electricity is available in few places in the country.

The uncertainty of its supply is a failure of government, for it is the government that, in India as in virtually every other country, has the responsibility for providing it. That failure, in turn, is part of a wider one, which is the major obstacle to the fulfillment of India's enormous economic potential. Both by what it does and what it fails to do, India's government at every level gives inadequate support to, and sometimes actively obstructs, productive economic activity. In India the political system drags down the economy.[83]

That political system is a democratic one. India has maintained democratic government, with one brief exception, since its independence from Great Britain in 1947. Democracy is one of the country's proudest and most important achievements, and has in fact made a major contribution to the economic progress that it has achieved. Like populism for Brazil and energy for Russia, however, democracy, as it is practiced in India, is not only an economic asset, it is also an economic liability.

India inherited many of the institutions of democracy from Great Britain, but the major credit for establishing it belongs to its first post-independence leaders and above all to its prime minister from 1947 to 1964, Jawaharlal Nehru. Educated in England and having seen Western democracy first hand, Nehru had a personal commitment to it. Beyond his own preferences, however, democracy was, and remains, a necessity for his country.

With its various ethnic groups, religions, rigid social categories known as castes, and seventeen major languages, India has the diversity of the entire European Union—but with twice as many people. Since independence, many of its constituent groups have agitated for changes in its public life, sometimes violently. Imperfectly, to be sure, and often after prolonged (but invariably localized) instability, Indian democracy has always managed to accommodate them. India has avoided full-scale civil war and the breakup of the country, which was the fate of Pakistan, the other sovereign state carved out of the British Empire on the Asian subcontinent. Without democracy, with its emphasis on compromise, the peaceful resolution of disputes, and the rights of minorities, a united India within its twenty-first-century borders would not exist.[84]

Nehru set India on a particular economic course as well: import-substituting industrialization, with the promotion of heavy industries such as steel through subsidies, foreign-exchange controls, and protective tariffs.[85] The government assumed the ownership and management of some parts of the economy and imposed regulations on much of the rest.[86] Nehru's policies did not seek to make

India an integral part of the revived international economic order. After World War II, globalization proceeded without major Indian participation.[87]

By the standards of its recent past the Indian economy performed respectably during the Nehru era. Yearly growth during the last decades of British rule had averaged 1 percent. Independent India raised that rate to 4.1 percent.[88]

Nehru's daughter Indira Gandhi became prime minister in 1966 and proceeded to bring the banking system as well as the oil and coal industries under state control. She so discouraged foreign investors that major international companies such as IBM and Coca-Cola abandoned their businesses in India. She also presided over an increase in the tangle of government-imposed regulations within which the Indian economy had to operate.[89]

As a result—and also because of external shocks such as a 1971 war with Pakistan and the steep increases in the price of oil in 1973–74 and 1979—India's economic growth rate declined. Between 1965 and 1981 it fell to 3.2 percent.[90] Even when the economy grew 4 percent annually, the country's population increased yearly by 2 percent, yielding per capita growth of only 2 percent, a performance that became known, disparagingly, as the "Hindu rate of growth."

In 1991, India's slow-growing economy experienced a foreign-exchange crisis. The country had reserves covering only a single month's imports. Confidence in India's international creditworthiness evaporated, and in July of that year it was forced, like other countries before and since, to apply to the International Monetary Fund for a loan.[91] In return for the loan the government in New Delhi, with the Cambridge- and Oxford-trained economist Manmohan Singh as finance minister, was obliged to reduce its deficit and to implement a series of measures that rolled back government controls on economic activity.

India lowered barriers to trade while making the rupee convertible on the current account. It lifted some restraints on foreign direct investment. It abolished many regulations and licensing requirements for businesses.[92] It began a program of selling state-owned economic assets to the private sector.

These reforms brought impressive results. Between 1988–1989 and 2007 the average annual growth rate was 6.3 percent. From 2007 through 2011 it was even higher: 7.7 percent.[93] Exports rose fourteen times between 1991 and 2007.[94] In the two decades following 1991 the country's total output quadrupled.[95]

Even with this more-than-respectable performance, however, India still qualified as an economic underachiever. It lagged well behind China, the only other country of comparable size, which had emerged from World War II at about the same economic level. China's economy is about four times as large as India's, and India has many more people living in poverty.[96] China plays a far bigger role in the international economy. Of course, China's economic reforms began a decade before India's, but that does not fully account for the gap between them. China's rate of economic growth has exceeded India's even in the years of India's best performance. Two features of the Indian economy in particular have kept it from reaching its full potential in achieving economic growth and reducing poverty.

The first is its unusual, lopsided configuration. Every modern economy has three sectors: agriculture, industry, and services.[97] As countries become richer, workers move from one sector to another, and almost always in a particular order: from the farm to the factory to the office. So it was for the country that blazed the trail of economic growth that virtually every sovereign state has sought to follow, Great Britain. So it is today with China.

India, however, has departed from this pattern. Despite its economic growth, and the decline of agriculture's share in its total output due to expansion in other sectors, its agricultural workforce has shrunk only modestly.[98] Its industrial sector has grown relatively slowly, contributing only 27 percent of the country's GDP in 2008, with 17 percent coming from manufacturing.[99] Services in India, by contrast, have expanded rapidly, rising from 32 percent of the GDP in 1970–1971 to 41 percent in 1990–1991 and 52 percent in

2004–2005.[100] In comparison with other countries at a similar stage of economic development, and compared with what has been normal in economic history since the Industrial Revolution, India is an anomaly: a country that seems to be skipping the industrial stage of economic advance.

The size of the service sector is in large measure a tribute to India's thriving information technology companies, which employ sophisticated computer programmers and software designers, as well as to the young Indians in call centers who respond in fluent English to questions from around the world about computer malfunctions and credit card bills.[101] While its exploitation of information technology is an economic asset for India, this has created relatively few jobs. In a workforce of almost 500 million people, the information technology industry employed, in the middle of the first decade of the twenty-first century, just over a million of them, or about 0.25 percent of the country's total pool of labor.[102] For this reason, although they raise the country's GDP, India's service industries do relatively little to reduce its massive poverty.

Only a robust industrial sector with growing manufacturing industries can do that, but Indian manufacturing suffers from a shortage of the industries, and therefore the jobs, that require unskilled labor. Such jobs offer the most accessible and surest route out of poverty for India's hundreds of millions of rural laborers and their families.[103] It is the route that China, and other countries before it, have taken.[104] The underdevelopment of its industrial sector is the first feature of India's economy that keeps it from its full potential.

The second, which the 2012 blackout vividly illustrated, is the shortage of the things that governments ordinarily provide—roads, bridges, ports, and schools as well as reliable supplies of electricity and clean water—on which economic growth depends. Poor infrastructure constrains the Indian industrial sector. Factories need reliable supplies of power to operate effectively, good roads and railways to gather inputs and distribute products, and, if they are to sell what they make to other countries, ports for cargo ships and airports for high-value items and business travel. China has these things in abundance. India does not.[105]

Not only are power outages normal, nearly half the country's households lack any electricity at all.[106] As for transportation, in 2007 only 9 percent of the country's national highways had four lanes.[107] In that year China had 25,000 miles of expressways while India had 3,700.[108] While in the United States a trucker can haul a load a thousand miles in about twenty hours, in India the equivalent trip takes four to five days.[109] Shorter journeys can also be time-consuming: to travel the nineteen miles from the airport serving Mumbai, for example, to the city's downtown financial center can take more than two hours.[110] For cargo ships in India's ports, export dwell time (the time it takes for the ship to load and depart) is three to five days and import dwell time is seven to fourteen days. The international norms for these functions are, respectively, less than 18 hours and less than 24 hours.[111]

The shortcomings of Indian education also hold back the country's economy, including its manufacturing sector. Even many unskilled factory jobs require rudimentary literacy, and as jobs become more complicated, higher levels of education are needed to do them. Many villages have only part-time teachers for their young children; some have none. In the middle of the first decade of the twenty-first century, India's overall literacy rate was 75 percent, compared with China's 92 percent. The lack of unskilled manufacturing jobs and the inadequacies of India's infrastructure and education have a common cause. Both stem from failures of governance, which is ultimately a failure of the country's political system. The major challenges to India's twenty-first-century economic prospects arise from the shortcomings of Indian democracy.

Several of the growth-limiting aspects of the country's democratic political system are specifically Indian. The quality of its governance has deteriorated since Nehru's time, a decline captured by the exaggerated but not entirely misleading observation that while in the country's first independent parliament every member had written a book, in the initial parliament of the twenty-first century none of the members had even read one.[112] Indian parliamentary life has become, if not a criminal enterprise, then certainly an enterprise for criminals: a quarter of the members of the national legislature in 2007 had criminal backgrounds.[113]

As for administering the laws, the British bequeathed to independent India a highly trained, competent, and honest cadre of elite civil servants, but over six decades it expanded in size and declined in efficiency, while corruption came to pervade both the national and the state governments.[114] An estimated two-thirds of the subsidized grain that the government reserves for the poor is either stolen or adulterated.[115] The legal system has become dysfunctional. In 2006 the courts had a backlog of 27 million cases, which would take, at the prevailing rate of adjudication, more than 300 years to clear. The Indian equivalent of bankruptcy proceedings takes, on average, ten years.[116] In addition, the country's national parliament has become politically fragmented, which makes decisive and coherent action of any kind, let alone action promoting economic growth, extremely difficult.

Moreover, hostility to free markets has deep roots in India and remains alive in Indian politics. Socialist arguments, often stressing the need for a large economic role for the government in order to promote equality, are still invoked in debates about economic policy, usually by those opposing further reform.[117] Still influential, as well, are the ideas of the most important leader of the independence movement, Mohandas Gandhi, who denigrated modern industry, exalted village life, and regarded small farmers as the backbone of Indian society.[118] Furthermore, India's caste system creates a social hierarchy in which people engaged in commerce, although hardly at the bottom, rank lower than priests (Brahmins) and warriors. Like socialism and the Gandhian perspective, the caste system does not confer high prestige on business, profit, entrepreneurship, markets, or trade.

A more general aspect of political democracy, found wherever it is practiced, however—indeed, one of its defining and in many ways most admirable features, which has made it possible to conciliate dissatisfied constituencies and so keep India united—also hinders economic development: the political space available to minorities of all kinds. People organize themselves on the basis of a common identity—race, religion, ethnicity—but also according to common economic interests. Such groups work politically to bring benefits to their members, but the benefits can come at the expense of the general welfare. India, like other democracies, is susceptible to the formation of these "distributional coalitions,"[119] which tend over time to grow in power and number, to the detriment of a country's economic well-being.

It is a political advantage but also, on occasion, an economic drawback of democratic government that sometimes, as in the erection of tariffs,[120] it is minorities rather than majorities that rule. Powerful minorities have helped to create India's two major economic problems—a too-small manufacturing sector and inadequate infrastructure and education—by imposing some policies and blocking others, in both cases harming the interests of the country as a whole.

While India abounds in workers with low (or no) skills, from 1967 until the reforms of the 1990s, regulations reserved to small-scale firms the manufacture of products requiring the intensive use of unskilled labor such as toys, furniture, simple electrical products, and plastics.[121] Even with the ending of these reservations and the opening of the country to trade, laws governing employment have the same effect. They make it all but impossible for large firms to fire workers,[122] which discourages hiring them in the first place and keeps such firms from entering industries that require large workforces. The biggest and most efficient Indian companies tend to avoid such industries,[123] which are precisely the ones that could, if established on a large scale, lift millions of Indians out of poverty. Similarly, laws restricting the use of land make it difficult in many places to build facilities such as factories and hotels that could employ large numbers of people.[124]

It is a particular kind of interest group—unions—that promotes and defends the laws that discourage large firms from entering industries that employ unskilled workers. These laws work to the benefit of union members, who make up a very small fraction of the total workforce, even as they penalize India as a whole.[125] Other interest groups obstruct the growth of employment-creating businesses in different ways. Local protesters, for example, sometimes prevent the use of land for industrial and other commercial purposes. In one well-known case in 2008, the Tata company, one of the biggest in the country, was stopped from building an automobile factory in the state of West Bengal.

Minorities also inhibit the building of the infrastructure and the development of the educational system that India needs by using the political process to divert resources to themselves that then cannot be used to build roads or pay teachers. Subsidies of various kinds, all of them the legislative achievements of interest groups, account for fully 2.4 percent of the country's GDP.[126] The Indian bureaucracy itself is a large, powerful, and voracious interest group. Its salaries consume resources that would be better devoted to more productive uses.[127] Special-interest spending leads to budget deficits; borrowing to finance these deficits drains yet more money from infrastructure and education.[128]

Despite these handicaps, India, like the other BRICs, will almost certainly grow more rapidly than the trilateral countries in the years ahead: the dynamics of convergence all but assure this. Whether it will reach the upper limit of its potential for growth, however, will depend on whether and to what extent it can cope with the obstacles that its democratic system presents.

India has two methods, both consistent with democracy, of dealing with its politically imposed obstacles to economic growth: removing them and bypassing them. The country's political system badly needs reform, and the impetus for political reform around the world often comes from the middle class:[129] propertied, salaried people who see government as an impersonal enforcer of the law and neutral arbiter of disputes rather than as a source of funds and favors.[130] Such a social stratum, although still a minority of the total population, is growing in India.[131] In 2011, an anticorruption movement led by the self-styled neo-Gandhian activist Anna Hazare attracted considerable middle-class support, although it did not succeed in forcing the national legislature to enact the clean-government laws it advocated.[132]

The middle class is largest in the south of India, where, not coincidentally, government functions, on the whole, more effectively than it does elsewhere. As the Indian middle class grows—and national economic growth will increase its number—the pressure to make public administration more transparent, more efficient, and more honest will increase as well, to the country's economic benefit.

Serious political reform may one day make government in India more friendly, or at least less unfriendly, to investment, production, and employment. In the meantime, Indians have found another way to deal with its failure to provide the infrastructure and the education that underpin long-term growth: privatization. In the private sector, competition creates the imperative for efficiency, since consumers have a choice of firms from which to buy a product or a service. Privatization in India has involved not only returning to private enterprise tasks that it usually performs in other countries—the production of steel and cement and the management of hotels, for example—but also opening to private participation activities customarily undertaken by the government.[133] Rather than reforming the government, privatization of this kind circumvents it.

Private investment in power-generating plants is growing, and the great blackout of 2012 will only increase it,[134] but privatization's greatest Indian success involves communications. The government monopoly in charge of telephone landlines performed poorly. Before the 1991 reforms very few Indians were connected to the national system and obtaining a private line took years. Once private cell-phone companies were permitted to operate, the number of people with access to telephone service mushroomed. In 1991 the country had only 5.1 million phones in aggregate. By November 2006, in stark contrast, an average of 5.2 million new telephones were going into service *each month*.[135] At that point India had 153.3 million of them. By May 2012 there were fully 960 million telephone subscribers, 929 million of them using mobile phones, in a population of 1.2 billion.

The government has also made far more extensive use of the private sector in transportation since 1991.[136] The most prominent initiative in this sector is the building of the Golden Quadrilateral—a series of four- and six-lane highways connecting the country's four largest cities, New Delhi, Mumbai, Chennai, and Kolkata, and as well as many cities located between pairs of them. The project is the country's most ambitious undertaking in infrastructure since the British built the national railway system in the nineteenth century.[137] Private provision is also beginning to have an impact on education. Private academies offering primary instruction have proliferated, even in villages, and a private sector has started in higher education as well.[138]

Just how effectively the Indian middle class can exert pressure for political reform, and the extent to which India can get around the political obstacles to economic progress by replacing or supplementing government programs with private initiatives, will determine how big a contribution it will make to twenty-first-century global economic growth, and how swiftly it will close the wide economic gap between itself and the rich countries.

How far and how quickly reform and privatization proceed will also help to determine how rapidly, if at all, India catches up with the country against which it most often measures itself—the final member of the BRICs and the largest, fastest-growing, and economically most important one: China.[139] As with the other BRICs, a particular feature of Chinese public life that has enhanced economic performance in the past threatens to retard it in the future. As in the case of India, China's political asset-turned-liability is its political system.

China: The Limitations of Autocracy

In late 2011 and early 2012 a remarkable series of events took place in the village of Wukan on China's southeast coast. In September villagers protested the sale of land by local Communist officials to real estate developers without paying proper compensation to them. The protests escalated, and in December the villagers forced the Communist Party leaders out of the village. A thousand police laid siege to it and the standoff received wide coverage in the Chinese and international press. The Chinese government is not reticent about using force against its citizens who defy its authority, but this particular case ended differently. Negotiations between officials and the residents of Wukan led to free elections, which are almost never held in China, for the village governing committee. These took place in February, and 5,000 of the village's 12,000 people voted.

Like the demonstrations against the Putin regime in Russia at about the same time, the Chinese protesters had a political agenda: they were opposing the arbitrary actions of China's authoritarian government. Also as in Russia, the Wukan events had implications for China's economic future. The continuation of the country's remarkable economic growth requires political changes similar to those that the Wukan villagers demanded and, in what is almost without precedent in the history of Communist China, succeeded in winning.[140]

Descriptions of China's economic performance since it began its transition from central planning to free markets at the end of the 1970s invariably feature superlatives, and rightly so. The country has sustained the highest annual economic growth rate of any major country—almost 10 percent—for three decades, which is the best performance in recorded history.[141] In so doing it has lifted well over 500 million people out of poverty.[142] It has become the world's largest exporter, the world's largest emitter of greenhouse gases, the world's largest market for automobiles, and the country with the largest store of hard-currency reserves. It has also become the world's second-largest economy and is on course to replace the United States as the global leader in total annual output.

Economic growth now matters to all governments, but it is particularly important for China's rulers, not only because the country still has hundreds of millions of people who must live on the equivalent of $2 a day or less but also because, having abandoned the version of Marxism-Leninism propagated by the country's first Communist leader, Mao Zedong, their claim to govern rests almost exclusively on Chinese economic performance. China's economic growth is important for the world as well because China is so large, so dynamic, and so deeply embedded in the integrated global economy.[143] More than on any other single country except the United States, the future of the global economy depends on how fast China can continue to grow.

China's autocratic government has not only presided over the country's three-decade run of resounding economic success, it has contributed to that success. It has excelled in installing infrastructure, building roads, ports, airports, and power plants rapidly and on a large scale. It has managed to give virtually all its citizens a basic education. It has conducted, on the whole, prudent macroeconomic policies: the country has experienced periods of inflation, but they have been less severe and prolonged than those that plagued, for example, twentieth-century Brazil. It coped with, by substantially reducing although not eliminating, an expensive legacy of the Maoist period, the large state-owned enterprises that became obsolete when the country abandoned central planning.[144] It also coped well with the economic crisis of 2008–2009. When the recession struck, the regime responded quickly, implementing, in November 2008, a stimulus package equal to 14 percent of the country's GDP, which cushioned the impact of the global downturn on China.

Its autocratic character probably helped the regime to carry out its growth-friendly policies. The fact that the authorities do not have to respect the liberties or the political opinions of those they govern made it easier to devote resources to building roads, schools, and power plants, to shut down inefficient factories (thereby putting many people out of work), and to respond quickly to economic shocks. Whatever the economic advantages China has derived from its autocratic political system, however, it is a wasting asset. For the tasks that are necessary to sustain high growth, in fact, autocratic rule counts as a liability.

To continue to grow at anything like the pace to which it, and the rest of the world, have become accustomed since the outset of the 1980s, China will have to do four things: achieve high productivity; add more value to the products that are made in the country; rely less on exports and more on domestic consumption; and maintain a stable political framework. To accomplish these tasks, the country will have to make political changes. Specifically, it will have to make its political system, if not necessarily a full-fledged democracy, then at least more democratic—as democracy is properly understood.

Democracy is a hybrid political form, the product of the merger of two political traditions that for most of recorded history were considered incompatible with each other. One is popular sovereignty—rule by the people through freely elected representatives—which makes the government accountable to the governed. The other is liberty, more commonly called freedom, which includes economic liberty in the form of private property, religious liberty—freedom of worship—and the political liberty embodied in the first ten amendments to the American Constitution, the Bill of Rights. All are protected in functioning democracies by the rule of law.[145] Each of the two traditions is relevant to China's economic agenda. Higher productivity, adding more value to what it produces, and shifting from selling to foreigners to selling to Chinese, will require more liberty. Higher domestic consumption will also need wider popular participation in the governance of the country as will the more purely political task of keeping the country stable enough for productive economic activity to take place.

Productivity—the capacity to produce more output per unit of input—drives economic growth. China has made major gains in productivity by shifting labor from less productive farmwork to more productive industrial employment, specifically in the low-skill-intensive industries that employ many Chinese but comparatively few Indians.

While China's supply of underemployed rural labor is large, it is not limitless; and it will be restricted in the future by the aging of the Chinese population, the result of the government-mandated policy, begun in the 1970s, of permitting couples to have only one child. As in the trilateral countries, the ratio of retirees and children to active workers in China will rise sharply.[146] By mid-century the country is expected to have seven dependents for every ten workers. While the trilateral countries are already wealthy, even as the overall size of China's economy approaches that of the United States its per capita income remains low. Its demographic trajectory raises the risk that China will grow old before it gets rich.[147] Under these circumstances, getting rich—that is, sustaining a high growth rate—will require improving the country's productivity in ways other than the rural-to-urban transfer of workers. It will require widening the scope of liberty, especially economic liberty, in China.

The greatest potential for enhancing productivity lies in the financial sector.[148] China allocates resources inefficiently because the government directs investment through its control of the country's major banks. It would do better by entrusting this task to private, profit-seeking organizations and individuals—private banks and investors—which would do it more effectively.[149] For the financial system to contribute more to economic growth, China also needs better-defined and more secure property rights, which are crucial for many of a market economy's functions, including capital allocation.

Private property has a "fuzzy,"[150] unstable status in China, which has evolved over time and varies from place to place and from one kind of asset to another. The status of property suffers in particular from the lack of the firmly established rule of law, which is the guarantor of property and the lack of which undercuts the confidence needed for a financial system to thrive. Chinese justice is neither blind nor deaf; it heeds the wishes of the Communist Party, which take precedence over whatever the country's actual laws say. Courts do not operate independently of the governing authorities as they do where market economies' complicated financial systems function smoothly.[151]

To maintain a high rate of economic growth, in addition to improving productivity China will have to rely less on the kind of unskilled manufacturing that has loomed so large in its economy for three decades. The factories along China's coast that employ so many people mainly assemble consumer products out of component parts, many of which are fashioned elsewhere and shipped into the country. "Made in China" more often than not means "Assembled in China."[152] Serving as the location for assembly is not particularly lucrative. For every $1,000 of the purchase price of a laptop computer that emerges from a Chinese plant and is sold overseas, for example, by one estimate only $30 or $40—3 to 4 percent of the total—remains in China with the owner of the facility and the workers who make it.[153] To continue to get richer, China needs to do better than this, or risk falling into the "middle income trap," with its goods caught between less expensive products made in lower-wage countries and products of higher quality from countries with higher wages but also greater skills.[154]

Moving to more lucrative stages in the production process involves inventing, designing, financing, packaging, and marketing rather than assembling products. It involves as well, as the Chinese government has recognized, participating in the cutting-edge industries of the twenty-first century—biotechnology, for example—which rely on scientific discovery and technological innovation and that are likely to yield the greatest economic gains in the years ahead.

Here, too, economic liberty matters. As important as secure property rights are for improving the financial system, they are also a prerequisite for innovation. Inventors and entrepreneurs take risks and spend time and money in search of new processes and devices and to found new companies when they are confident that they will reap the financial rewards if they are successful. They cannot have such confidence in China, where businesses must have governmental approval and give government officials a share of their profits in order to operate.[155]

The Chinese government will have to permit greater liberty in Chinese society in other ways in order to move the Chinese economy beyond agriculture and assembly. The more ingenuity and creativity a job requires, the greater will be the freedom that must be available to do it well. Factory workers assembling computers need nimble hands and a basic level of literacy, but they do not need broad latitude to experiment and to meet and discuss their work with their colleagues. Designers and inventors do. Scientific advances require institutions—in the West most of them are universities—in which freedom of inquiry is taken for granted.

China sells many of the products it assembles to foreign customers. Along with increasing productivity and contributing more to the overall value of what it makes, the country will have to reduce its reliance on exports to continue its record-breaking rate of economic growth. Its chief customer, the United States, is buying less from China because Americans are saving more and consuming less, and this pattern will continue. If the Chinese currency rises in value, the country's exports will become more expensive; and the cost of Chinese labor will rise as well.[156] The prices of Chinese-made products will correspondingly increase, and other countries with lower wages will likely make inroads into China's markets. Just as Western countries have lost jobs to China, so China, as it grows more prosperous, will lose some of the jobs its factory workers now perform to Bangladesh, Vietnam, Cambodia, India, and perhaps ultimately to countries in Africa.

Chinese sales abroad will not come to a halt. The country has expanded its reach beyond the United States and Europe—to Brazil, India, and other emerging markets—and it is likely to remain the world's leading exporter. But to sustain an elevated rate of economic growth, the Chinese themselves will have to buy more Chinese-made goods and services, which would also help to reduce the large and potentially dangerous imbalances in the global economy.[157] For the purpose of raising domestic consumption China can usefully make two changes, each involving one of democracy's component parts.

One change is to establish rural property rights—to extend, that is, this form of liberty to those living outside China's cities. While almost all urban dwellings, most of them apartments, are privately owned, farmers usually cannot get unrestricted title to the land they work.[158] Without clear ownership rights they cannot use the land as collateral for borrowing, as do farmers all over the world. If they could borrow more, they would spend more. China's rural sector has untapped potential for consumption.

The other change is to expand the social safety net. Most of what countries everywhere spend on social programs they spend at home. The more generous social welfare programs become, the greater China's domestic consumption will be and the less the Chinese people will feel they must save. In Western countries, public pressure, the result of democracy's other defining feature, popular sovereignty, led to the programs of social protection that all now enjoy. The origins and growth of old-age pensions and unemployment insurance coincided with the expansion of the franchise. To be sure, Chinese authorities are already committed to spending more on health care. But if the Chinese people do gain a measure of political power, they are likely to use it to press for more spending on social welfare programs. They might also oppose the government's investing so much of the national wealth in low-yielding American securities simply for the purpose of assisting exporters by depressing the exchange rate, preferring to have that money spent on themselves. They could also exert pressure for opening up the financial system so that the state-dominated banks no longer control the nation's savings. In this way, too, greater democracy in China could contribute to the reorientation of the country's economy away from exports and toward domestic consumption.

For China to shift its economic policies and modify its institutions to sustain a high rate of growth assumes the maintenance of the stable political framework that all markets—global, national, and local—require. In the Chinese case, stability cannot be assumed. While the country's extraordinary three-decades-long economic performance has benefited hundreds of millions of people, as with the normal workings of free markets everywhere tens of millions have also been displaced, disoriented, and dispossessed in the process. Economic growth, with its particular Chinese characteristics, has created discontent, public expressions of which have become, over the years, increasingly frequent. Although the outcome of the events at Wukan in 2011–2012 was unusual, the protests that began them were scarcely unique.

In 1994 the number of disturbances of the public order reported by the authorities (who have an incentive to understate the total) was 10,000, with a total of 730,000 people taking part in them. A decade later the number had reached 74,000, involving 1.3 million individuals. In 2005, 82,000 were officially acknowledged. By 2010 estimates ranged up to 180,000.[159] Many of these episodes arise from labor disputes[160] and some have involved large groups: in 2005, 17 protests were reported to have involved more than 10,000 people.[161]

The government has developed a three-pronged strategy for coping with this mounting unrest. First, it has worked to keep protests localized. Second, it has launched programs to distribute the benefits of reform more widely, in the belief that prosperity is an antidote to discontent. Third, it has cracked down vigorously and promptly on demonstrators, jailing many and killing some. These tactics have contained the unrest but have not eliminated it because they cannot eliminate a major, common, underlying cause: China's unelected, unrepresentative, unresponsive, and unaccountable government.

To contain and ultimately reduce the rising level of publicly expressed discontent that, if not checked, has the potential to shake the political foundations of China's economic growth, a more accountable government is needed. Accountability comes about through the rule of law and through transparency in the conduct of public business, for which a free press is crucial. China has neither.

Accountability also comes about through the power of the people to replace their rulers peacefully through free elections: that is, through the popular sovereignty that is one of democracy's two constituent elements. Accountable government is particularly relevant to dealing with the two problems that give rise to popular protests: pollution and corruption.

As in other countries during comparable stages of economic advance, China's surging economic growth has befouled its environment. According to official figures, at the end of 2005 the drinking water of 300 million people was contaminated and 90 percent of China's cities suffered from polluted water.[162] According to World Bank estimates, sixteen of the twenty cities worldwide with the most polluted air are in China and about 500,000 Chinese die every year from diseases linked to air pollution.[163] Many of China's mass protests have been directed against environmental degradation of one kind or another.[164]

China's problems of environmental pollution stem ultimately from the country's lack of political accountability. The national government has promulgated laws and regulations to prevent environmental abuse, but local authorities frequently disregard them. These authorities allow factories to continue to discharge toxic material into the air and water because to stop them would in many cases forfeit economic growth and therefore jobs, tax revenues, and bribes.[165]

Officials are able to ignore illegal pollution because they face no sanction for lax enforcement. They are accountable to no one: in theory not to the people who are injured by their inaction and in practice not even to the central government.[166] To reduce the damage China's frenetic economic growth does to the country requires the creation of channels of accountability. The most prominent of these are free elections.

The absence of accountability in government lies at the heart of another corrosive feature of Chinese society that promotes growth-threatening political instability: rampant corruption. Anger at officials abusing their positions for personal gain provoked the Wukan uprising and has been responsible for many other protests as well. China ranks as one of the most corrupt countries in the world.[167] As with pollution, China's rulers have sought to combat corruption with Communist-style Party-led campaigns, which consist of slogans, exhortation, and a few token punishments to give the impression of seriousness.

This approach has done little to solve the problem. As with pollution, reducing corruption requires generating public pressure on officials who abuse their power. A free press that can bring abuses to light is one source of pressure. Another is investing the public with the power to remove corrupt officials through free elections.

As with the other BRICs, whether China overcomes the chief obstacle to fulfilling its potential will depend on the outcome of a political struggle. Unlike in Brazil and India, which are democracies, and Russia, whose political system has some democratic elements, the Chinese contest, over whether the country will have wider liberty and more accountable government, will not take place mainly in the open, with the clash of organized interest groups and lively public debates. The crucial decisions are likely be discussed and made secretly, within the ranks of China's ruling Communist Party.

Most officials will oppose both features of democracy—liberty and popular sovereignty—because the more of each there is in China, the less they will have of what they value most: power. That does not mean, however, that democratic reforms are impossible. Some Party offiicals surely favor them; if that were not so, free elections would not have taken place in Wukan. More importantly, the post-Maoist Communist Party has shown itself to be eminently practical. It has discarded most of the ideology that Mao imposed.

"It doesn't matter whether a cat is black or white," Mao's successor Deng Xiaoping decreed in making this point, "as long as it catches mice." It has governed instead for three decades on the basis of trial and error—the Chinese phrase "crossing the river by feeling the stones" describes this approach—with the promotion of economic growth as the consistent goal.

Over those three decades the Chinese Communist Party has been willing to do whatever has seemed necessary to secure growth, including relinquishing some of its own prerogatives: it has given up some of its power in order to retain the rest. If it concludes that only more democratic governance can deliver the growth that will preserve its leadership of the country and the political stability needed to underpin that growth, then China is likely to become more democratic, with wider liberties available, especially in economic matters, and a greater measure of public participation in public life. Whether and to what extent this happens will have a great deal to do with China's role in the global economy in the first half of the twenty-first century. Because other countries have come to depend so heavily on Chinese economic growth, the whole world, not only the people of China, has a stake in Chinese democracy.

•   •   •

One of the best-known exchanges in Arthur Conan Doyle's celebrated Sherlock Holmes stories occurs in "Silver Blaze" when Holmes calls attention to "the curious incident of the dog in the night-time." "But the dog did nothing in the night-time," the Scotland Yard detective says. Holmes replies, "That was the curious incident." Sometimes what does not happen is as significant as what does. The great financial crisis and deep economic recession of the first decade of the twenty-first century produced a non-event that has important consequences for the economic futures of the BRIC countries.

The worst shock to the global economy since the Great Depression at first seemed to bypass Brazil, India, and China, although output in Russia did fall sharply. By 2012, however, the economic performances of all three had declined.[168] Each was growing more slowly than before 2008. One major consequence of the Great Depression was to give credibility to forms of economic organization other than globalization-friendly free-market capitalism. The central planning that Communist governments in Russia and China and the import-substituting economic strategy that Brazil and India had practiced until the 1990s became attractive to them in no small part because, in the 1930s, free markets had so calamitously failed to deliver prosperity.

After World War II, by contrast, free markets and globalization had done so well in creating wealth that the BRIC countries, and many others, decided to make them the basis of their own economic orders, triggering their own impressive subsequent growth. In 2008 and thereafter the Western approach to economic management seemed to have failed again. Even so, history did not repeat itself. The BRICs did not abandon the basic economic course they had set for themselves. They remained committed to market economics and cross-border trade and investment.

No doubt this had something to do with the fact that the economic damage in the twenty-first century, while considerable, fell short of the devastation of the 1930s.[169] In addition, the obvious alternatives to globalization and free markets—the models the BRICs had already tried in the twentieth century—had been discredited, and the world had, at least for the moment, no other models of economic organization that the BRICs could readily adopt. Whatever, the reasons, free markets and globalization could accurately be described, in the twenty-first century, as Winston Churchill had once characterized democracy: the worst system except for all the others.

In the wake of the near-meltdown of global finance, the steep decline in global output, and their own diminished growth rates, Brazil, Russia, India, and China remained on the path of globalization that they had previously chosen. Just how far and how fast they will proceed along that path as the twenty-first century unfolds will depend on the outcome of the domestic political struggles over Brazilian populism, Russian energy, Indian democracy, and Chinese autocracy. But they have all chosen to stay with globalization; there will be no turning back.

FAULT LINES

On November 1, 1755, All Saints' Day, a powerful earthquake struck Portugal's capital city of Lisbon. It did immense damage. As many as 50,000 people were killed. An estimated 85 percent of the city's buildings collapsed. The shock was felt as far away as Finland. The disaster affected the way Europeans saw their world and themselves. It triggered reflections among both religious and secular thinkers: Voltaire and Rousseau, two of the eighteenth century's leading intellectual lights, wrote about its meaning.

It also inspired another of the century's most influential thinkers, Immanuel Kant, to propose a theory of the causes of earthquakes. And the prime minister of Portugal, Sebastião de Melo, ordered the collection of all information available on the shock and its effects. Their response to the event marks the beginning of the systematic study of earthquakes, which is now called seismology, just as the publication of Adam Smith's treatise *The Wealth of Nations*, twenty-one years later, in Edinburgh, marks the beginning of the systematic study of economics in general and the global economy in particular. The two enterprises have important features in common.

In the two and one half centuries since seismology and economics began, a great deal has been learned about earthquakes and economies. Students of each have come to a sophisticated understanding of how they work. Earthquakes turn out to be caused by the movement of what are known as tectonic plates, composed of the two sublayers of the Earth's crust beneath its surface, a theory that achieved consensus among scientists, it should be noted, only in the 1960s, long after Adam Smith had set down the basic workings of a market economy.

Earthquakes are episodes of instability in the Earth's surface. The global economy is prone to instability of a different kind. In both cases, though, the locations from which instability emanates are known. Earthquakes occur along faults—fractures in the Earth's surface. Shocks to the global economy come from its own version of fault lines: the equivalent of the tectonic plates whose movements cause earthquakes are the domestic politics of the major countries. Politics pervades economics, as Adam Smith, who called his field of study "political economy," well understood.[1] It is politics, and specifically the outcomes of political conflicts, that set off economic tremors: so it is domestic politics that will determine the future of the world's economy.

Seismologists have discovered the location of the principal faults in the Earth's surface. Similarly, on the basis of the 150-year history of globalization it is possible to identify the four major fault lines in the global economy, and the domestic politics that underlie them.

The first of them is the framework, consisting of the services known as "global public goods," that any economy needs to function smoothly. The public good of security will be provided to the world by the United States or it will not be provided at all. The United States must assure sufficient calm to permit productive economic activity in East Asia and the Middle East by keeping in check the two inherently aggressive countries in those regions, North Korea and Iran. The United States also bears the responsibility for discouraging China from pursuing its territorial claims on Taiwan and in the seas off its coast in ways that could cripple trade, investment, and production in East Asia. If America does not perform these tasks, no other country or group of countries will do so. And, indeed, the United States, fatigued by long, frustrating wars in Afghanistan and

Iraq, saddled with a large and growing national debt, and facing rising financial obligations to its older citizens in the years ahead, may fail to perform them. If it does fail, the world will be a less stable, less prosperous place.

Whether and to what extent the United States will continue to police East Asia and the Middle East will depend on American domestic politics, as will the American capacity to supply the strictly economic services on which the global economy relies—a market for others' exports and a currency that others use as a reserve. These need not come from the United States alone; but whether other countries will contribute to supplying them—whether Germany, Japan, and China will consume more (and save less) and the euro and the renminbi will join the dollar as currencies that every country is content to hold—will depend on the domestic politics of these countries. Those politics will be contentious: in every case, the policies favorable to the global economy as a whole violate strongly held and vigorously defended preferences of well-established domestic interests.

A conflict of interests also lies beneath the global economy's second fault line—the ongoing, inevitable clash between the winners and the losers from the cross-border movement of money, people, and goods. For much of the twentieth century, global capital flows had a bad reputation: international investment in land, factories, or shares of enterprises provoked serious opposition. In the twenty-first century this is no longer the case. Once shunned as the instrument of imperial domination, capital investment of this kind is now welcomed, above all in the places that once rejected it, such as China, as the fertilizer of economic growth.

As for the movement of people—immigration—it has the potential to administer the largest *positive* shock to the global economy. Flinging open the gates of the rich countries to workers from the poor ones would produce a dramatic surge in global output. No such thing will happen, however, because no matter how positive immigration's economic impact, many citizens experience it as an assault on aspects of their lives even more precious than wealth: their country's customs, its values, its very identity.

In the two places where it causes the most controversy, the politics of immigration are likely to play out in different ways. In the United States, with its two-hundred-year history of welcoming and absorbing immigrants, the resistance will abate, although not disappear. The flow of people to the United States will be in the future, as in the past, a source of economic strength.

In Europe, by contrast, lacking America's tradition in this regard and with recent and glaring failures to assimilate newcomers in countries across the continent, immigration and immigrants will encounter increasing resentment and resistance. The political backlash against them will not attain the intensity of the ethnic, national, and religious conflicts that erupted in the Balkans in the 1990s and that plague the Middle East today, however, and so will likely have a negligible effect on global economic activity. The greatest economic impact will be in gains foregone: successful immigration would raise economic growth in Europe and therefore in the world as a whole.

The third cross-border flow, of products and services, should be the least controversial. Trade, because of the principle of comparative advantage, always brings net benefits to all countries engaging in it. Yet trade has never been entirely free. It is freer now than at any time in the past but does have the potential for major disruptions in the commerce between the United States and to a lesser extent Europe, on the one hand, and China and India on the other.

Sino-American trade brings benefits to both countries but is vulnerable to a political backlash in the United States for three reasons: it aggravates, although is by no means the sole cause of, economic inequality in America; China is seen by many Americans as violating the norms of fair trade—by keeping its currency artificially cheap, for example; and the two countries have political disputes in East Asia that, if they should become more pronounced and especially if they lead to open hostilities, would cause an interruption in commerce. A trade war between the world's two biggest economies would cause serious injury to the entire global economy.

America's political relations with India, a fellow democracy, are less fragile than those with China; but the political backlash against commerce with India could be far greater. This is so because, while the United States has lost jobs to both countries, China has captured mainly blue-collar, factory jobs, while it is white-collar, office jobs, which make up a far greater proportion of total American employment, that have migrated to India. The number of such jobs that have actually crossed the Pacific is modest, and may remain modest. If it becomes substantial, however, as it might, this could touch off the political equivalent of an earthquake in the United States, and in other countries similarly affected. If they felt sufficiently vulnerable, tens of millions of the citizens of the rich countries could act to protect their livelihoods, which could in turn seriously disrupt the global economy as a whole.

The first two equivalents, for the global economy, of seismic faults have been less active since World War II than in the previous hundred years. Major wars and trade protectionism occurred more often, and did more damage to the global economy, before than after 1945. The third kind of shock, stemming from finance, has, by contrast, been more frequent in recent years.

Financial shocks arise from the combination of the two most powerful negative human emotions—greed and fear—and the fundamental design of the free-market economy, which means that the potential for them cannot be eliminated. The larger the market and the fewer the safeguards against financial crises, the more frequent and more severe they will be. In globalization's third era, markets expanded and safeguards decreased.

In the wake of the huge, destructive financial shock of 2008, governments began trying to restore some safeguards: capital requirements and size limits for financial institutions, restrictions on cross-border capital flows, and other regulations governing their financial industries. The implementation of such measures met stiff political resistance everywhere, however, from those, mainly in the financial sector, who stood to lose from them. Moreover, to be effective in curtailing the frequency and severity of financial crises, something politically difficult to achieve—the international coordination of financial policy—is required. The relevant measures would have to be adopted everywhere, lest one country's lax financial regime permit shocks that spread to others.

To put an end to the ongoing disruption of the global economy caused by the other major financial crisis of globalization's third era, the one involving the euro, an even greater degree of international political cooperation is needed. That crisis arose from the economic differences, with their roots in politics and culture, between the northern and the southern European countries. The principal symptom of the crisis was the difficulty the southerners had in borrowing money to finance their national deficits. The cure for it is far closer political integration among them—the establishment of effective governance for the entire euro area. This, however, would entail relinquishing important parts of what all regard as the supreme political value: national sovereignty. Sovereignty will not be given up anywhere without a strenuous political struggle. The global economy's third fault line thus runs through the domestic politics of the major economic powers and the members of Europe's common currency. The fourth and final one cuts across the domestic affairs of a different group of countries. The BRICs—Brazil, Russia, India, and China—are the most important of the emerging market countries, the ones with the greatest potential for economic growth in the decades to come. All have made the basic choice to organize their national economies along free-market lines and to take part in cross-border trade and investment. The magnitude of their respective contributions to the global economy in the future now depends on whether and to what extent they adopt policies conducive to rapid growth. To put it in the language of computing, all have installed the basic operating system for globalization: what remains for them to do is to make use of the most appropriate programs.

Implementing growth-promoting policies will be difficult because it involves in each case discarding, minimizing, or resisting the pull of traditions and institutions that once favored, but now obstruct, economic expansion. Optimal economic performance entails, as with the other three fault lines, political struggle: in Brazil to overcome the impulse of populism; in Russia to circumvent the negative effects of its endowment of energy; in India to repair the flaws in its democratic political system; and in China to democratize its autocracy.

All four countries can reasonably be expected to lift the global economy by growing faster than the trilateral countries for the next several decades. Just how much faster they grow will depend on the outcome of these four domestic political contests. This raises an obvious question: how are these conflicts, and the other political conflicts within the United States, China, and Europe that will determine the world's economic future, likely to turn out? That question leads back to the study of earthquakes, and another similarity between it and the understanding of the global economy.

For all the progress they have achieved, neither can make precise, accurate predictions. In neither case does that inability stem from lack of trying. Successfully predicting earthquakes is the ultimate prize for seismologists, but despite the advances in the field, it has proven to be out of reach. Accurate economic predictions are potentially so valuable that trying to make them has become a multimillion-dollar industry. Even though the people who make them are paid, sometimes handsomely, for their work, their predictions seldom match reality.[2]

The shortcoming of seismology comes from a lack of detailed information. Although the geophysical processes that produce earthquakes are well understood, they occur ten miles underground, so they cannot be closely observed and precisely measured.[3] The various elements that make up a modern market economy can be observed and measured, but there are millions of them and they interact in multiple and complicated ways, which makes it difficult to predict what the sum of their many interactions will be. What makes consistently accurate economic prediction even more difficult—indeed impossible—is its inevitable entanglement in politics.

Politics is unpredictable because it is based on human behavior, and human beings do not now behave, and have never behaved, in standard, unvarying ways. The tectonic plates that cause earthquakes cannot change their minds about their movements. Human beings can and do. So the accurate predictions to which the natural sciences aspire and that they often achieve are not possible for the future of the global economy. This does not mean, however, that its future is entirely opaque. On the basis of a familiarity with its history and an understanding of its main political fault lines—on the basis, that is, of the preceding chapters—some elements of that future can be foretold with confidence.

Ongoing improvement in the technologies of transportation and especially communication will enhance the global economy's potential to grow in scope by incorporating ever-increasing numbers of people. It will also enhance the potential for the movement of goods, money, and people across sovereign borders to grow in volume and value. The inherent tendency of free markets to expand their reach will ensure that at least some of that potential is fulfilled. The technological and economic momentum of globalization will remain powerful in the twenty-first century, as it was for most of the nineteenth and twentieth.

Political momentum will continue as well, for two reasons. First, the expansion of cross-border trade, investment, and immigration will continue to be associated, on the whole, with economic growth, and most people and most governments will continue to put economic growth at the top of their personal and national agendas. Second, there is no attractive alternative to free markets at home or global integration abroad. The other two approaches to economic organization most frequently adopted in the last century—central planning and import-substitution—which do not lend themselves to full participation in the globalized international economy, failed to produce growth as effectively as globalization does. Nothing else is currently available.

At the same time, the global economy will experience disruptions emanating from its four principal fault lines. It cannot be made entirely shockproof. As with earthquakes, some shocks will be more serious than others; but just as few earthquakes in all of history have been as powerful as the one that struck Lisbon in 1755, so the economic shocks in the next decades will have modest effects on the cross-border movement of goods, money, and people. They will, happily, fall far short, in the economic damage they inflict, of the two world wars of the first half of the twentieth century, the Great Depression of the 1930s, and even the financial crisis of 2008.

Putting these near-certainties together leads to a final observation. The global economy of the twenty-first century is to its original version, which dates to the repeal of the Corn Laws in 1846, what a modern automobile is to the earliest models built at the outset of the twentieth century. The present version is larger, more sophisticated, more powerful, more versatile, and can carry more passengers: today's integrated world economy is transporting, in one way or another, the majority of the planet's 7 billion inhabitants. In the years ahead this contemporary vehicle will not come to a halt, veer sharply off the road, or hurtle into a fatal collision. Globalization will surely continue on its upward path; but for the billions of people on board, the ride will just as surely be a bumpy one.

NOTES

CHAPTER ONE: THE ROOF

1. Quoted in John Darwin, *Unfinished Empire: The Global Expansion of Britain*, New York: Bloomsbury Press, 2012, p. 29.
2. Dani Rodrik, *The Globalization Paradox: Democracy and the Future of the World Economy*, New York: W. W. Norton and Company, 2011, p. 12.
3. Martin Wolf, "The world's hunger for public goods," *Financial Times*, January 25, 2012, p. 11.
4. This is the theme of one of the earliest and most influential modern accounts of government, Thomas Hobbes's *Leviathan*, published in 1651.
5. Public goods are things that no one can be excluded from consuming. For that reason, no one has an incentive to pay for them. It is in everyone's interest to let others pay and become a nonpaying, public-goods-consuming "free rider." When everyone attempts to ride free, however, no one pays anything and, as a consequence, the public good is not supplied. Government can supply them because, with its monopoly of force, it can *compel* everyone to pay.
6. Michael Mandelbaum, *The Case for Goliath: How America Acts as the World's Government in the Twenty-first Century*, New York: PublicAffairs, 2006, pp. 8–9.
7. The French have an unusually strong distaste for global economic integration, evidence of which is a French word of recent coinage that is not found in other languages: *démondialisation*—deglobalization. While its citizens preach it, France, as a charter and stalwart member of the European Union, does not practice it.
8. John Mueller, *Quiet Cataclysm*, New York: HarperCollins, 1995, Chapter 8.
9. Michael Mandelbaum, *The Ideas That Conquered the World: Peace, Democracy, and Free Markets in the Twenty-first Century*, New York: PublicAffairs, 2002, pp. 121–133.

10. The idea that trade fosters peace goes back to the nineteenth century. In that era it gained particular currency in Great Britain, the world's major trading state. Trade did not, of course, prevent World War I.

11. Michael Mandelbaum, *Democracy's Good Name: The Rise and Risks of the World's Most Popular Form of Government*, New York: PublicAffairs, 2007, Chapter 4.

12. This is a prominent theme of Steven Pinker, *The Better Angels of Our Nature: Why Violence Has Declined*, New York: Penguin, 2011.

13. Cited in Neal Ascherson, "How Millions Have Been Dying in the Congo," *The New York Review of Books*, April 5, 2012, p. 68.

14. For historical, cultural, and geopolitical reasons, the United States has gone to war more frequently than any other country since the end of the Cold War. This record notwithstanding, the United States is neither inherently bellicose nor free of the sentiment of war-aversion.

15. Dmitri Trenin, *Post-Imperium*, Washington, D.C.: Carnegie Endowment for International Peace, 2011.

16. Michael Mandelbaum, "Modest Expectations," *The American Interest*, May/June 2009.

17. Paul Kennedy, *The Rise and Fall of the Great Powers: Economic Change and Military Conflict from 1500 to 2000*, New York: Random House, 1987, traces this pattern over five centuries.

18. Paul Kennedy, *The Rise of the Anglo-German Antagonism, 1860–1914*, London: George Allen & Unwin, 1982, especially p. 469.

19. " . . . consider history—especially the parallel between China's rise and that of imperial Germany over a century ago. Back then nobody in Europe had an economic interest in conflict; but Germany felt that the world was too slow to accommodate its growing power, and crude, irrational passions like nationalism took hold. China is reemerging after what it sees as 150 years of humiliation, surrounded by anxious neighbors, many of them allied to America. In that context, disputes about clumps of rock could become as significant as the assassination of an archduke." "Could Asia really go to war over these?" *The Economist*, September 22, 2012, p. 13. See also "Locked On," *The Economist*, February 9, 2013, p. 41.

20. Michael Mandelbaum, "Arms Competition: The Nuclear Arms Race and the Anglo-German Naval Rivalry," Chapter 4 in Mandelbaum, *The Nuclear Revolution: International Politics Before and After Hiroshima*, New York: Cambridge University Press, 1981.

21. The mainland government also probably fears that Taiwanese independence would generate pressure from the country's non-Han-Chinese regions—largely Muslim Xinjiang and mainly Buddhist Tibet—to follow suit. Although thinly populated compared to the country's heartland, these regions comprise almost 40 percent of China's territory.

22. China conducts considerable trade with Taiwan, partly, no doubt, in the hope that this will draw the island politically closer to the mainland without war.

23. Mandelbaum, *The Case for Goliath*, pp. 31–42.

24. North Korea is particularly prone to bellicose rhetoric. In March 2013, for example, its young dictator, Kim Jong Un, "threatened the United States with nuclear Armageddon, promising to rain missiles on mainland America and military bases in Hawaii and Guam; [and] declared a 'state of war' with South Korea. . . ." "Korean roulette," *The Economist*, April 6, 2013, p. 13.

25. Walter Laqueur, *The New Terrorism: Fanaticism and the Arms of Mass Destruction*, New York: Oxford University Press, 1999, Chapter 1.

26. The Japanese cult Aum Shinrikyo released sarin gas in a Tokyo subway station in 1995. Thousands of people were affected but only twelve died.

27. The opportunities and obstacles confronting a terrorist group seeking nuclear weapons are assessed in Charles D. Ferguson, "Preventing Catastrophic Nuclear Terrorism," New York: The Council on Foreign Relations, CSR No. 11, March 2006.

28. "What if?" *The Economist*, May 29, 2004, p. 69; Patrick Clawson and Simon Henderson, *Reducing Vulnerability to Middle East Energy Shocks: A Key Element in Strengthening U.S. Energy Security*, Washington, D.C: The Washington Institute for Near East Policy, Policy Focus No. 49, November, 2005, pp. 7–8; Gal Luft, "An Energy Pearl Harbor?" "Outlook," *The Washington Post*, March 5, 2006, p. B2; Michael Slackman, "Saudis Round Up 172, Citing a Plot Against Oil Rigs," *The New York Times*, April 28, 2007, p. A1. Iran has a history of trying to disrupt the world's oil supply. During its war with Iraq in the 1980s it attacked neutral oil tankers in the Persian Gulf. Clawson and Henderson, *op. cit.*, p. x.

29. "In 2001 Americans were using more than eleven times more oil per person than the Chinese. Indeed, if the Chinese were ever to consume at the American levels of 2001, they would need to guzzle three times the world's total consumption." James Kynge, *China Shakes the World: A Titan's Rise and Troubled Future—and the Challenge for America*, Boston: Houghton Mifflin, 2006, p. 134.

30. "Each of the last five major downturns in global economic activity has been immediately preceded by a major spike in oil prices." Gavyn Davies, quoted in Martin Wolf, "Arab freedom is worth a short shock," *Financial Times*, March 2, 2011, p. 9.

31. The United States would surely side with the Saudi government against an internal rebellion, as it did not with the equally pro-American Egyptian government in 2011. That is the difference that oil makes. Whether in such circumstances American support would extend to dispatching Ameri-

can troops to the Arabian peninsula to defend the House of Saud from its own subjects is uncertain.

32. Making it even more acute will be the rising interest costs from the national debt that the government will be obliged to pay.

33. This is the theme of Michael Mandelbaum, *The Frugal Superpower: America's Global Leadership in a Cash-Strapped Era*, New York: PublicAffairs, 2010.

34. These points are made in Robert J. Lieber, *Power and Willpower in the American Future*, New York: Cambridge University Press, 2012.

35. Charles Kindleberger, *The World in Depression: 1929–1939*, Berkeley, California: University of California Press, 1973. "In these circumstances, the international economic and monetary system needs leadership, a country which is prepared, consciously or unconsciously, under some system of rules that it has internalized, to set standards of conduct for other countries; and to seek to get others to follow them, to take on an undue share of the burdens of the system, and in particular to take on its support in adversity by accepting its redundant commodities, maintaining a flow of investment capital and discounting its paper. . . . It is the theme of this book that part of the reason for the length, and most of the explanation for the depth of the world depression, was the inability of the British to continue their role of underwriter to the system and the reluctance of the United States to take it on until 1936." p. 28.

36. This is discussed below, pp. 33–35.

37. This is the subject of Chapter 3.

38. Robert Samuelson, "The Next Big Spenders," *The Washington Post*, March 1, 2006, p. A11. The American share of global output as a whole was less than half that percentage.

39. While Nixon's desire to raise employment in advance of a presidential election precipitated his decision, the basic weakness of the Bretton Woods system, which would have ended it eventually, was economic in nature and was built into its design. The dollar played two contradictory roles: it provided global liquidity, which required an ongoing *expansion* of the world's supply of dollars to underwrite global economic growth; but it also served as the primary reserve currency, which required that it maintain its value in relation to gold by *limiting* the creation of dollars. By the time Nixon terminated the system, the United States did not have enough gold to redeem every dollar in circulation at the prescribed rate, as it was obliged to do under the Bretton Woods conditions. (By the system's rules only governments, not individuals, were entitled to demand this exchange.) This contradiction became known as the "Triffin dilemma," after the Belgian-American economist Robert Triffin, who first called attention to it.

40. Barry Eichengreen, *Exorbitant Privilege: The Rise and Fall of the Dollar and the Future of the International Monetary System*, New York: Oxford University Press, 2011, pp. 66–68.

41. In 2012 about 62 percent of the world's reserves were in dollars.

42. The temptation to inflate it away was all the greater because a majority of the American debt was held by foreigners. Eichengreen, *op. cit.*, p. 119.

43. A nonmonetary alternative to the dollar as a place to store wealth is gold, whose price rises when confidence in the dollar falls, and vice versa. In the second decade of the twenty-first century, the price of gold soared.

44. This issue is discussed in Chapter 3, pp. 108–118. Even before the crisis of the euro, and despite the fact that its architects saw the common currency as a rival to the dollar, member countries had reservations about its use as a global reserve. The wider its usage, the greater the demand for the euro and thus the higher its value would be. A strong euro would negatively affect exports, upon which several members of the eurozone, notably Germany, depended. See Jean-Pisani Ferry and Adam S. Posen, "Why the Euro Is Not the Next Global Currency," *Financial Times*, October 19, 2009, http://www.piie.com/publications/opeds/print.cfm?doc=pub&research/ID=1313.

45. On this subject see Chapter 4, p. 159.

46. Keynes proposed to call the global currency equivalent the "bancor."

47. At the outset of 2010 the currencies and their proportions of the total were as follows: US dollars, 44 percent; euros, 34 percent; Japanese yen, 11 percent; and British pound sterling, 11 percent.

48. See Benn Steil, "Why There Will Be No New Bretton Woods," *The Wall Street Journal*, February 27, 2013, p. A15.

49. The U.N. sanctioned the war to oust the Taliban from power in Afghanistan in 2001, but the initial combat was exclusively an American affair. NATO members contributed modestly to the fight against the insurgency that developed after the Taliban's ouster.

50. Members of the multinational coalition that evicted Iraq from Kuwait defrayed the financial costs of the war (the United States made a small profit) but did not bear much of the military burden.

51. "European nations used to provide near to 40 per cent of Nato's defence spending; now that figure is closer to 20 per cent and is likely to fall further as austerity kicks in." Geoff Dyer, "Washington can focus on Asia only with a robust Nato," *Financial Times*, May 22, 2012, p. 2. See also Gideon Rachman, "A disarmed Europe will face the world on its own," *Financial Times*, February 19, 2013, p. 9. The Europeans' percentage of NATO's total defense spending overstates their military capacities, because their forces are less readily deployable than those of the United States: they get less bang for the buck.

52. These are discussed in Chapter 3, p. 105–107.

53. Eichengreen, *op. cit.*, pp. 150–152.

54. " . . . actual greenhouses do not produce the 'greenhouse effect'; they mainly trap the air that is warmed by contact with the ground that is warmed by the sun." Thomas C. Schelling, "It's Getting Warmer," *The Wall Street Journal*, February 23, 2006, p. A16.

55. Global warming could, by triggering the disintegration of governments overwhelmed by the problems it creates and through the dislocations that arise out of it, lead to actual wars. These issues are discussed in *National Security and the Threat of Climate Change*, Alexandria, Virginia: The CNA Corporation, 2007. See also *Impacts of Climate Change: A System Vulnerability Approach to Consider the Potential Impacts to 2050 of a Mid-Upper Greenhouse Gas Emissions Scenario*, San Francisco: Global Business Network, 2007. According to Steven Chu, a Nobel Prize–winning physicist and secretary of energy in the first Obama administration, "Climate change [of five degrees Celsius] will cause enormous resource wars over water, arable land, and massive population displacement. . . . We're talking about hundreds of millions to billions of people being flooded out, permanently." Charles Homans, "The Experiment," *The New Republic*, February 16, 2012, p. 11.

56. The precise sensitivity of the global temperature to greenhouse gas emissions—that is, the amount of warming produced by a particular volume of greenhouse gas in the atmosphere—came into question in 2013. "A sensitive matter," *The Economist*, March 30, 2013, p. 77.

57. There is another relevant difference. For one country to defend itself successfully does not necessarily require that others defend themselves as well, or even assist in its defense. But for one country to get the benefits of reducing its greenhouse gas emissions, others must also reduce their own emissions.

58. Quoted in "All Free Traders Now?" *The Economist*, December 7, 1996, p. 21.

CHAPTER TWO: THE GATES

1. Ben S. Bernanke, "Global Economic Integration: What's New and What's Not? Remarks at the Federal Reserve Bank of Kansas City's Thirtieth Annual Economic Symposium, Jackson Hole, Wyoming, August 25, 2006. http://www.federalreserve.gov/boarddocs/speeches/2006/20060825/default.htm.

2. Joseph Schumpeter, *Capitalism, Socialism, and Democracy*, New York: Harper & Brothers Publishers, 1942, pp. 82–83.

3. In almost every country some goods and people evade these gates and enter illegally. The illegal movement of money often involves leaving rather than entering a country.

4. See Peter Gourevitch, *Politics in Hard Times: Comparative Responses to International Economic Crises*, Ithaca, N.Y.: Cornell University Press, 1986, and Ronald Rogowski, *Commerce and Coalitions*, Princeton, N.J.: Princeton University Press, 1990.

5. According to the chairman of the American Federal Reserve Board, Ben S. Bernanke, "the influence of globalization on inequality has been moderate and almost surely less important than the effects of skill-based technological change." Martin Wolf, "Why America will need some elements of a welfare state," *Financial Times*, February 13, 2007.

6. Since Ricardo first proposed it, the principle of comparative advantage has been subjected to a number of challenges, notably from the "infant industry" theory, which holds that countries can benefit economically by protecting new industries from international competition until they grow strong enough to compete without protection. Germany, the United States, and Japan did protect their young industries in the nineteenth century and did prosper. It is not clear, however, that the protected industries that flourished owed their success to the protection they received, or that they would have failed without it, or that governments are consistently capable of adopting the policies necessary to nurture infant industries. See Douglas Irwin, *Against the Tide: An Intellectual History of Free Trade*, Princeton, N.J.: Princeton University Press, 1996, Chapter 8.

7. " . . . income redistribution is the other side of the gains from trade." Dani Rodrik, *The Globalization Paradox*, New York: W. W. Norton, 2011, p. 56.

8. In theory, those who lose their jobs can and should get work in thriving industries, acquiring new skills for this purpose if necessary. In practice, this often does not happen.

9. The pattern is not confined to trade. Advocates of restricting imports belong to a broad category that the economist Mancur Olson called "distributional coalitions:" groups that lobby successfully for economic policies that favor them at the expense of the economic interests of the country as a whole. Olson, *The Rise and Decline of Nations: Economic Growth, Stagflation, and Social Rigidities*, New Haven, Conn.: Yale University Press, 1982, pp. 43–47.

10. "It has been said that voting for freer trade is an unnatural act for a politician because they [*sic*] are taking away tangible benefits for some in exchange for uncertain benefits for others." Douglas Irwin, *Free Trade Under Fire*, Third Edition, Princeton, N.J.: Princeton University Press, 2009, p. 97.

11. This is true as long as trade issues are not of major importance in national politics. The repeal of the Corn Laws is the occasional instance of trade becoming a highly visible and important political matter.

12. Polls frequently show majorities skeptical of, if not outright opposed to, free trade. See, for example, Rodrik, *op. cit.*, p. 51.

13. Workers benefited from the repeal as well, but had no political power because they could not vote.

14. "The future of globalization," *The Economist*, July 29, 2006, p. 11.

15. Paul Markillie, "The physical internet: a survey of logistics," *The Economist*, June 17, 2006, p. 9. "For one particular car produced by an American manufacturer . . . 30 percent of the car's value can be attributed to its assembly in Korea, 17.5 percent to components from Japan, 7.5 percent to design from Germany, 4 percent to parts from Taiwan and Singapore, 2.5 percent to advertising and marketing services from Britain, and 1.5 percent to data processing in Ireland. In the end just 37 percent of the production value of this 'American' car comes from the United States." Douglas A. Irwin, "Trade and Globalization," in Michael M. Weinstein, editor, *Globalization: What's New?* New York: Columbia University Press, A Council on Foreign Relations Book, 2005, p. 24. See also Thomas L. Friedman, *The World Is Flat: A Brief History of the Twenty-first Century*, New York: Farrar, Straus & Giroux, 2005, pp. 414–419.

16. Moises Naim, "The Trade Paradox," *The Washington Post*, September 9, 2007, p. B7.

17. The total gains from the Doha Round, were it to be completed, were modest, reducing the incentive to complete it. ". . . the deal 'on the table' [in the Doha negotiations] would boost *global* GDP by $114 billion . . ." Matthew Adler, Claire Brunei, Gary Clyde Hufbauer, and Jeffrey J. Schott, "What's on the Table? The Doha Round as of August, 2009," Washington, D.C: The Peterson Institute for International Economics, Working Paper Series, August 2009 p. 4. The world's total output in 2011 was an estimated $79 trillion. "The reason for US disinterest is very simple . . . the formula cuts of farm subsidies and tariffs and industrial tariffs currently on the table in the Doha Round would expand total US exports by a munificent $6 billion to $7 billion. The number is so embarrassingly small that no US industry or firm has lobbied the administration of Congress on the Round during the entirety of the Obama administration (or for some time before)." C. Fred Bergsten, "US Trade Policy and the Doha Round: An Alternative View," VoxEU.org, May 18, 2011.

18. One effort to reach a deal in the Doha Round in July 2008 failed because "China and India insisted on their right to protect their fragile farming sectors." Peter Coy, "Free Trade: After the Impasse," *Businessweek*, August 11, 2009, p. 29.

19. In 2001 there were 49 such agreements in place. By 2009 there were 167. "Doing Doha down," *The Economist*, September 5, 2009, p. 15.

20. The case against bilateral, or "preferential" trade agreements is made in Jagdish Bhagwati, *Termites in the Trading System: How Preferential Agreements Undermine Free Trade*, New York: Oxford University Press, 2008, especially Chapter 3.

21. "One basic condition for improving international labour standards is economic growth and a rising standard of living. . . . Solid gains in labour standards do not come through a foreign government using the threat of trade penalties." Andrew C. Brown et al., "US workers and labour standards," *Financial Times*, June 7, 2007, p. 10. On the impact of trade on labor and environmental standards, see Martin Wolf, *Why Globalization Works*, New Haven, Conn.: Yale University Press, 2004, Chapter 10, and Jagdish Bhagwati, *In Defense of Globalization*, New York: Oxford University Press, 2004, Chapters 10 and 11.

22. "But the real reason Democrats oppose trade has little to do with foreigners' stances on union rights or endangered species and a lot to do with the fact that trade harms some U.S. workers." Sebastian Mallaby, "Breaking the Trade Deadlock," *The Washington Post*, November 20, 2006, p. A17.

23. James Kynge, *China Shakes the World: A Titan's Rise and Troubled Future—and the Challenge for America*, Boston: Houghton Mifflin, 2006, pp. xii–xiii. "China is the world's largest manufacturing power. Its output of televisions, smart phones, steel pipes and other things you can drop on your foot surpassed America's in 2010. China now accounts for a fifth of global manufacturing. Its factories have made so much, so cheaply that they have curbed inflation in many of its trading partners." "The end of cheap China," *The Economist*, March 10, 2012, p. 75.

24. Kynge, *op.cit.*, Chapters 4 and 5.

25. Ronald Findlay and Kevin H. O'Rourke, *Power and Plenty: Trade, War, and the World Economy*, Princeton, N.J.: Princeton University Press, 2007, pp. 536–537.

26. "From 1993 to 2010, the incomes of the richest 1 percent of Americans grew 58 percent while the rest had a 6.4 percent bump." Eduardo Porter, "Inequality Undermines Democracy," *The New York Times*, March 21, 2012, p. Bl. "A recent study by the Congressional Budget Office found that the after-tax incomes of the top 1 percent of U.S. households almost quadrupled in real terms between 1979 and 2007. The income of the median household—again after taxes and transfers, and adjusted for inflation—went up just 35 percent. On the same basis, incomes of the lowest 20 percent of households managed an increase of only 18 percent." Clive Crook, "Look Past Taxes to Fix Global Puzzle of Inequality," http://www.bloomberg.com/news/print, December 27, 2011. "America's Gini

[the measure of national inequality] for disposable income is up by almost 30% since 1980 . . ." Zanny Minton Beddoes, "For richer, for poorer," *The Economist*, October 13, 2012, p. 4. Because Chinese-made goods are cheap, they also benefit less affluent Americans. "The authors [of an economic study] reckon that low-cost imports from China alone offset more than a quarter of the measured rise in income inequality since 1994." "Cheap and cheerful," *The Economist*, July 20, 2008, p. 90.

27. Martin Wolf, "Grim truths Obama should have told Hu in Beijing," *Financial Times*, November 18, 2009, p. 9. See also C. Fred Bergsten, "Correcting the Chinese Exchange Rate: An Action Plan," Testimony before the Committee on Ways and Means, U.S. House of Representatives, March 24, 2010, Washington, D.C: The Peterson Institute for International Economics.

28. Just what the appropriate value of the Chinese currency was at any time— that is, how far it was "overvalued"—and the extent to which Beijing's policies, as distinct from other factors (especially the low rate of savings in the United States) were responsible for the Chinese surpluses, were matters of debate among economists and economic officials in the West. See, for example, "Is China a Currency Manipulator?" New York: The Council on Foreign Relations, cfr.org, April 15, 2010. Nor, for a variety of reasons, was it certain that a sharp increase in the value of the renminbi would cause the Sino-American trade imbalance to shrink dramatically. For a skeptical view see Robert C. Pozen, "Bashing Beijing Will Not Help Our Trade Deficit," *The Wall Street Journal*, August 20, 2010, p. A13. In 1985, Japan revalued its currency under the terms of an agreement among the major free-market economies known as the Plaza Accord, but this did not markedly diminish its trade surplus with the United States.

29. Another motive is to fortify China against a currency crisis like the one that struck several Asian countries at the end of the 1990s. This bypassed China because the Chinese currency was not convertible. On this crisis, see Chapter 3, p. 89.

30. Justin Scheck and Evan Perez, "FBI Traces Trail of Spy Ring to China," *The Wall Street Journal*, March 9, 2012, p. A1; Richard A. Clarke, "How China Steals Our Secrets," *The New York Times*, April 3, 2012, p. A23; Nicole Perlroth, "Hacking Case Based in China Is Given a Face," *The New York Times*, March 30, 2012, p. A1.

31. "Getting ugly," *The Economist*, February 23, 2012, p. 12.

32. See Alan Beattie, "Trading blows," *Financial Times*, July 6, 2010, p. 8.

33. "For perspective, the trade surpluses of Japan, Taiwan, and South Korea taken together are $141 billion, only slightly smaller than China's." Tyler Cowen, "Reversal of Fortunes," *The New York Times Book Review*, August 12, 2012, p. 14.

34. A December 8, 2009 op-ed article in the staunchly pro-free-trade *Financial Times* by Robert Aliber, an emeritus professor of international economics and finance at the University of Chicago—an institution whose economists are notable for their devotion to free-market principles, including free trade—recommended imposing a 10 percent surcharge on all Chinese imports, with a provision that it rise by 1 percent each month until China's trade surplus shrinks to an acceptable level. The author argued that this would persuade the Chinese government to allow its currency to appreciate. Robert Aliber, "Tariffs can persuade Beijing to free the renminbi," *Financial Times*, December 8, 2010, p. 11. See also Robert J. Samuelson, "Obama's Tire Tariff: Bad Policy, Right Message," *The Washington Post*, September 21, 2009, p. A19, Samuelson, "Standing up to China," *The Washington Post*, September 27, 2010, p. A15, and Clive Crook, "Time to get tough with China," *Financial Times*, October 11, 2010, p. 11.

35. On the economics of carbon tariffs, see "Free exchange: Air Trade," *The Economist*, February 23, 2013, p. 72.

36. James Politi, "Race for the rustbelt," *Financial Times*, September 27, 2012, p. 11.

37. See, for example, Joshua Chaffin, "Tempestuous trade winds," *Financial Times*, May 29, 2012, p. 7.

38. So did the campaign promise by former Massachusetts governor Mitt Romney, the presidential candidate of the political party most closely associated with free trade—the Republicans—that he would brand China a "currency manipulator" and impose tariff penalities on his first day as president.

39. In 2007 the Chinese current account surplus was more than 10 percent of GDP. In 2011 it was about 2.8 percent. Eduardo Porter, "China's Trade Imbalance Is Vanishing," *The New York Times*, May 2, 2012, p. B1.

40. According to American businessman Bruce Cochrane, "Back in 2000, the average wage in China was about 50 cents an hour, now it's $3.50." Ed Crooks, "Companies attracted to US again as Asia loses its edge," *Financial Times*, January 18, 2012, p. 4. In the year 2012 private sector wages rose 14 percent. Tom Orlick, "Rising Wages Rose Dilemma for China," *The Wall Street Journal*, May 18–19, 2013, p. A7.

41. Keith Bradsher, "Hello, Cambodia," *The New York Times*, April 9, 2013, p. B1.

42. " . . . the US has made a huge leap in industrial competitiveness. Unit production costs are down 11 percent over the past 10 years. . . . The differences in labour costs compared with China are narrowing." Roger Altman, "How the American economy could surprise us all," *Financial Times*, September 4, 2012, p. 11.

43. Paul Markillie, "A third industrial revolution," *The Economist*, April 21, 2012, p. 4. See also Charles Fishman, "The Insourcing Boom," *The Atlantic*, December 2012; and Tamzin Booth, "Here, there, and everywhere," *The Economist*, January 19, 2013, pp. 1–9.

44. "China is estimated to control nearly half of all U.S. treasuries in the hands of official foreign owners. Some 65 percent of China's $2.5 trillion of reserves are in dollar-denominated assets." Barry Eichengreen, *Exorbitant Privilege: The Rise and Fall of the Dollar and the Future of the International Monetary System*, New York: Oxford University Press, 2011, p. 135.

45. The consensus of later research is that Germany did in fact want to fight, but only a limited, continental war, not one against Great Britain, let alone the United States. See, for example, David Fromkin, *Europe's Last Summer: Who Started the Great War in 1914?* New York: Alfred A. Knopf, 2004.

46. Services were exchanged internationally before the digital revolution. Firms and individuals in one country routinely bought insurance and clothing designs, for example, from other countries.

47. Alan Blinder, "Offshoring: Big Deal or Business as Usual?" in Jagdish Bhagwati and Alan Blinder, *Offshoring of American Jobs: What Response from U.S. Economic Policy?* Cambridge, Mass.: MIT Press, 2009, p. 20. Much of the analysis that follows is drawn from this essay.

48. "Ritu Solanki, a 28–year-old lawyer . . . is in Gurgaon, a high-rise satellite city on Delhi's edge, where she works for CPA Global, a legal-outsourcing company. A lawyer with similar experience at a London law firm might charge up to $400 an hour for the sort of work Ms. Solanki does; her labour costs around $50 an hour." "Passage to India," *The Economist*, June 26, 2010, p. 69.

49. Michael Spence, *The Next Convergence: The Future of Economic Growth in a Multispeed World*, New York: Farrar, Straus & Giroux, 2011, pp. 65, 200.

50. Blinder, *op. cit.*, pp. 36–37.

51. "Police officers will not be replaced by electronic monitoring, but some security guards will be. Janitors and crane operators are probably immune to foreign competition; accountants and computer programmers are not. In short, the dividing line between the jobs that produce services that are suitable for electronic delivery (and are thus threatened by offshoring) and those that do not does not correspond to traditional distinctions between high-end and low-end work." Alan Blinder, "Offshoring: The Next Industrial Revolution?" *Foreign Affairs*, March/April 2006, pp. 119.

52. " . . . despite fears of offshoring, mature economics are running increasing surpluses in services, particularly in knowledge-intensive services . . ." Charles Roxburgh, James Manyika, Richard Dobbs, Jan Mischke, *Trading Myths: Addressing Misconceptions About Trade, Jobs, and Competitiveness*, McKinsey Global Institute, May, 2012, p. 3.

53. J. Bradford Jensen, "Opportunities for US Exports of Business Services," Peterson Institute for International Economics, http://www.piie.com/publications/interstertitial.cfm?ResearchID=2220.

54. Friedman, *The World Is Flat*, pp. 28–29.

55. See J. Bradford Jensen, *Global Trade in Services: Fear, Facts, and Offshoring*, Washington, D.C.: The Peterson Institute for International Economics, 2011, especially Chapter 4. See also Booth, *op. cit.*, pp. 16–20.

56. Blinder, "Offshoring: Big Deal," p. 41.

57. Sometimes a fourth factor of production is listed: enterprise, or entrepreneurship, which also depends on human beings.

58. Robert Guest, *Borderless Economics: Chinese Sea Turtles, Indian Fridges, and the New Fruits of Global Capitalism*, New York: Palgrave Macmillan, 2011, p. 16.

59. Christopher Caldwell, *Reflections on the Revolution in Europe: Immigration, Islam, and the West*, New York: Doubleday, 2009, p. 9.

60. Political refugees do not move for economic reasons, but do have an economic impact on the countries to which they flee.

61. "By the end of the 1990s, Chinese and Indian engineers were running 29 percent of the Valley's technology businesses." Philippe Legrain, *Immigrants: Your Country Needs Them*, London: Little, Brown 2006. "A recent study carried out by Duke University showed that, while immigrants make up an eighth of America's population, they founded a quarter of the country's technology and engineering firms." "The magic of diasporas," *The Economist*, November 19, 2011, p. 13.

62. The large-scale transatlantic migration in the nineteenth century raised wage levels in the European countries from which people left and lowered them, compared to what they would have been without immigration, in North America. Kevin H. O'Rourke and Jeffrey G. Williamson, *Globalization and History: The Evolution of a Nineteenth-Century Atlantic Economy*, Cambridge, Mass.: MIT Press, 1999, p. 119.

63. "It is estimated that more than half of known [university] graduates from the world's poorest nations are living abroad. About one-third of R&D professionals from developing countries are estimated to be residing in OECD countries." TheGlobalist.com, October 19, 2006.

64. "According to a World Bank internal document, a quarter of a trillion dollars in remittances were wired around the world in 2006; if you add unrecorded flows, they account for more funds than all the foreign direct investment in the world, and are more than double the level of international aid." Caldwell, *op. cit.*, p. 56. "Some countries depend heavily on remittances. In Tajikistan, they are a staggering 46 percent of the economy. In Tonga they are 39 percent; in Lesotho, 28 percent. . . ." Guest, *op. cit.*, p. 116.

65. Devesh Kapur, *Diaspora, Development, and Democracy: The Domestic Impact of International Migration from India*, Princeton, N.J.: Princeton University Press, 2010, Chapter 4. See also Guest, *op. cit.*, Chapters 4 and 5.

66. George Borjas, "Globalization and Immigration," in Weinstein, editor, *op. cit.*, p. 79. An estimated 43 percent of all American immigrants lived in just four metropolitan areas: Los Angeles, New York, Miami, and Chicago. Only 15 percent of all natives lived in those areas. *Ibid.*

67. Rodrik, *op. cit.*, p. 268; Michael A. Clemens, "Economics and Emigration: Trillion-Dollar Bills on the Sidewalk?" *Journal of Economic Perspectives* 25:3, Summer 2011.

68. Guest, *op. cit.*, p. 17.

69. *Ibid.*, p. 18; Legrain, *op. cit.*, pp. 64–65.

70. Cited in David Pilling and Kathrin Hille, "The new melting pot," *Financial Times*, July 9, 2007, p. 7.

71. See Rafaela M. Dancygier, *Immigration and Conflict in Europe*, New York: Cambridge University Press, 2010.

72. "The social, spiritual, and political effects of immigration are huge and enduring, while the economic effects are puny and transitory." Caldwell, *op. cit.*, p. 39.

73. "In 44 of 47 countries polled by Pew Research Center last fall, majorities supported further restrictions on immigration." Bob Davis, "Rise of Nationalism Frays Global Ties," *The Wall Street Journal*, April 28, 2008, p. A16.

74. Ethan Bronner, "Israeli Plan Cracks Down on Migrants from Africa," *The New York Times*, December 12, 2011, p. A7.

75. Richard Jackson and Neil Howe, *The Graying of the Great Powers: Demography and Geopolitics in the 21st Century*, Washington, D.C.: Center for Strategic and International Studies, 2008, Chapter 2.

76. Caldwell, *op. cit.*, p. 49. Much of the analysis of immigration in Europe draws on this book. "In Sweden only 51% of non-Europeans have a job, compared with over 84% of native Swedes. . . . In Sweden 26% of all prisoners, and 50% of prisoners serving more than five years, are foreigners. Some 46% of the jobless are non-Europeans, and 40% of non-Europeans are classified as poor, compared with only 10% of native Swedes." Adrian Wooldridge, "Northern Lights," *The Economist*. February 2, 2013, p. 7.

77. "In a Pew Research poll of Muslims conducted last spring, 81 percent of British Muslims said they were Muslim first and British second, compared with only 46 percent of French Muslims saying they are Muslim first, French second." Jonathan Paris, "Letters to the Editor: Europe and Its Muslims," *Foreign Affairs* 86:1, January/February 2007, p. 182.

78. Caldwell, *op. cit.*, Part II.

79. *Ibid.*, p. 15.

80. "For every depressing statistic about integration—France's prisons hold nine times more young men with North African fathers than ones with French fathers—there are several reassuring ones: a quarter of young Muslim Frenchwomen are married to non-Muslim men; Muslims are flocking to British universities and even popping up in white bastions like the Tory party." "Tales from Eurabia," *The Economist*, June 24, 2006, p. 11. See also Jytte Klausen, *The Islamic Challenge: Politics and Religion in Western Europe*, New York: Oxford University Press, 2005.

81. Caldwell, *op. cit.*, Chapters 3 and 4.

82. "Multikulturell? Wir?" *The Economist*, November 13, 2010, p. 59.

83. "On the march," *The Economist*, March 9, 2011, p. 60. These parties typically also express more skepticism about the European Union and its common currency than the mainstream parties, which are usually deeply committed to both.

84. Bobby Duffy, "Europe's Anti-Immigrant Voters," *The Wall Street Journal*, May 22, 2012, p. A15.

85. " . . . the United States accounts for 40 percent of all net immigration worldwide." Stijn Hoorens, "Midnight in Munich," *Rand Review*, Winter, 2011–2012, p. 26.

86. "The degree of success may hinge in part on the cultural distance between minorities and majorities. The distance between Hispanics and the U.S. majority is arguably less than between Muslims and the European majority." Jackson and Howe, *op. cit.*, p. 125.

87. France is a partial exception to this rule, accepting and successfully assimilating a large number of immigrants—most from eastern Europe—in the first half of the twentieth century and a substantial number, again largely of European origin, from former French colonies that became independent in the 1950s and 1960s. See David Bell, "The Shorn Identity: Why the French Forgot How to Assimilate," *The New Republic*, November 28, 2005.

88. See Aristide Zolberg, *A Nation by Design: Immigration Policy in the Fashioning of America*, Cambridge, Mass.: Harvard University Press, 2006, especially Chapters 7 and 8.

89. New York: Simon & Schuster, 2004.

90. Official estimates tend to be lower. In 2003, for example, the Immigration and Naturalization Service reported that 7 million people resided in the United States illegally, with an estimated annual flow of 350,000. Borjas, *op. cit.*, p. 798. People are not the only things that move illegally across borders. See Moises Naim, *Illicit: How Smugglers, Traffickers, and Copycats Are Hijacking the Global Economy*, New York: Doubleday, 2005.

91. In the United States there is a "pervasive disjunction between public opinion, which tends to favor less immigration and more restricted ac-

cess to government benefits, and the balance of political forces that has allowed an alliance of business groups and ethnic minorities to sustain policies that generally mean more immigrants." Jack Citrin and Matthew Wright, "Defining the Circle of We: American Identity and Immigration Policy," *The Forum* 7:3, 2009, Article 6, Berkeley Electronic Press, http://www.bepress.com/forum/vol17/iss3/art6.

92. Linda Chavez, "The Great Assimilation Machine," *The Wall Street Journal*, June 5, 2007, p. A23. See also Legrain, *op. cit.*, pp. 243–244.

93. "The Pew Hispanic Center reported last summer that Mexican immigration to the U.S. from spring 2008 to spring 2009 was only one-quarter the level of 2004–2005. The Center for Immigration Studies (CIS) estimates that the number of illegals in the U.S. dropped to 10.8 million in spring 2008 from 12.5 million in summer 2007—a decline of 14% . . . the CIS estimates that 1.2 million illegals returned to Mexico in 2006–09, more than twice as many as in 2002–05." Michael Barone, "Immigration Reform: The New Third Rail," *The Wall Street Journal*, April 16, 2010, p. A19. "The flow has already stopped, Douglas Massey of the Mexican Migration Project at Princeton recently told The New York Times. The net traffic has gone to zero and is probably a little bit negative." Barone, "New Reality Emerging on Illegal Immigration," realclearpolitics.com, July 14, 2011.

94. See Thomas L. Friedman and Michael Mandelbaum, *That Used to Be Us: How America Fell Behind in the World It Invented and How We Can Come Back*, New York: Farrar, Straus & Giroux, 2011, pp. 226–229.

95. This is the subject of Chapter 3, pp. 90–100.

96. David M. Marchick and Matthew J. Slaughter, "Global FDI Policy: Correcting a Protectionist Drift," CSR No. 34, New York: The Council on Foreign Relations, The Maurice Greenberg Center for Geoeconomic Studies, June 2008, p. 6.

97. "Being eaten by the dragon," *The Economist*, November 13, 2010, p. 81.

98. Siobhan Gorman, "China Tech Giant Under Fire," *The Wall Street Journal*, October 8, 2012, p. A1. On a related episode in 2013, see Spencer E. Ante, Danny Yadron, and Thomas Gryta, "China Worries Arise in Sprint Deal," *The Wall Street Journal*, March 28, 2013, p. A1.

99. On these concerns about foreign investment in the United States, see Theodore H. Moran, *Three Threats: An Analytical Framework for the CFIUS Process*, Washington, D.C.: Peterson Institute for International Economics, 2009.

100. The most comprehensive account of sovereign wealth funds is Edwin M. Truman, *Sovereign Wealth Funds: Threat or Salvation?* Washington, D.C.: Peterson Institute for International Economics, 2010. The discussion of this subject owes a great deal to this book and to a summary of

its findings—Edwin M. Truman, *In Brief: Sovereign Wealth Funds: Threat or Salvation?* Peterson Institute for International Economics, September 2010.

101. David Pilling, "China's spending spree deserves three cheers," *Financial Times*, May 12, 2011, p. 9.
102. Truman, *Sovereign Wealth Funds*, p. 43.
103. *Ibid.*, pp. 158–159.
104. *Ibid.*, p. 46.
105. *Ibid.*, p. 40.
106. *Ibid.*, p. 7.
107. Joseph B. White and Norihiko Shibouzu, "In the Heart of the Rust Belt, Chinese Funds Provide the Grease," *The Wall Street Journal*, February 11–12, 2012, p. A1.

CHAPTER THREE: THE RIVER

1. Edward Carr, "Greed—and fear," *The Economist*, January 24, 2009, p. 6.
2. Gordon Brown, "How the west can reverse a decade of decline," *Financial Times*, December 9, 2012, p. 13.
3. "Charles McKay, in his discussion of the South Sea Bubble, mentioned the case of a banker who purchased 500 pounds' worth of South Sea stock in the third subscription list of August 1720 saying, 'when the rest of the world are mad, we must imitate them in some measure.'" Charles Kindleberger and Robert Aliber, *Manias, Panics, and Crashes: A History of Financial Crises*, Fifth Edition, New York: John Wiley & Sons, 2005, p. 42.
4. "Economists do not have a terribly good idea of what kinds of events shift confidence and of how to concretely assess confidence vulnerability." Carmen M. Reinhart and Kenneth S. Rogoff, *This Time Is Different: Eight Centuries of Financial Folly*, Princeton, N.J.: Princeton University Press, 2009, p. xliii.

   While not offering a way to predict sudden losses of confidence, Charles Kindleberger, building on the work of the economist Hyman Minsky, identified a broad pattern common to the inflating and bursting of bubbles: a change in the economy leads to a new investment opportunity, euphoria and manic trading result, then something changes investor psychology, sowing distress and then revulsion as investors sell the asset as fast as they can. Kindleberger and Aliber, *op. cit.*, Chapters 1 and 2.

   Bubbles pose a difficult problem for public policy because it is hard to know when one is forming—as distinct from a justified and sustainable increase in the price of an asset—until *after* it has burst, when it is too late for preventive action. Michael Spence, *The Next Convergence: The Future of Economic Growth in a Multispeed World*, New York: Farrar, Straus & Giroux, 2011, p. 152. Where bubbles are concerned, hindsight is 20/20 but foresight is blind.

5. Kindleberger lists the ten biggest ones at the time his book was written, seven of which occurred in the twentieth century. Kindleberger and Aliber, *op. cit.*, p. 9. Reinhart and Rogoff list many more in the appendixes to their book. Their analysis includes sovereign debt crises as well as banking crises. Reinhart and Rogoff, *op. cit.*, pp. 295–392.

6. The importance of debt in financial crises is a central theme of Reinhart and Rogoff, *op. cit.* ". . . without easy credit creation a true bubble cannot occur. That is why so many bubbles have their origins in the sins of omission and commission of central banks." Neil Ferguson, "Wall Street Lays Another Egg," www.vanityfair.com/politics/features/2008/12banks200812, p.3.

7. Reinhart and Rogoff, *op. cit.*, p. xliv.

8. Barry Eichengreen, *Exorbitant Privilege: The Rise and Fall of the Dollar and the Future of the International Monetary System*, New York: Oxford University Press, 2011, p. 34.

9. *"Periods of high international capital mobility have repeatedly produced international banking crises, not only famously, as they did in the 1990s, but historically."* Reinhart and Rogoff, *op. cit.*, p. 155. Italics added for emphasis in the original.

10. Matthew Rees, "Why Money Can Now Make Its Way Around the World," *The Wall Street Journal*, February 17, 2007, p. D12. See also Martin Wolf, "The new capitalism," *Financial Times*, June 19, 2007, p. 11.

11. The flight seems, in retrospect, more the product of investor psychology than of fundamental economic problems in Asia. See Dani Rodrik, *The Globalization Paradox: Democracy and the Future of the World Economy*, New York: W. W. Norton, 2011, p. 93.

12. When a country receiving an investment from abroad lowers the value of its currency, the foreign investor suffers a loss. The anticipation of devaluation can therefore cause money to flee. When exchange rates are not fixed but allowed to vary—that is, to float—anticipated changes in the inflation rate can have the same effect. Kindleberger and Aliber, *op. cit.*, p. 287.

13. The Asian financial crisis is described in Paul Blustein, *The Chastening: Inside the Crisis That Rocked the Global Financial System and Humbled the IMF*, New York: PublicAffairs, 2001. "In 1998, Thailand, South Korea, Malaysia and the Philippines each saw economic activity fall by between 8 per cent and 13 per cent. . . . The lost output of 1998 was never recovered and the Asian Development Bank calculates that the post-crisis average growth rates 'have slipped by an average 2.5 [percentage points] in the five

countries that were most directly affected.'" Chris Giles, "Wrong lessons from Asia's crisis," *Financial Times*, July 2, 2007, p. 7.

14. Reinhart and Rogoff, *op. cit.*, p. 75.

15. Robert Skidelsky, *John Maynard Keynes: The Return of the Master*, New York: PublicAffairs, 2009, p. 5.

16. "The International Monetary Fund estimates that holders of U.S. mortgage and other debt lost $2.7 trillion in the U.S. phase of the global crisis. . . . American homes are worth nearly $7 trillion less than they were five years ago, a 25% decline." David Wessel, "Dividing the Tab Prolongs Pain," *The Wall Street Journal*, November 10, 2011, p. A4.

17. The American International Group, an insurance company, had a reported $2.7 trillion in exposure in housing-related instruments, with 12,000 separate contracts. Of this total $1 trillion was with twelve major financial institutions. This meant that "if AIG went under, it could take the entire financial system along with it." Andrew Ross Sorkin, *Too Big to Fail*, New York: Viking, 2009, p. 184.

18. A week later the Washington Mutual Bank failed after a classic run on its assets in which depositors, behaving like a herd of panicked gazelles, withdrew $16.7 billion. Skidelsky, *op. cit.*, p. 9.

19. The recession officially began in 2007 but the near-meltdown of 2008 substantially worsened it.

20. An excellent overview and analysis of the causes is Alan Blinder, *After the Music Stopped: The Financial Crisis, the Response, and the Work Ahead*, New York: Penguin Press, 2013, Part II.

21. Other forms of debt, on credit cards and for student loans for example, were also turned into securities.

22. "[Investment banker Ralph] Schlosstein picked out the growth of credit-default swaps, a type of derivative often used purely for speculative purposes. When an investor or financial institution buys this kind of swap, it doesn't purchase a bond itself; it just places a bet on whether the bond will default. At the height of the boom, for every dollar banks issued in bonds, they might issue twenty dollars in swaps. 'If they did a hundred-million-dollar bond issue, two billion dollars of swaps would be created and traded,' Schlosstein said." John Cassidy, "What Good Is Wall Street?" *The New Yorker*, November 29, 2010. AIG wrote $3 trillion in derivatives such as credit-default swaps "while reserving precisely zero dollars against future claims." Barry Ritholtz, "What caused the financial crisis? The Big Lie goes viral," *The Washington Post*, November 6, 2011, p. G6.

23. "From 2003, senior officials at the BIS (Bank for International Settlements) in Basel . . . repeatedly warned that risk dispersion might not always be benign. However, such warnings were largely kept out of public view, partly because the US Federal Reserve was convinced that financial

innovation had changed the system in a fundamentally beneficial way." Gillian Tett, "A year that shook faith in finance," *Financial Times*, August 4, 2008, p. 9.

24. At their peak, the two owned or guaranteed fully 55 percent of the $11 trillion American mortgage market. Sorkin, *op. cit.*, p. 184.

25. Paul Volcker, the chairman of the Federal Reserve between 1979 and 1987 and a critic of the way the financial system had evolved since his time in office, described the shadow banking system in this way: "the nondepository banks, hedge funds, insurers, money market funds, and other largely unregulated entities that grew enormously in size after 2000—a system that by June 2008 was roughly the size of the traditional banking system." Paul Volcker, "Financial Reform: Unfinished Business," *The New York Review of Books*, November 24, 2011, p. 74.

26. On this point see Richard Posner, *A Failure of Capitalism: The Crisis of '08 and the Descent into Depression*, Cambridge, Mass.: Harvard University Press, 2009, pp. 259–260; John Cassidy, *How Markets Fail: The Logic of Economic Calamities*, New York: Farrar, Straus & Giroux, 2009, Part III; and Skidelsky, *op. cit.*, pp. 38–42. The most prominent and influential proponent of this point of view was Alan Greenspan, the chairman of the U.S. Federal Reserve Board. After the crash he confessed his error: "Those of us who have looked to the self-interest of leading institutions to protect shareholders' equity—myself especially—are in a state of shocked disbelief." He had come to the conclusion, he went on, that there had been "a flaw in the model that I perceived as the critical functioning structure that defines how the world works." Quoted in John Lanchester, "Heroes and Zeroes," *The New Yorker*, February 2, 2009, p. 73.

27. The phrase is from Skidelsky, *op. cit.*, p. 4.

28. " . . . no other financial crisis since the Great Depression has been nearly as global in nature." Reinhart and Rogoff, *op. cit.*, p. 201.

29. Posner, *op. cit.*, p. 38; Niall Ferguson, *The Ascent of Money: A Financial History of the World*, New York: Penguin Press, 2008, pp. 335–336. "When China bought a Treasury bond from an American insurance company or bank, it provided the pension fund or bank with funds to invest in riskier assets that offered a higher yield than Treasury bonds." Brad Setser, "Read Brender and Pisani's 'Globalised Finance and Its Collapse,'" June 16, 2009, http://blogs.cfr.org/setser/2009/06/16/read-brender-and-pisani.

30. Sorkin, *op. cit.*, p. 222. Foreigners also bought credit default securities. Ferguson, *op. cit.*, p. 269.

31. Johan A. Lybeck, *A Global History of the Financial Crash of 2007–2010*, New York: Cambridge University Press, 2011, p. 96; Reinhart and Rogoff, *op. cit.*, p. 244.

32. The contribution of financial engineering in the United States to the housing bubble by attracting foreign capital is a major theme of Anton Brender and Florence Pisani, *Globalised Finance and Its Collapse*, Brussels, Belg.: Dexia Asset Management, 2010 (English translation). See also Posner, *op. cit.*, pp. 39, 55. "About one-fifth of securities issued by Fannie, Freddie and a handful of much smaller quasi-governmental agencies, some $1.4 trillion worth, were held by foreign investors at the end of March [2008]." Heather Timmons, "Trouble at Fannie and Freddie Stirs Concern Abroad," *The New York Times*, July 21, 2008, p. C1.

33. Evidence of the global character of the financial crisis was the increased demand for American Treasury bills. This seems counterintuitive: the United States was, after all, the epicenter of the crisis: why would foreigners rush to hold its currency? The reason is that, as the crisis spread to other countries, the United States, even with all its problems, came to appear to global investors a safer place for their money than the alternatives. Harold James, *The Creation and Destruction of Value: The Globalization Cycle*, Cambridge, Mass.: Harvard University Press, 2012, p. 196.

34. "The crude figures show that, on average, emerging Asia's exports amount to 47% of their GDP, up from 37% ten years ago. The share varies from 14% in India to 186% [*sic*] in Singapore." "Troubled tigers," *The Economist*, January 31, 2009, p. 76.

35. " . . . many of Asia's tiger economies seem to have been hit harder than their spendthrift Western counterparts. In the fourth quarter of 2008, GDP probably fell by an average annualised rate of around 15% in Hong Kong, Singapore, South Korea and Taiwan; their exports slumped more than 50% at an annualised rate." *Ibid.*

36. The Group of Twenty was initially established as a venue for finance ministers to meet in 1999. It superseded the Group of Eight in the wake of, and because of, the economic crisis of 2008. The membership consists of Australia, Canada, Saudi Arabia, the United States, India, Russia, South Africa, Turkey, Argentina, Brazil, Mexico, France, Germany, Italy, Great Britain, China, Indonesia, Japan, and South Korea as well as the European Union.

37. Kindleberger and Aliber, *op. cit.*, Chapter 11.

38. Robin Harding, Matt Kennard, and Suzanne Kapner, "Fed data reveal how it helped European Banks," *Financial Times*, April 1, 2011, p. 3.

39. Posner, *op. cit.*, p. 204.

40. Sorkin, *op. cit.*, pp. 519–528.

41. *Ibid.*, p. 510; Skidelsky, *op. cit.*, pp. 10–11.

42. Skidelsky, *op. cit.*, p. 11; Peter Coy, "Enough Shock Treatment?" *Businessweek*, December 1, 2008, p. 27. An exception was the tiny country of

Iceland. Over the years it had built up a sizable banking sector, which, when the crash came, it lacked the resources to rescue. "In early 2008 the total assets of the three [large Icelandic] banks was almost eleven times the Icelandic GDP." Howard Davies, "Fish stocks up bank stocks down," *TLS*, December 11, 2009, p. 26.

43. Krishna Guha, "Monetary chiefs in historic harmony," *Financial Times*, October 9, 2008; Skidelsky, *op. cit.*, p. 11. "Coordinated interest-rate changes by multiple central banks are scarcer than hens' teeth. To a first approximation, they *never* happen because each central bank does what it thinks best for its own country, not for the world. So the coordinated rate cuts of October 8, 2008, were stunning. They symbolized, first, that the problem was global and, second, that it was no longer just financial. The health of the world economy was at stake." Blinder, *op. cit.*, p. 172.

44. This was the retrospective judgment of the chairman of the American Federal Reserve, Ben Bernanke (who was himself, to be sure, deeply involved in the response to the financial crisis and so had a vested interest in thinking well of it). "Without these speedy and forceful actions, last October's panic would likely have continued to intensify, more major financial firms would have failed, and the entire global financial system would have been at serious risk." Quoted in Martin Wolf, "Why it is still too early to start withdrawing stimulus," *Financial Times*, September 9, 2009, p. 9.

45. The recession began in 2007, but the acute financial crisis of 2008 almost certainly made it deeper and longer than it would otherwise have been. A study by two prominent economists found that without government spending economic output in the United States would have been 6.5 percent lower than it actually was in 2010. Sewell Chan, "In Study, 2 Economists Say Intervention Helped Avert a 2nd Depression," *The New York Times*, July 28, 2010, p. B8.

46. Not coincidentally, given the subject's aspirations and the impact of his thought, the second volume of Robert Skidelsky's three-volume biography of Keynes is entitled *The Economist as Savior*. New York: Allen Lane, The Penguin Press, 1994.

47. David Pilling, "Asia's Keynesians take pride in prudence," *Financial Times*, July 22, 2010, p. 9. "According to the Fitch rating agency, fiscal stimulus packages as a percentage of gross domestic product amounted to 6.9 per cent for Vietnam, 7.7 per cent for Thailand, 8 per cent for Singapore, 13.5 per cent for China, and a whopping 14.8 per cent for Japan." *Ibid.* By way of comparison, the stimulus package the American Congress passed in February 2009 was worth 5.7 per cent of 2009 GDP. Martin Wolf, "Obama's mistake was being too cautious in fearful times," *Financial Times*, September 1, 2010, p. 7.

48. James, *op. cit.*, p. 124.

49. "Waiting for Armageddon," *The Economist*, March 29, 2008, p. 81.

50. Posner, *op. cit.*, pp. 281–282; Peter Boone and Simon Johnson, "The Next Financial Crisis," *The New Republic*, September 23, 2009, p. 25. "The primary rationale for noninterference is the moral hazard that the more interventionist the authorities are with respect to the current crisis, the more intense the next bubble will be, because many of the market participants will believe that their possible losses will be limited by government measures." Kindleberger and Aliber, *op. cit.*, p. 81.

51. In the United States the opposite trend occurred. ". . . 'half of the entire banking industry's assets' are concentrated in five institutions whose combined assets amount to almost 60 percent of the gross domestic product. And 'the top 10 banks now account for 61 percent of commercial banking assets, substantially more than the 26 percent of only 20 years ago.'" George F. Will, "Break Up the Banks," *The Washington Post*, October 14, 2012, p. A21.

52. See Introduction, p. xvii.

53. Rodrik, *op. cit.*, pp. 260–266. "Among the leaders of the major countries, there is universal agreement that a coordinated global regulatory system is needed—and little will to get such a system in place. They talk globally when the Group of 20 meets, and act locally when they return home." Floyd Norris, "A Retreat from Global Banking," *The New York Times*, July 24, 2009, p. B6.

54. "But the United States and Europe are increasingly pursuing their own— sometimes clashing—paths to reform, potentially undermining the regulatory overhauls taking shape on both sides of the Atlantic. If this continues, a resulting patchwork of reforms could allow companies to continue exploiting national differences by moving operations to countries where conditions are most favorable and thwart the efforts of regulators to spot financial threats early on." Anthony Faiola and Brady Dennis, "Nations go their own way on global financial reform," *The Washington Post*, May 26, 2010, p. A1. "'There is a mismatch between the brave G20 announcements of global solutions and the messy practicalities of national authorities, scrambling to protect their own national interests,' says Jon Pain, a former UK regulator . . ." Brooke Masters, "Conflicting signals," *Financial Times*, April 2, 2012, p. 7.

55. "Christopher J. Dodd, the Connecticut Democrat who shepherded the [financial reform] legislation through the Senate, said on Friday that improving regulation made more sense than restraining an industry that was critical to the American economy and that faced fierce competition from foreign banks, which would not be placed under similar restrictions." Binyamin Appelbaum, "Rules Grow, Banks Stay Same Size," *The New York Times*, May 24, 2010, p. B7. See also Clive Crook, "Designs that ignore a wider terrain," *Financial Times*, March 22, 2010, p. 11.

56. Reinhart and Rogoff, *op. cit.*, p. 282.

57. Even regulation that is global in scope might not be effective. "The Basel Committee on Banking Supervision, the global club of bank regulators, has been widely hailed as the apogee of international financial cooperation, but has produced largely inadequate agreements." Rodrik, *op. cit.*, p. 224.

58. "Tide barriers," *The Economist*, October 6, 2012, p. 90.

59. This is the finding of William R. Cline, *Financial Globalization, Economic Growth, and the Crisis of 2007–2009*, Washington, D.C: Peterson Institute for International Economics, 2009.

60. On some of the difficulties, see Sebastian Mallaby, "The genie of global finance is out of the bottle," *Financial Times*, October 12, 2010, p. 11.

61. Martin Wolf, "Who are the villains and the victims of global capital flows?" *Financial Times*, June 13, 2007, p. 11.

62. Eichengreen, *op. cit.*, pp. 160–167; C. Fred Bergsten, "The Dollar and the Deficit," *Foreign Affairs*, November/December 2009, pp. 29–31.

63. The Middle Eastern oil-exporting countries accumulated large surpluses. "Petrodollar profusion," *The Economist*, April 28, 2012, p. 83.

64. Bergsten, *op. cit.* pp. 32–33.

65. In general, in order to rebalance, deficit countries "have to produce more than they consume and save more than they invest; they also have to increase exports and reduce imports. The domestic political economy of this sort of adjustment cannot be popular, involving as it does reduced consumption and lower real wages." Jeffry A. Frieden, "Global Imbalances, National Rebalancing, and the Political Economy of Recovery," New York: Council on Foreign Relations, Working Paper, Center for Geoeconomic Studies, October 2009, p. 5. "There are three questions, therefore, about [the United States] shifting to a new growth model. First, can the American economy grow as fast by investing and exporting as it did by consuming and building houses? Second, is it flexible enough to switch without any permanent loss in output. And, third, how much pain will there be during the transition?" Robin Harding and James Politi, "A new way forward," *Financial Times*, August 13, 2010, p. 5.

66. According to German chancellor Angela Merkel, speaking in March 2009: "The German economy is very reliant on exports, and this is not something you can change in two years." Quoted in Martin Wolf, "Why G20 leaders will fail to deal with the big challenge," *Financial Times*, April 1, 2009, p. 11. "The transition from an export-led economy to a domestic consumption-led model involves a long restructuring of the financial system and household behaviour, and a major reversion away from political structures and industrial policies that powered growth in the past." Michael Pettis, "Asia needs to ditch its growth model," *Financial Times*, May 20, 2009, p. 9.

67. "Stuck in neutral," *The Economist*, August 15, 2009, p. 65.

68. " . . . most Chinese are what Dragonomics, a research firm, calls 'survivors,' whose purchases of basic food and clothing are meaningless for multinationals or global demand. Only about 150m are part of 'consuming China,' although this may double to 300m by 2015." David Pilling, "Chinese consumption is a disappearing act," *Financial Times*, April 9, 2009, p. 9.

69. "The Beijing government is acting: it doubled spending on health care, education, and social security between 2005 and 2008. But the total amount remains low at only 6% of GDP, compared with an average of around 25% in OECD countries." "The spend is nigh," *The Economist*, August 1, 2009, p. 9.

70. The story is told in Robert Skidelsky, *John Maynard Keynes: Volume Three, Fighting for Freedom, 1937–1946*, New York: Viking, 2000. See also Eichengreen, *op. cit.*, pp. 45–49.

71. The economic motivation for the euro is a theme of Harold James, *Making the European Monetary Union*, Cambridge, Mass.: Harvard University Press, 2012. "For what it was worth, statistical analysis suggested that adopting a common currency had big effects on trade, which suggested in turn large economic gains. Unfortunately, this optimistic assessment hasn't held up very well since the euro was created: the best estimates now indicate that trade among euro nations is only 10 to 15 percent larger than it would have been otherwise. That's not a trivial number, but neither is it transformative." Paul Krugman, "Eurotrashed," *The New York Times Magazine*, January 16, 2011, p. 28.

72. "Economists have long understood that significant labour mobility is not nearly enough. A sustainable currency union requires other country-like features, including a centralised fiscal authority that has at least as much power to collect taxes as the constituent states. A central financial regulator is also essential, at least absent an adequate global regulator. Finally, the centre cannot be endowed with so much power without the legitimacy that can only come from political union. Currency union without political union is an unstable halfway house." Kenneth Rogoff, "A euro parable: the young couple with a joint account," *Financial Times*, April 24, 2012, p. 9.

73. "Inside the eurozone, adjustment of imbalances remains essential. But it is also vastly difficult, because the exchange rate has gone. In its place, comes adjustment via depression and default." Martin Wolf, "There is no sunlit future for the euro," *Financial Times*, October 19, 2011, p. 11.

74. See, for example, Eichengreen, *op. cit.*, p. 75.

75. Tony Barber, "Tall ambition, flawed foundations," *Financial Times*, October 12, 2010, p. 9.

76. Andrew Moravcsik, "Europe After the Crisis: How to Sustain a Common Currency," *Foreign Affairs*, May/June 2012, pp. 58–59.

77. " . . . the 'sudden stops' in private inflows . . . occurred during the global
crisis of 2008 (affecting Greece and Ireland), in the spring of 2010 (affecting Greece, Ireland, and Portugal) and, finally, in the second half of 2011
(affecting Italy, Portugal, and Spain)." Martin Wolf, "Why the Bundes-
bank is wrong," *Financial Times*, April 11, 2011, p. 9.

78. "The problem [with Italy] isn't the debt itself but, rather, the soaring
interest rates, and these are driven more by fear than by economic funda-
mentals. Investors have become far more skittish than they once were. . . ."
James Surowiecki, "An Avoidable Crisis," *The New Yorker*, December 5,
2011, p. 30.

79. "Ten years of pretending that loans to southern European governments
carried as little risk as loans to the German government left Europe's
banks with nearly $2 trillion worth of claims on those riskier borrowers.
For the purposes of 'stress tests,' it was assumed that these claims were
worth 100 cents on the dollar when the marketplace implies substantially
lower values. The large sovereign-debt holdings by European banks pose
a threat to the solvency of many of those banks that rises in proportion to
doubts about governments' ability to service those loans." John H. Makin,
"The Eurozone Crisis and the US Economy: What Has Gone Wrong?"
Washington, D.C.: The American Enterprise Institute, October, 2011, p. 3.

80. "The real danger was and remains a collapse of Europe's financial system
and the slump this would trigger. A sovereign default could easily have
repercussions exceeding even those of the Lehman bankruptcy. . . ." "Making eurozone safe from failure," *Financial Times*, October 13, 2010, p. 10.

81. Sebastian Mallaby, "Europe's Optional Catastrophe: The Fate of the
Monetary Union Lies in Germany's Hands," *Foreign Affairs*, July/August
2012, p. 7.

82. " . . . the eurozone had no effective way to sustain banking systems, finance countries in trouble, or secure adjustment by creditor and debtor
economies. We see improvisation instead: the eurozone's aircraft is being
redesigned while crashing." Martin Wolf, "The Union outlived de Toc-
queville," *Financial Times*, April 18, 2012, p. 9. See also Roger C. Altman,
"Europe on the brink," *The Washington Post*, June 5, 2012, p. A17.

83. "According to one German political leader, 'Four years ago we increased
our pension age to 67. In Greece it is 55. We cannot persuade our people
that we will give the Greeks money to finance their state spending when
they have not carried out their most urgent reforms." Quentin Peel and
Gerrit Wiesmann, "Germany wants Athens to lift its chin to the bar," *Financial Times*, February 13/February 14, 2010, p. 2.

84. " . . . the domestic German debate assumes, wrongly, that the answer [to
the problems of the euro] is for every member to become like Germany
itself. But Germany can be Germany—an economy with fiscal discipline,

feeble domestic demand and a huge export surplus—only because others are not." Martin Wolf, "The eurozone crisis is now a nightmare for Germany," *Financial Times*, March 10, 2010, p. 11. If Germany were Germany with national, floating exchange rates, its own currency would strengthen to the extent needed to achieve balance.

85. "The proportion of young people between the ages of 15 and 25 who are now without a job is 51 per cent in Greece and Spain, 36 per cent in Portugal and Italy, and 30 per cent in Ireland." Martin Wolf, "What Hollande must tell Germany," *Financial Times*, May 9, 2012, p. 9.

86. "Inherently there are two conflicting economic tensions in the rescue packages. The first is that the austerity programmes needed to cut deficits are killing the growth needed to make debt bearable. . . . The other inherent tension is that the steps needed to improve competitiveness within the euro require prices and wages to be held down, making it even harder to cope with debt." "A second wave," *The Economist*, June 18, 2011, p. 31.

87. "'Without doubt, we need more and not less Europe,' Ms. Merkel declared, 'That's why it's necessary to create a political union, something that wasn't done when the euro was launched.'" Quentin Peel, "A very federal formula," *Financial Times*, February 10, 2012, p. 7.

88. "The Germans know what they do not want: no transfer union, no Eurobonds, and no transformation of the European Central Bank into a lender of last resort." "And then there was one," *The Economist*, January 21, 2012, p. 60.

89. See Anders Aslund, "Why a Breakup of the Euro Area Must Be Avoided: Lessons from Previous Breakups," *Policy Brief Number PB12–20*, Washington, D.C: The Peterson Institute for International Economics, August 2012. "If Spain and Italy were to exit [the euro] there would be a collapse of systemically important financial institutions throughout the European Union and North America and years of global depression." Willem Buiter, "The terrible consequences of a eurozone collapse," *Financial Times*, December 8, 2011, p. 11.

90. The case that the governments of the eurozone will always, eventually, come to the currency's rescue is made in C. Fred Bergsten, "Why the Euro Will Survive: Completing the Continent's Half-Built House," *Foreign Affairs*, September/October 2012.

91. Reinhart and Rogoff, *op. cit.*, pp. xliv–xlv.

92. On the impact of financial crises on the amount of public debt see *ibid.*, pp. 163–170.

93. Nathaniel Popper, "Old Economies Rise as Emerging Markets' Growth Falter," *The New York Times*, August 15, 2013, p. B1.

94. The details are in Richard Jackson and Neil Howe, *The Graying of the Great Powers: Demography and Geopolitics in the 21st Century*, Washington,

D.C: Center for Strategic and International Studies, 2008, Chapters 2 and 3.

95. "Today, one in five Japanese and Europeans is over age 65. In 2050, it will be one in three." David Wessel, "The Shifting Demographics Driving Nations' Wealth," *The Wall Street Journal*, August 12, 2010, p. A4.

96. Jackson and Howe, *op. cit.*, pp. 108–118.

97. The American birth rate falls just below the "replacement rate" of 2.2 live births per female, which is needed to avoid population decline.

98. In Japan, for example, the working-age population, "from a peak of 87m in 1995 . . . is expected to fall to about 52m by 2050, leaving it close to its level at the end of the second world war." "The Japan Syndrome," *The Economist*, November 20, 2010, p. 18.

99. See Tyler Cowen, *The Great Stagnation*, New York: Dutton, 2011, especially Chapter 1.

100. Rich countries tend to be more productive for quantitative as well as qualitative reasons: they have more capital invested per worker than poorer countries. For the poorer ones, therefore, investment can be a way of catching up. Poorer countries tend to get bigger payoffs for increased investment. For speculation that increases in productivity may be smaller in the future than they have been in the past, see Martin Wolf, "Is the age of unlimited growth over?" *Financial Times*, October 3, 2012, p. 13.

101. On the importance of institutions for economic growth, see the work of Douglass North, for example *Structure and Change in Economic History*, New York: W. W. Norton, 1981, and Daron Acemoglu and James Robinson, *Why Nations Fail: The Origins of Power, Prosperity, and Poverty*, New York: Crown Business, 2012.

102. Blinder, *op. cit.*, Chapter 11.

103. See Anat Admati and Martin Hellwit, *The Bankers' New Clothes: What's Wrong with Banking and What to Do About It*, Princeton, N.J.: Princeton University Press, 2013.

CHAPTER FOUR: THE BRICS

1. Samuel Brittan, "The long foreshadowed decline of western dominance," *Financial Times*, January 4, 2013, p. 7.

2. Michael Spence, *The Next Convergence: The Future of Economic Growth in a Multispeed World*, New York, Farrar, Straus & Giroux, 2011, p. 6.

3. John Kay, "Why India cannot take economic growth for granted," *Financial Times*, January 9, 2008, p. 11.

4. *Global Economics Paper No: 66*, London, Goldman Sachs, November 30, 2001.

5. In December 2010, South Africa became a member of the group, changing it from BRIC to BRICS.

6. China grew by an annual average of almost 10 percent per year from the early 1980s through the first decade of the twenty-first century. After its economic reorientation in 1991, India averaged almost 7 percent growth annually. For most of the first decade of the new century, Russia grew at a 6 percent yearly rate. Brazil did not do as well, but still grew at close to 3 percent from 1997 to 2007.

7. "In 2002–08 more than 85% of developing economies grew faster than America's compared with less than a third between 1960 and 2000, and virtually none in the century before that." "How to grow," *The Economist*, October 9, 2010, p. 3.

   "Two decades ago economic models treated the developing world like a dog's tail, wagged this way and that by rich countries but too small to affect them. Now the tail wags the dog. Their greater weight and speed mean emerging markets drive global growth, commodity prices, and inflation." "Economics focus: Why the tail wags the dog," *The Economist*, August 6, 2011, p. 66.

8. By one estimate, between 2012 and 2035 the developing countries will account for 68 percent of global growth. Stephen P. A. Brown and Joel Darmstader, "Energy and Natural Resources," in Bertelsmann Foundation, *Megatrends in Global Interaction*, Gutersloh, Germany, 2012, p. 149.

9. See Chapter 3, pp. 120–122.

10. "The Boston Consulting Group (BCG) predicts that there will be nearly a billion middle-class Chinese and Indians—some 320m households—by 2020. McKinsey & Co, another consultancy, points out that consumption tends to follow an 'S' curve. When people's income hits a certain point, demand for consumer goods surges." "Mammon's new monarchs," *The Economist*, January 5, 2013, p. 59.

11. Jim O'Neill, *The Growth Map*, New York: Portfolio/Penguin, 2011, p. 26.

12. *Ibid.*, p. 4; Jim Yardley, "For Group of 5 Nations, Acronym Is Easy, but Common Ground Is Hard," *The New York Times*, March 29, 2012, p. A4.

13. Ruchir Sharma, "Broken BRICs," *Foreign Affairs*, November/December 2012, p. 2; Sebastian Mallaby, "Beware membership of this elite club," *Financial Times*, December 5, 2012, p. 9.

14. The billion-plus Chinese and billion-minus Indians include many underemployed rural dwellers—although the supply does have limits in each country—who can become more productive, and thus increase national output, simply by moving to and working in cities. This source of growth is not available to the already urbanized societies of the rich world and is available only on a far smaller scale to the other two BRIC countries.

15. The country's rain forest also counts as a major asset. "If Brazil disappeared from the face of the earth, the rest of humanity would probably miss the Amazon rainforest most. It is one of the world's biggest reservoirs of carbon dioxide, the principal greenhouse gas, as well as a rain factory for all of South America and, possibly, a vital regulator of the world's weather." Brooke Unger, "Dreaming of glory: A special report on Brazil," *The Economist*, April 14, 2007, p. 10. The rain forest's ecological significance is a potential source of revenue. Under the terms of one proposal, "Brazil would be compensated for reducing deforestation below a certain baseline according to the market value of the carbon sequestered in the rainforest." *Ibid.*, p. 11.

16. Populist economics began as a defensive response to the Great Depression of the 1930s. In the preceding decades, Brazil had been relatively well integrated into the international economy through its agricultural exports, principally coffee. When the market for coffee collapsed, the government stepped in to bolster its price and support those who depended on it. Werner Baer, *The Brazilian Economy: Growth and Development*, Sixth Edition, Boulder, Colo.: Lynne Rienner, 2008, pp. 37–38. After 1945, Brazil joined many other non-Communist countries outside the trilateral regions in adopting import-substitution. Lincoln Gordon, *Brazil's Second Chance: En Route Toward the Second World*, Washington, D.C.: The Brookings Institution, 2003, p. 46.

17. Baer, *op. cit.*, pp. 220, 223–224. "By the end of the 1970s Brazil had established no fewer than 654 state firms, including 28 of the 30 largest companies in the country." Michael Reid, *The Forgotten Continent: The Battle for Latin America's Soul*, New Haven, Conn.: Yale University Press, 2007, p. 118.

18. By one definition populism is "an approach to power that depends on giving away money." Jorge G. Castaneda, "Latin America's Left Turn," *Foreign Affairs* 85:3, May/June 2006, p. 34.

19. The Brazilian with the longest twentieth-century tenure in power, Getúlio Vargas, ruled as a dictator from 1930 to 1945 but was also elected president in 1950. (He died by suicide in 1954.) The populist presidents Juscelino Kubitschek, Jânio Quadros, and João Goulart came to office through elections, although the last of them was deposed by a military coup in 1964, inaugurating two decades of military rule.

20. Baer, *op. cit.*, p. 66.

21. Spence, *op. cit.*, p. 203

22. The figures for the 1950s and 1960s are calculated on the basis of the numbers in Table A5 of Baer, *op. cit.*, p. 410. For the succeeding decades the figures are from Gordon, *op. cit.*, p. 3.

23. Baer, *op. cit.*, p. 82.

24. Riordan Roett, *The New Brazil*, Washington, D.C: The Brookings Institution, 2010, p. 151.

25. Between October 1991 and December 2005 more than 120 state-owned enterprises were sold. Baer, *op. cit.*, p. 232.

26. *Ibid.*, p. 205.

27. *Ibid.*, p. 133.

28. *Ibid.*, pp. 88–89.

29. "As of 2011, Brazil had possibly the most overvalued currency of the BRICs." O'Neill, *op. cit.*, p. 48.

30. *Ibid.*, p. 402.

31. Ruchir Sharma, "Bearish on Brazil," *Foreign Affairs*, May/June 2012, pp. 80–83.

32. Baer, *op. cit.*, pp. 147–148; Gordon, *op. cit.*, pp. 188–192.

33. "Tick, tock," *The Economist*, March 24, 2012, p. 38.

34. Paolo Leme, "The 'B' in BRICs: Unlocking Brazil's Growth Potential," *BRICs and Beyond*, London: Goldman Sachs Global Economic Group, 2007, p. 90. ". . . the total federal wage bill more than doubled in nominal terms between 2003 and 2009, while inflation was less than 50%." "Flying too high for safety," *The Economist*, May 22, 2010, p. 41.

35. "Many political scientists say that the rootlessness of elected officials helps to explain why Brazil never seems to fulfill its vast economic potential." Matt Moffett, "In Brazil, the Party Line is Often Blurry," *The Wall Street Journal*, June 20, 2006, p. A8.

36. Baer, *op. cit.*, p. 267.

37. Cited in Mary Anastasia O'Grady, "Brazil: Still the Country of the Future," *The Wall Street Journal*, August 25, 2006, p. A15. "The Constitution of 1988, drafted by an assembly composed of elected members of Congress (deputies and senators) and containing 245 articles and 70 'transitional provisions,' reflected a populist reaction against the military regime. It gave constitutional protection not only for vital civil rights and liberties but also for social and economic privileges for a large array of special interest groups." Gordon, *op. cit.*, pp. 3–4.

38. Gordon, *op. cit.*, pp. 121–123. In 1989, Brazil had 35 percent of Latin America's population and 45 percent of those in poverty. *Ibid.*, p. 130.

39. "The number of people living in poverty has fallen by 20m under Lula, from 49.5m (or 28.5% of the total) in 2003 to 29m (16% of the total) in 2008. . . ." "In Lula's footsteps," *The Economist*, July 3, 2010, p. 35. Of course, the bulk of this progress came from private growth, but government programs contributed to it as well.

"Last year, the [Family Allowance] program offered monthly subsidies of about $50 to some 11 million families, representing 40 million to 50 million voters." Alexei Barrionuevo, "A Resilient Leader Trumpets Brazil's

Potential in Agriculture and Biofuels," *The New York Times*, September 23, 2007.

40. "Almost continuously since 2003, federal-government spending has gone only one way, rising at an annual average rate of 8% in real terms." "Joining in the carnival spirit," *The Economist*, February 13, 2010, p. 41.

41. "Business investment was being depressed by the interest rates needed to finance the fiscal deficits." Gordon, *op. cit.*, p. 187. Brazilian taxes amount to 36 percent of the country's GDP, twice the proportion in China and India. "A moment of truth for Dilma," *The Economist*, August 18, 2012, p. 11.

42. "Government spending is growing faster than the economy as a whole, but both private and public sectors still invest too little.... Too much public money is going on the wrong things. The federal government's payroll has increased by 13% since September, 2008. Social-security and pension spending rose by 7% over the same period although the population is relatively young." "Brazil takes off," *The Economist*, November 14, 2009, p. 15.

43. Baer, *op. cit.*, pp. 171–174; "Still a lot to learn, *The Economist*, June 6, 2009, p. 36. "[2010 presidential candidate José] Serra likes to say that Brazil holds three negative world records: it has the highest interest rates in the world, the heaviest tax burden of any emerging country and one of the lowest rates of public investment." "In Lula's footsteps," p. 36; "Facing headwinds, Dilma changes course," *The Economist*, August 18, 2012, p. 32.

44. "'Admitting to liberalism explicitly,' wrote Roberto Campos, a Brazilian politician, diplomat, and swimmer against the tide . . . 'is as outlandish in a country with a dirigiste culture as having sex in public.' His observation still holds for Brazil, where economic liberals (in the British, free-market sense, not the socialistic America one) are as scarce as snowflakes." "The almost lost cause of freedom," *The Economist*, January 30, 2010, p. 46. Campos was known in Brazil as "Bob Fields," the English translation of his name, to denote his Anglo-American and, in the Brazilian context, anomalous political and economic views.

45. "If the ambitious plans of Petrobras, the national oil company, come to fruition, by 2020 Brazil will be producing 5m barrels per day, much of it from new offshore fields. That might make Brazil a top-five source of oil." "The devil in the deep-sea oil," *The Economist*, November 5, 2011, p. 17.

46. Anders Aslund, *Russia's Capitalist Revolution: Why Market Reform Succeeded and Democracy Failed*, Washington, D.C: Peterson Institute for International Economics, 2007, pp. 68–70. In late 1993 the rate of price increase in Russia approached the standard for hyperinflation—50 percent per month. *Ibid.*, p. 111.

47. Marshall I. Goldman, *Petrostate: Putin, Power and the New Russia*, New York: Oxford University Press, 2008, p. 106.

48. Privatization proved controversial and unpopular, and this was especially the case for an episode that occurred after it had been largely completed: the "loans for shares" scheme. In 1995 some of Russia's wealthiest men loaned money to the revenue-starved central government and took as collateral valuable state-owned properties, including oil companies. When the government failed to repay the loans, the lenders got the right to auction off the properties. The auctions were rigged and the original lenders got control of the assets. The loans-for-shares scheme is described in Goldman, *op. cit.*, pp. 63–69. Aslund, *op. cit.*, p. 164, offers a generally favorable assessment of the scheme's ultimate economic consequences. So wealthy and so influential politically did this windfall make several of the lenders-turned-purchasers that they came to be known as Russia's "oligarchs." The oligarchs acquired a largely unfavorable reputation in Russia and abroad. For a more positive verdict, see Aslund, *op. cit.*, p. 106.

49. Aslund, *op. cit.*, pp. 173–180. See also Daniel Treisman, *The Turn: Russia's Journey from Gorbachev to Medvedev*, New York: Free Press, 2010, pp. 230–231.

50. Aslund, *op. cit.*, pp. 197.

51. Timothy Frye, "Corruption and the Rule of Law," in Anders Aslund, Sergei Guriev, and Andrew C. Kuchins, editors, *Russia After the Global Economic Crisis*, Washington, D.C.: Peterson Institute for International Economics, Center for Strategic and International Studies, New Economic School (Moscow), June 2010.

52. The Russian think tank is Indem; the assessment comes from sociologist Georgyi Satarov. Both are cited in Chrystia Freeland, "The Next Russian Revolution," *The Atlantic*, October 2011, p. 64.

"Escaping the draft, registering a company, buying an apartment, getting into school, passing an exam, being acquitted of criminal charges, trumped up or valid, receiving medical treatment may all require the bribery of public officials. The kickback plague is endemic, inflating by as much as 50 per cent the cost to the state of everything from weapons to highway construction." Stephen Holmes, "Fragments of a Defunct State," *London Review of Books*, http://www.lrb.co.uk/v34/no01/stephen-holmes/fragments-of-a-defunct-state.

53. "The sad truth is that Russia cannot build much infrastructure until the government manages to control corruption in public procurement. For large public infrastructure projects, kickbacks of 50 percent appear standard and cases of 90 percent are cited. This is one reason that the total length of paved roads has not been expanded since 1997. A regime that cannot build roads cannot have a great future." Anders Aslund, "Putin

Represents What Is Wrong with Russia," *Moscow Times*, September 29, 2010, http://www.piie.com/publications/opeds/print.cfm.

54. Treisman, *op. cit.*, p. 236.

55. In time, the government's treatment of him "turned Mr. Khodorkovsky into a symbol of property rights, just as Andrei Sakharov became a symbol of human rights in the Soviet Union." "Another great leap forward?" *The Economist*, March 13, 2010, p. 28. Khodorkovsky was reconvicted, on equally specious charges, in 2010. At the time of his initial arrest he was not, for most Russians, an attractive figure, and his fate initially evoked little in the way of popular sympathy, let alone protest. He had gained control of Yukos through the loans-for-shares scheme and had consolidated his hold over it in ruthless fashion. However, he had begun to change the way he operated the company to make it more transparent, more accountable, and generally in closer conformity with international legal and corporate norms. Nor did the regime move against him because of his past misdeeds. His arrest was motivated by fear of and anger at his political activities, which the Putin group saw as a challenge to their power, as well as by the prospect that a large share of Yukos would be sold to Western energy companies, thereby weakening the Russian government's influence over the use of the country's energy resources. The Yukos affair is discussed in Aslund, *op. cit.*, pp. 234–241; Goldman, *op. cit.*, pp. 105–124; and Treisman, *op. cit.*, pp. 95–96.

56. By the standards of the countries that had once been part of the Soviet Union, Russia's economic gains during Putin's first two terms were not particularly impressive. Between 1999 and 2007 "the economies of 11 of the 15 former republics of the Soviet Union expanded by more than Russia's. Indeed, only Kyrgystan did markedly worse." Martin Wolf, "Why Putin's rule threatens both Russia and the west," *Financial Times*, February 13, 2008, p. 9.

57. Sergei Guriev and Aleh Tsyvinski, "Challenges Facing the Russian Economy After the Crisis," in Aslund, Guriev, and Kuchins, *op. cit.*, p. 12.

58. Aslund, Guriev, and Kuchins, *op. cit.*, Introduction, p. 1.

59. Goldman, *op. cit.*, pp. 36–37; Guriev and Tsyvinski, *op. cit.*, p. 13.

60. Oil production increased from 6 million barrels per day to 9 million barrels per day between 2000 and 2004. Aslund, *op. cit.*, p. 236; Goldman, *op. cit.*, p. 80.

61. In the first decade of the twenty-first century, Russia had the world's largest proven reserves and was the world's largest exporter (mainly to Europe) of natural gas.

62. Goldman, *op. cit.*, p. 13; Aslund, *op. cit.*, p. 252; Wolf, *op. cit.*

63. Guriev and Tsyvsinski, *op. cit.*, p. 14.

64. Cited in Philip Hanson, *The Sustainability of Russia's Energy Power: Im-*

plications for the Russian Economy, London: UCL Centre for the Study of Economic and Social Change in Europe, Economics Working Paper No. 84, December 2007, p. 4.

65. Putin "had the good luck to come to office just as the positive effects of his predecessor's reforms and the ruble's devaluation were kicking in, and as the oil price was rising. . . . He won his exceptional ratings in the lottery." Treisman, *op. cit.*, p. 251.

66. See Terry Lynn Karl, *The Paradox of Plenty*, Berkeley: University of California Press, 1997, especially Part I.

67. Philip Hanson, "The Russian economic puzzle: going forwards, backwards, or sideways?" *International Affairs* 83:5, 2007, p. 875. For a somewhat different view, see Michael L. Ross, *The Oil Curse: How Petroleum Wealth Shapes the Development of Nations*, Princeton, N.J.: Princeton University Press, Chapter 6.

68. Goldman, *op. cit.*, p. 12.

69. Hanson, "The Russian economic puzzle," p. 875; Hanson, "The Sustainability of Russia's Energy Power," p. 16.

70. Treisman, *op. cit.*, p. 99. "From 2000 to 2012, the number of state officials increased by more than 65 percent—from 1.3 million to 2.1 million." Ivan Kraster and Vladislav Inozemtsev, "Putin's Self-Destruction," *Foreign Affairs*, June 9, 2013, http://foreignaffairs.com/print/136643.

71. Paul Collier, *The Bottom Billion*, New York, Oxford University Press, 2007, Chapter 6.

72. Ross, *op. cit.*, pp. 90–93.

73. See Michael Mandelbaum, *Democracy's Good Name: The Rise and Risks of the World's Most Popular Form of Government*, New York: PublicAffairs, 2007, pp. 222–223.

74. Russia is an example of what Daron Acemoglu and James Robinson call "extractive economies," whose growth potential is limited. To create a more growth-friendly "inclusive" economic system generally requires a more open—that is, more democratic—political system. Daron Acemoglu and James Robinson, *Why Nations Fail: The Origins of Power, Prosperity, and Poverty*, New York: Crown Business, 2012. The book's argument is summarized in Chapter 15.

75. Before the economic downturn of 2007–2009 Russia had "a dynamic services sector and a manufacturing sector that at least provides a wide range of import-substitutes, even if it is not competitive as a producer of exports. Some diversification has been taking place." Hanson, *The Sustainability of Russia's Energy Power*, p. 16. "There is a fair amount of industry left in Russia that has prospects of competing on global markets, if given a chance. Potential strengths include aircraft, helicopters, engines, turbines, industrial gear such as pumps and compressors, and, inevitably, military

equipment." "A chance to get down to business," *The Economist*, July 14, 2012, p. 11.

76. "In Qatar, if the value of all oil and gas produced in 2006 had been divided among the emirate's residents, each would have received a cheque for $45,000. In Russia, the cheques would have been for only $2800, about the same as in Venezuela." Treisman, *op. cit.*, pp. 363–364.

77. Russia has natural gas as well as oil, of course, but the new technology of natural gas extraction, known as "fracking," will greatly expand the global supply and so reduce Russia's earnings from exporting it.

78. Richard Jackson and Neil Howe, *The Graying of the Great Powers: Demography and Geopolitics in the 21st Century*, Washington, D.C: Center for Strategic and International Studies, 2008, pp. 150–152.

79. Charles Clover, "Russians braced for an end to surpluses," *Financial Times*, October 4, 2012, p. 5; Anders Aslund, "Gazprom's crisis casts a shadow over Putin's future," *Financial Times*, September 28, 2012, p. 11.

80. According to Mikhail Dmitriev, the head of a Russian think tank, "At prices below $80 per barrel, this system would receive a blow from which it could not survive." Quoted in Charles Clover, "A Kremlin of crude calculations," *Financial Times*, February 24, 2012, p. 7. In the words of Charles Robertson, chief economist at Renaissance Capital, a Moscow investment bank, "If Russia didn't have oil and gas I'd already expect it to be a strong democracy." Quoted in *ibid.* It is within the realm of possibility that the Putin regime, under the pressure of falling revenue from energy, will undertake to reform itself. Thane Gustafson, "Putin's Petroleum Problem," *Foreign Affairs*, November/December 2012, pp. 95–96.

81. Jim Yardley and Gardiner Harris, "India Staggered by Power Blackout; 670 Million People in Grip," *The New York Times*, August 1, 2012, p. A1.

82. "In India, about a quarter of all power generated is either stolen or lost in transmission, five times the figure for China. Still more is given away to farmers, while the rest is sold to consumers at a loss, pushing state electricity companies toward bankruptcy and resulting in the rolling blackouts that afflict almost the entire nation every day. . . ." Simon Denyer, "In India, power corrupts," *The Washington Post*, October 5, 2012, p. A7.

83. This is a major theme of Gurcharan Das, *India Grows at Night: A Liberal Case for a Strong State*, New Delhi: Allen Lane, 2012, especially Chapter 4.

84. On this general point, see Ramachandra Guha, *India After Gandhi: The History of the World's Largest Democracy*, New York: HarperCollins, 2007, pp. 71, 418, 741.

85. *Ibid.*, pp. 213–218, 683.

86. Arvind Panagariya, *India: The Emerging Giant*, New York: Oxford University Press, 2008, pp. 31–41.

87. While Nehru did not favor deep engagement in the global economy,

during his years as prime minister the Indian government did permit a measure of cross-border trade and foreign investment. ". . . India had a relatively liberal trade and foreign investment regime in the 1950s. This liberalism owed much to the benign neglect of trade policy and active defense of an open foreign investment policy by Prime Minister Nehru." *Ibid.*, p. 24.

88. *Ibid.*, p. xvii. The period of 4.1 percent growth lasted from 1951 to 1968. *Ibid.*, p. 5.

89. *Ibid.*, Chapter 3. On regulations, see pp. 59–71.

90. *Ibid.*, p. 5.

91. *Ibid.*, p. 103.

92. "On licensing, the new policy explicitly stated, 'Industrial licensing will henceforth be abolished for all industries, except those specified, irrespective of levels of investment.'" *Ibid.*, p. 104.

93. The figures are based on data from the World Bank. http://data.worldbank.org/indicator/NY.GDP.MKTP.KD.ZG.

94. Tushar Poddar and Eva Yi, "India's Rising Growth Potential," in *BRICs and Beyond*, p. 15.

95. James Lamont, "An economic vulnerability undermines Singh's record," *Financial Times*, August 15, 2011, p. 2.

96. "A bumpier but freer road," *The Economist*, October 2, 2012, p. 76; ". . . China has lifted over 400 million of its 1.3 billion citizens out of poverty in the last twenty years. India's 7.5 percent average growth has brought an estimated 100 million out of poverty since 1991." Jayshree Bajora, "Inequalities in Asia's Giants," New York: Council on Foreign Relations, November, 2007, at http://www.cfr.org/publication/14706.

97. See Chapter 2, p. 59.

98. " . . . the proportion of the workforce employed in agriculture in the Republic of Korea fell from 68 percent in 1960 to 50 percent in 1970 and to 34 percent in 1980. In India, the decline has been far more attenuated: from 67 percent in 1991 to 58 percent in 2001. In terms of rural-urban split, the data give an even more pessimistic picture: Rural population fell from 79 percent of the total population in 1991 to just 77 percent in 2001." Panagariya, *op. cit.*, p. 259.

99. *Ibid.*, p. 283.

100. *Ibid.*

101. Thomas L. Friedman, *The World Is Flat: A Brief History of the Twenty-first Century*, New York: Farrar, Straus & Giroux, 2004, pp. 21–32, 103–113, 184–191.

102. Edward Luce, *In Spite of the Gods: The Strange Rise of Modern India*, London: Little, Brown, 2006, p. 48.

103. According to Manmohan Singh, "Our biggest single problem is the lack

of jobs for ordinary people. We need employment on a large scale, and it is not happening to anything like the degree we are witnessing in China." Quoted in Luce, *op. cit.*, p. 4. ". . . the type of growth matters for how much poverty reduction a given aggregate growth delivers. Rapid growth of unskilled-labor-intensive sectors is likely to create many more opportunities for the poor than rapid growth of capital- and skilled-labor-intensive sectors." Panagariya, *op. cit.*, p. 282.

104. Panagariya, *op. cit.*, p. 264. "Some 280 million Chinese work in factories; fewer than 45 million Indians do so, and India's industrial output is about the same as Spain's." Mehul Srivastava, "What's Holding India Back," *Businessweek*, October 19, 2009, p. 40.

105. "China's authoritarian leaders have built world-class infrastructure; India's infrastructure and bureaucracy are both considered woefully outdated." Jim Yardley, "Where Growth and Dysfunction Have No Boundaries," *The New York Times*, June 9, 2011, p. A1.

106. Panagariya, *op. cit.*, p. 384.

107. Joe Leahy, "Digging for votes among Mumbai's neglected poor," *Financial Times*, February 1, 2007, p. A8.

108. Steve Hamm, "The Trouble with India," *Businessweek*, March 19, 2007, p. 51.

109. "Wal-Mart in India," *The Wall Street Journal*, August 11—12, 2007, p. A8.

110. "Shares and shovels," *The Economist*, August 5, 2006, p. 66.

111. Panagariya, *op. cit.*, p. 401.

112. On the quality of parliament see Luce, *op. cit.*, p. 355.

113. Jo Johnson, "The criminalisation of Indian democracy," *Financial Times*, May 3, 2007, p. 11; Luce, *op. cit.*, pp. 7, 118. Of the 522 members of the parliament in 2007, "120 are facing criminal charges; around 40 of these are accused of serious crimes, including murder and rape." James Astill, "An elephant, not a tiger," *The Economist*, December 13, 2008, p. 5. In the parliament elected in 2009, 72 members had been charged with serious crimes. "Singh when you're winning," *The Economist*, May 23, 2009, p. 31.

114. "At almost every point where citizens are governed, at every transaction where they are noted, registered, taxed, stamped, licensed, authorised or assessed, the impression of being open for negotiation is given." New Delhi political scientist Pratap Bhanu Mehta, quoted in Luce, *op. cit.*, p. 79. See also Guha, *op. cit.*, p. 568, Panagariya, *op.. cit.*, p. 364, and "Battling the babu raj," *The Economist*, March 18, 2008, pp. 27–30.

115. "Identifying a billion Indians," *The Economist*, January 29, 2011, p. 61.

116. Luce, *op. cit.*, p. 94; Panagariya, *op. cit.*, pp. 293–294.

117. See, for example, Jo Johnson, "Uphill struggle: why transport turmoil is threatening a dead-end to India's boom," *Financial Times*, February 13, 2006, p. 11. "India's suspicion of foreign capital goes back to colo-

nial times, and those who question the unwelcoming official attitude to Walmart and Tesco are briskly reminded by Indian commentators of the commercial depredations of the British East India Company." Victor Mallet, "Indian corporate comedy fails to get them rolling in retailer's aisles," *Financial Times*, October 23, 2012, p. 2. See also Jagdish Bhagwati and Arvind Panagariya, *Why Growth Matters: How Economic Growth in India Reduced Poverty and the Lessons for Other Developing Counries*, New York: PublicAffairs, 2013, Part I.

118. Luce, *op. cit.*, pp. 10–12, 41–42; Joseph Lelyveld, *Great Soul: Mahatma Gandhi and His Struggle with India*, New York: Alfred A. Knopf, 2011, p. 260.

119. The term is from Mancur Olson, *The Rise and Decline of Nations: Economic Growth, Stagflation, and Social Rigidities*, New Haven, Conn.: Yale University Press, 1982, pp. 43–47.

120. See Chapter 2, pp. 46–47.

121. Panagariya, *op. cit.*, p. 65.

122. The laws apply to the "organized" sector of the economy, which includes firms that have ten or more employees if they use power and twenty or more if they do not. The organized sector encompasses the largest and best-established Indian companies, but firms in this sector employ only 10 percent of the Indian workforce. Panagariya, *op. cit.*, pp. 273, 283, 288–289. On the difficulty of firing workers, see Nandan Nilekani, *Imagining India: The Idea of a Renewed Nation*, New York: The Penguin Press, 2009, p. 305, and Gurcharam Das, "The Indian Model," *Foreign Affairs*, July/August 2006, p. 9. See also Bhagwati and Panagariya, *op. cit.*, Chapter 8.

123. India's major manufacturing firms concentrate on products that make intensive use of skilled labor and capital. Some of these firms do well in both the domestic and international markets, demonstrating that India can compete in the industrial sector and adding to the country's overall output and its exports. But skilled-labor-intensive and capital-intensive Indian industries must compete with firms located in wealthy countries, where skilled labor and capital are more abundant and thus often cheaper; and the operations of these Indian firms do little to reduce the country's vast supply of poor people. Panagariya, *op. cit.*, pp. 264, 445.

124. Panagariya, *op. cit.*, p. 68; Niraj Seth, "India Tourism Booms, but Just Try Finding a Hotel," *The Wall Street Journal*, April 24, 2008, p. A8; Bhagwati and Panagariya, *op. cit.*, Chapter 9.

125. Luce, *op. cit.*, p. 346; Panagariya, *op. cit.*, pp. 288–289.

126. "Unfinished journey," *The Economist*, March 24, 2012, p. 28.

127. "Including those at central, state, and local government and state-owned enterprise levels, the civil service numbers about 18m people—a figure approaching the population of Australia. That size also makes them the most

important group of workers in the country." Joe Leahy, "India's public sector needs decent incentives," *Financial Times*,, April 3, 2008, p. 9. See also Luce, *op. cit.*, p. 89 and Panagariya, *op. cit.*, p. 416.

128. "The central government's deficit has been 5–6.5% of GDP. Add in spending by the states, and India's overall budget deficit has been running at a wild 8–10% of GDP." "A walk on the wild side," *The Economist*, February 23, 2013, p. 37.

129. By one definition, people enter the middle class when they "have a third of their income left for discretionary spending after providing for basic food and shelter. This allows them not just to buy things like fridges or cars, but to improve their health care or plan for their children's education." John Parker, "Burgeoning bourgeoisie," *The Economist*, February 14, 2009, p. 6.

130. *Ibid.*, p. 20. "What is new is the arrival of a group of floating middle class voters who swing between parties depending on how they perform, not on promises of rewards for their particular group. Mostly young, urban, literate, mobile, and privately employed, they are increasingly well-informed thanks to cable news, social media and mobile phones." Adam Roberts, "Aim higher," *The Economist*, September 29, 2012, p. 7.

131. "Defined most broadly, to include all households with an annual income in excess of 70,000 rupees a year (at 1998–1999 prices), the middle class consists of as many as 250 million Indians. Defined most narrowly, to exclude those who earn less than 140,000 rupees a year, it consists of only 55 million Indians." Guha, *op. cit.*, p. 689.

132. Gurcharan Das, "India Says No to $80 Toilet Paper," *The Wall Street Journal*, September 3–4, 2011, p. C2.

133. Panagariya, *op. cit.*, pp. 299–305, 351–352.

134. "An area of darkness," *The Economist*, August 4, 2012, p. 35.

135. Panagariya, *op. cit.*, pp. 370–382.

136. For example, airports in New Delhi and Mumbai were turned over to private management. *Ibid.*, p. 303.

137. Poddar and Yi, *op. cit.*, p. 18.

138. Panagariya, *op. cit.*, Chapter 20. ". . . one government survey found that 30 percent of the 187 million students in grades 1 through 8 now attend private schools. Some academic studies have suggested that more than half of all urban students now attend private academies." Vikas Bajaj and Jim Yardley, "Many of India's Poor Turn to Private Schools," *The New York Times*, December 31, 2011, p. A9. Private firms also provide post-school training. "To recruit 31,000 graduates last year, Infosys considered 1.3m applications; only 65,000 passed a basic test. To address the skills shortage, the company is investing a whopping $450m in training. 'We are building India's human resources,' says Mohandas Pai, Infosys's chief of human resources." "With reservations," *The Economist*, October 6, 2007, p. 81.

139. Vikas Bajaj, "A One-Sided Rivalry," *The New York Times*, September 1, 2011, p. B1. "India is about fourteen years behind China. India's per capita income is presently about one-third that of China." Spence, *op. cit.*, p. 48.

140. A year later the practice of genuinely free elections had not spread and there was some disillusionment about their results in Wukan itself. "A revolution fizzles," *The Economist*, October 20, 2012, p. 41.

141. "It took England fifty-eight years to double its GDP starting in 1780; the United States needed forty-seven years starting in 1839; Japan doubled its GDP in thirty-four years starting in 1885; South Korea doubled the size of its economy in a remarkable eleven years starting in 1966; and then China came along to set a new record—it doubled its per capita GDP in just nine years starting in 1978, then doubled it again by 1996. Robyn Meredith, *The Elephant and the Dragon: The Rise of India and China and What It Means for All of Us*, New York: W. W. Norton, 2007, p. 145.

   "How does an average growth rate of 9 or 9.9 percent compare with other major historical cases? As it turns out, whether we take the top or the bottom end of the range, China is a world record holder. Over its peak thirty-year growth period, Japan grew 'only' at an average real rate of nearly 8 percent, and between 1960 and 1995 the high-growth Asian 'tigers' expanded at paces of 7.8 percent in Hong Kong, 8.3 percent in Singapore and 8.9 percent (the previous record) in Taiwan." Jonathan Anderson, "Beijing's Exceptionalism," *The National Interest*, March/April 2009, p. 20.

142. According to the World Bank, the number of poor people in China fell by half a billion between 1981 and 2004. Cited in Richard McGregor, *The Party: The Secret World of China's Communist Rulers*, New York: Harper-Collins, 2010, p. xvii. "Between 1987 and 2010 [China] lifted a stunning 680m people out of poverty—more than the entire population of Latin America." "Not always with us," *The Economist*, June 1, 2013, p. 23.

143. "The global economy increasingly depends on China for growth. An expanding Chinese economy creates demand for commodities from many developing countries and for industrial products and services from the wealthy ones. China . . . has also become one of the world's leading destinations for foreign investment." Tom Orlik and Bob Davis, "China's Growth Engine Declines," *The Wall Street Journal*, January 17, 2012, p. A1.

144. This is described in Nicholas Lardy, *China's Unfinished Revolution*, Washington, D.C.: Brookings Institution Press, 1998.

145. Michael Mandelbaum, *Democracy's Good Name: The Rise and the Risks of the World's Most Popular Form of Government*, New York: PublicAffairs, 2007, Chapter 1.

146. "Peak toll," *The Economist*, January 26, 2013, p. 41.

147. Helen (Hong) Qiao, "Will China Grow Old Before Getting Rich?" in *BRICs and Beyond*, pp. 48–51.

148. Hong Liang, "China's Investment Strength Is Sustainable," in *BRICs and Beyond*, pp. 61, 70; Dwight Perkins, *The Challenge of China's Growth*, Washington, D.C.: The American Enterprise Institute, 2007, pp. 21–22. On the Chinese financial system see Barry Naughton, *The Chinese Economy*, Cambridge, Mass.: MIT Press, 2006, Chapter 19.

149. "[China's] banking system is still relatively primitive. Credit does not flow easily to small businesses or to service industries that might generate large numbers of jobs, and China's central bank does not yet rely on interest rates as a lever to guide the economy." Jeff Sommer, "In Currency Games, the Prize May Be a Trade War," *The New York Times*, April 11, 2010, "Business section," p. 5. Reform of the financial system is also necessary if the Chinese currency is to play a wider international role. See Barry Eichengreen, *Exorbitant Privilege: The Rise and Fall of the Dollar and the Future of the International Monetary System*, New York: Oxford University Press, 2011, pp. 143–147. On other aspects of Chinese financial reform, see Nicholas Lardy, *Sustaining China's Economic Growth: After the Financial Crisis*, Washington, D.C.: The Peterson Institute for International Economics, 2012, pp. 78–94.

150. The term is Barry Naughton's. *The Chinese Economy*, p. 121.

151. Minxin Pei, *China's Trapped Transition: The Limits of Developmental Autocracy*, Cambridge, Mass.: Harvard University Press, 2006, p. 8; Perkins, *op. cit.*, p. 24; C. Fred Bergsten, Bates Gill, Nicholas R. Lardy, and Derek Mitchell, *China: The Balance Sheet*, New York: PulicAffairs, 2006, pp. 69–70.

152. "Indeed, to call China a manufacturing economy is something of a misnomer. In reality, it is the world's biggest final assembly shop, with minimal local value-added." Guy de Jonquières, "Myths about Chinese manufacturing," *Financial Times*, April 4, 2006, p. 15.

153. James Fallows, "China Makes, the World Takes," *The Atlantic*, July/August, 2007, pp. 68–69. ". . . on average, about two-thirds of the value of these so-called 'processed exports' originates outside China, mostly in other Asian countries." *China: The Balance Sheet*, p. 90.

154. "Now for the soft part," *The Economist*, October 6, 2012, p. 50.

155. Yasheng Huang, "China is no haven for entrepreneurs," *Financial Times*, February 2, 2007, p. 13; McGregor, *op. cit.*, p. 267.

156. "The number of young people of workforce entry age (15 to 24) is projected to fall by one-third over the next 12 years. With young workers more scarce, wages have nowhere to go but up. This is already happening: Last month, Guangdong province (China's main export hub) raised its

minimum wage by 20 percent." Arthur Kroeber, "5 Myths about China's economic power," *The Washington Post*, April 11, 2010, p. B3; Enid Tsui and Simon Rabinovitch, "Chinese cities raise minimum wage," *Financial Times*, January 5, 2012, p. 2.

157. See Chapter 3, pp. 104–107.

158. "In China, the state officially owns all land, and in the countryside it is very difficult for peasant farmers to sell or trade the family plots they lease from the government of the local collective." Jamil Anderlini, "Beijing's fear of social nightmare slows fulfilment of urban dream," *Financial Times*, July 21, 2011, p. 2.

159. Ian Johnson, "China's Lost Decade," *The New York Review of Books*, September 27, 2012, p. 84.

160. A riot at an electronics factory in northern China in September 2012 required 5,000 police to quell. Paul Mozur and Tom Orlik, "Chinese Factory Erupts," *The Wall Street Journal*, September 25, 2012, p. B1. In 2013, Foxconn, a large contract manufacturer whose biggest customer is Apple, agreed to genuinely representative elections in its plants for the first time. Kathrin Hille and Rahul Jacob, "Foxconn workers in landmark China vote," *Financial Times*, February 4, 2013, p. 1.

161. James Kynge, *China Shakes the World*, New York: Houghton Mifflin Harcourt, 2007, p. 202; Guy Sorman, "The Truth About China," *The Wall Street Journal*, April 20, 2007, p. A15; Albert Keidel, "China's Social Unrest: The Story Behind the Stories," Carnegie Endowment for International Peace Policy Brief 48, September, 2006; *China: The Balance Sheet*, pp. 40–41; Rahul Jacob, "Beijing frets as local injustices swell rising tide of incidents," *Financial Times*, June 16, 2011, p. 2.

162. Richard McGregor and Fiona Harvey, "The polluter pays: how environmental disaster is straining China's social fabric," *Financial Times*, January 27, 2006, p. 11. The country also suffers from serious water shortages. *Ibid.* "China's disadvantage, compared with the United States, is that it has a smaller water supply yet almost five times as many people. China has about 7 percent of the world's water resources and roughly 20 percent of its population. It also has a severe regional water imbalance, with about four-fifths of the water supply in the south." Jim Yardley, "Under China's Booming North, the Future is Drying Up," *The New York Times*, September 28, 2007, p. A14.

163. Shai Oster and Andrew Batson, "Beijing Reorders Priorities," *The Wall Street Journal*, March 12, 2008, p. A6. Dirty air and water exact a substantial economic toll. By one estimate total pollution costs amounted, in the first decade of the twenty-first century, to $54 billion per year, fully 8 percent of the country's GDP. Naughton, *op. cit.*, p. 493. The costs of pol-

lution are examined in detail in Elizabeth Economy, *The River Runs Black: The Environmental Challenge to China's Future*, Ithaca, N.Y., and London: Cornell University Press, 2004, Chapter 3.

164. For examples of such protests, see "Mobilised by mobile," *The Economist*, June 23, 2007, pp. 48–49; Andrew Batson, "Dissent Slows China's Drive for Massive Dam Project," *The Wall Street Journal*, December 19, 2007, p. A1; and Maureen Fan, "Shanghai's Middle Class Launches Quiet, Meticulous Revolt," *The Washington Post*, January 26, 2008, p. A1.

165. Economy, *op. cit.*, p. 20. ". . . pollution is worsening across the country in large part because local officials protect polluting factories. They have many reasons for doing so. Promotions are mostly based on economic performance. Local officials often get kickbacks from factories. In some cases, industries provide needed jobs." Shai Oster, "In China, Activism Is Risky Pursuit," *The Wall Street Journal*, September 28, 2007, p. A4.

166. McGregor, *op. cit.*, Chapter 6. "While the outside world imagines an authoritarian Communist party firmly imposing its will on the whole of China and its 1.3m inhabitants, the reality is that national policies and directives announced with great fanfare in Beijing are frequently ignored by party leaders at the provincial and city levels, even though these local leaders may themselves aspire to national office." Victor Mallet, "An enduring dysfunctional relationship," *Financial Times*, Special report: China, October 9, 2007, p. 3. See also Andrew Batson and Jason Leow, "Hu's Big Challenge: Getting Provinces on Board," *The Wall Street Journal*, October 23, 2007, p. A6.

167. "The Transparency International Index places China tied for no. 78 out of a total of 159 countries. . . . China is grouped with a large number of very corrupt nations even if it is near the top of the list of the very corrupt." Perkins, *op. cit.*, p. 10. "Based on the conservative assumption that 10 percent of the land lease revenues, fixed investments, and government spending is stolen or misued, the *direct* costs of corruption in 2003 could be 3 percent of GDP, roughly $86 billion, an amount exceeding the government's entire spending on education in 2006." Minxin Pei, "Corruption Threatens China's Future," Washington, D.C.: The Carnegie Endowment for International Peace Policy Brief 55, October 9, 2007, p. 2.

168. "All the Brics are slowing sharply. China's economy has slowed from an average annual growth rate of 11% in the last decade to less than 8% in 2012. That has taken the wind out of economies that set sail by selling raw materials to China, particularly Brazil and Russia, where GDP growth slipped to 1% and 3.5% respectively, last year." Ruchir Sharma, "BRICS Summits Are So Last Decade: All Members Are Slowing Down, with Conflicting Interests Leaving Them Less Willing to Cut Deals," *Times of India*, April 1, 2013, http://timesofindia.indiatimes.come/home/

opinion/edit-page/BRICS; "Growth of gross domestic product [in India] is expected to fall to 5 per cent in the fiscal year to the end of this month, the lowest for a decade." Victor Mallet, "Brics summit faces big challenges on growth," *Financial Times*, March 26, 2013, p. 5.

169. "By most measures the current recession is far milder than the Great Depression." Paul Swartz, "Quarterly Update: The Recession in Historical Context," New York: Council on Foreign Relations Center for Geoeconomic Studies, June 5, 2009. The report includes a number of graphs plotting important economic indicators during the two periods. See also Allan H. Meltzer, "What Happened to the 'Depression'?" *The Wall Street Journal*, September 1, 2009, p. A17. The peak-to-trough declines in GDP in 2008–2009 for the largest rich countries were as follows: Japan, 8.4 percent, Germany, 6.7 percent, Italy, 6.5 percent, the UK, 5.9 percent, the United States, 3.8 percent, France, 3.5 percent. Chris Giles, "Recession to leave permanent scars," *Financial Times*, November 24, 2009, p. 4.

CONCLUSION: FAULT LINES

1. It was only at the end of the nineteenth century that its practitioners began to label it "economics," implying to the world and often assuming in their own work a clear separation between matters of profit and loss and considerations of power—a separation that does not exist in reality.

2. On earthquake prediction, see Nate Silver, *The Signal and the Noise: Why So Many Predictions Fail—but Some Don't*, New York: Penguin, 2012, Chapter 5. On economic predictions, see *ibid.*, Chapter 6.

3. *Ibid.*, p. 162.

INDEX

Michael Mandelbaum is the Christian A. Herter Professor of American Foreign Policy at The Johns Hopkins School of Advanced International Studies (SAIS) in Washington, D.C. He is the author of thirteen previous books, including *The Ideas That Conquered the World: Peace, Democracy, and Free Markets in the Twenty-first Century* (2002), *The Meaning of Sports: Why Americans Watch Baseball, Football, and Basketball and What They See When They Do* (2004), and, with Thomas L. Friedman, *That Used to Be Us: How America Fell Behind in the World It Invented and How We Can Come Back* (2011).